TRAMPING TO SUCCESS

Story of The Great Eastern Shipping Company Limited

TRAMPING TO SUCCESS

Story of The Great Eastern Shipping Company Limited

S.N. Sanklecha

POPULAR PRAKASHAN
BOMBAY

POPULAR PRAKASHAN PVT. LTD
35-C, Pandit Madan Mohan Malaviya Marg
Popular Press Bldg., Opp. 'Roche'
Tardeo, Bombay - 400 034

First published in 1994

(3554)

ISBN 81-7154-784-2

PRINTED IN INDIA

By Tejas Enterprises, B-1/7, Laxmi Nivas
J. K. Sawant Marg, Mahim, Bombay - 400 016
and Published by Ramdas Bhatkal for Popular
Prakashan Pvt. Ltd., 35-C, Pandit Madan
Mohan Malaviya Marg, Tardeo
Bombay - 400 034

Dedicated to the revered memory of

Vasantbhai

Preface

Shipping is a complex international business. Therefore it is no mean achievement for The Great Eastern Shipping Company to have earned the reputation of being one of the most dynamic and successful shipping companies in the world. In India, Great Eastern is not only the largest shipping company in the private sector, but financially the most successful amongst the private sector and public sector shipping companies.

Great Eastern started in 1948 as a small one ship company with a modest capital of Rs. 20 lakh and began its operations in a hostile shipping environment. Indian shipping companies at that time participated in the coastal trade or aspired for a share in the country's overseas liner trades. The coastal trade of India was not large enough to accommodate a large Indian fleet. India's overseas liner trades were controlled by liner conferences which were dominated by foreign shipping lines. The liner conferences gave a meagre share of the trade to a couple of Indian companies as members of the conferences in the important liner trades.

Indian shipping companies were blissfully ignorant that the shipping scenario had changed after the Second World War. Bulk cargo trades (known as tramp trades at that time), both dry as well as liquid, had become important internationally and offered great scope for employment of ships. India's own overseas trade was, volumewise, predominantly in bulk cargoes. It is the volume or quantity of cargo rather than value of cargo which gave employment to ships. But the established Indian shipping companies did not appreciate the potential of large growth offered by bulk cargoes at that time. Indian shipping companies in the immediate post-Independence years held as their model the British shipping industry, which for historical and other reasons controlled a substantial part of the liner trades in the world. They overlooked the continued decline of the British shipping industry that had been taking place. The tonnage of ships registered in the U.K. declined from 45 per cent of world shipping tonnage in the year 1900 to 16 per cent of world tonnage in 1960. The decline continued thereafter also. In the post war years, that is, late 1940s and 1950s, it was the Greek and the Norwegian shipowners who participated in the bulk cargo trades who prospered and expanded their shipping fleets. Government policies, were influenced by the thinking of established liner-minded Indian shipping companies. These policies not only ignored the requirements of tramp shipping but by their controls, restrictions and procedures were harmful to the growth of tramp shipping.

It was in this difficult climate that Great Eastern became a pioneer in tramp shipping. It advocated the freedom of operation for tramp shipping, and despite the government controls and regulatory procedures, managed to establish a nucleus tramp shipping fleet.

Great Eastern's prime architect and builder, the late Vasant J. Sheth, was not only an entrepreneur of exceptional abilities but an outstanding visionary. Through Great Eastern Chairman's speeches, memoranda submitted to the government from time to time on various aspects of shipping policies, and discussions with ministers and government officials, he endeavoured his utmost to educate Indian shipowners and the government on the importance of freedom of operation for Indian shipping to enable it to compete successfully in international shipping. He did succeed to some extent in his campaign, which he waged with dedication for over four decades.

Great Eastern, with its profitable operations, was able to reward its shareholders with handsome dividends and issue of bonus shares from time to time. This made shipping shares popular among investors and also encouraged the starting of more shipping companies in India.

It was Mr. Vasant Sheth's conviction that if the story of Great Eastern is written and published it will not only make available a record of the important events in the company's career but would also be of interest to those concerned with Indian shipping. He felt that if the story of Great Eastern would briefly deal with the demand and supply factors in respect of shipping and special events and problems which had an important bearing or influence on Indian shipping, it would be of interest to all those interested in the development of Indian shipping. Further, it would prove useful to future historians who will write the history of modern Indian shipping. It was in 1979 that he briefly summarized the important happenings and events of the three decades 1948-1958, 1958-1968 and 1968-1978 from the Annual Reports and Accounts of the company and his own memory and marked the same to me and asked me to discuss it with him. In the discussions we had, he asked me to prepare a brief summary of happenings and events from the speeches as delivered by the Chairmen of Great Eastern to the company's shareholders. He told me that this material would be useful in future for writing the story of Great Eastern. This was the origin of the writing of this book.

It was at a farewell dinner party arranged for me by Great Eastern in September 1990 after my retirement from the company that Mr. Vasant Sheth in his speech requested me to write the story of Great Eastern, which he would call "The Adventures of A Tramp." Accordingly, I undertook the project. I was in constant contact with Mr. Vasant Sheth, showing him the drafts of the chapters and finalising the chapters after taking his suggestions into account. After giving a brief account of the family of the promoters of the company in the first chapter, I covered the decade-wise story of the four decades (1948 to 1988) in four chapters. Mr.Vasant Sheth went through the five chapters, approved them and asked me to cover the period subsequent to 1988 and also to cover the Company's plans and prospects for the future. He wanted me to analyse Great Eastern shares from the investors' and stock exchange operators' view point. He also wanted me to give a comparative account of the public sector company Shipping Corporation of India and Great Eastern. He was keen that a chapter should be devoted to Great Eastern's campaign for freedom of operation for shipping by quoting relevant extracts from the Chairmen's speeches at the General Meetings of the shareholders. It was his suggestion that a chapter on Great Eastern's strengths and weaknesses as compared with other companies should be prepared.

I prepared a draft of the important chapter dealing with the beginnings of the 5th decade and the future (Chapter 10) and handed it over to him before he went to the U.S.A. for a second heart bypass surgery. On the day of his departure for the U.S.A. he told me that after his operation, during convalescence, he would go through the material handed over to him. Unfortunately that was not to be. A few days after his operation, he passed away on 13 May 1992.

I therefore could not have the benefit of his suggestions in regard to Chapters 6, 7, 8, 9 and 10. I am sure these chapters and especially Chapter 10 would have been far better if Mr. Vasant Sheth's advice and guidance would have beeen available. As a person who worked closely with Mr. Vasant Sheth for over four decades in Great Eastern, I was fully aware of his views and convictions. I have tried to keep them in view in writing these chapters. As I have no close knowledge of the stock exchange trading and operations I could not write the chapter suggested by Mr.Vasant Sheth which would have been useful to investors and stock exchange operators.

Since it is a story of Great Eastern, I have endeavoured to record the important corporate events and developments. I have also briefly dealt with the founders, directors and executives who were concerned with the founding, operations and growth of the company. I have provided at the end a chapter on Mr. Vasant Sheth because of the pivotal role he played in the building of the Company.

I would like to state that the responsibility for errors, whether of fact or interpretation, is entirely mine and not of any of the persons who assisted me in preparing this book. My aim has been to produce a record of important happenings and events as accurately as possible. At the same time I could not ignore the wise words of the ancient author of *History of Chinese Writing,* Tai T'ung, quoted by a friend of mine Mr. V.J. Taraporewala in his publication on a legal subject: "Were I to await perfection, my book would never be finished."

Before I close, I bow in salutation to all those, afloat and ashore, departed and living, who have kept the Great Eastern flag flying high with dedication, faith and courage.

S. N. SANKLECHA

Jiwan 11-B
Nepean Sea Road,
Malabar Hill
Bombay 400 006

14 November 1993

Acknowledgements

It was the late Vasant J. Sheth who requested me to write the story of Great Eastern. He took a keen interest in the project and gave me advice and guidance from time to time in the completion of the work undertaken by me. He made invaluable suggestions in regard to those chapters which were written in his lifetime. The chapters which were finalised after his death also are based broadly on his ideas as to what should be covered in this story. I owe a deep and abiding debt of gratitude to the late Vasant Sheth.

Mr. K.M. Sheth, the present Chairman of Great Eastern, in spite of his heavy preoccupation with the company's work, went through the drafts of the chapters of the book and made most useful and valuable suggestions. I am deeply indebted to Mr. K.M. Sheth.

I express my deep sense of gratitude to Mr. Sudhir Mulji, Great Eastern's Deputy Chairman, for his most valuable suggestions made in the course of the discussions I had with him.

Mrs. Asha Sheth, who was entrusted by the company's Board of Directors to initiate and see the project through, was most helpful. I am most grateful to Mrs. Asha Sheth and Miss Ketaki Sheth (daughter of Mr. Vasant Sheth) who put in a lot of effort to ensure that the designing and production of the book was of the requisite standard and the book was published in good time. The discussions with my erstwhile colleagues in Great Eastern, Mr. B.N. Adappa, Mr. P.C. Jain, Mr. D.G. Khatri and Mr. P.R. Naware, were most useful and I convey my grateful thanks to them for their very valuable assistance.

Mr. B.V. Nilkund, Chief Executive and Secretary of Indian National Shipowners Association and Editor of *Indian Shipping* gave me all the information and data required in regard to the Indian shipping industry. I had discussions with him from time to time and these were most useful. I express my deep sense of gratitude to Mr. Nilkund. Mr. T.R. Nair, Deputy Secretary of Indian National Shipowners Association, readily provided me with all the data regarding the financial results of the various Indian shipping companies over the years and I am most thankful to him.

Last but not the least, Mr. V.H. Krishnan, who most willingly typed and retyped the drafts of the chapters and meticulously typed the final manuscript, has made an excellent contribution to the preparation of this book. I record my sincere thanks to him.

S. N. Sanklecha

Bombay
November 14, 1993

Contents

1.	Heritage	1
2.	The Beginnings and First Decade 1948-1958	13
3.	The Second Decade 1958-1968	43
4.	The Third Decade 1968-1978	75
5.	The Fourth Decade 1978-1988	109
6.	Change in Scenario for Shipping in Distress	147
7.	Great Eastern's Advocacy of Freedom of Operation For Shipping	159
8.	Areas in which Great Eastern Scored	193
9.	Shipping in Public Sector	205
10.	Beginnings of Fifth Decade 1988-1992 and Future	225
11.	Vasant J. Sheth	251

1

Heritage

Ujamshi Mulji was born in 1850 in Wadhwan, which was then a princely state in Saurashtra, and which is now in the state of Gujarat. He served as a post-master for some time in Wadhwan. At a young age, he gave up the job and migrated to Natal in South Africa sometime in the second half of the nineteenth century. He set up his own business in Natal. The family was therefore known as "Natalia." He had three sons—Chunilal, born in 1880, Maneklal, born on 24 July 1884, and Jagjiwan, born on 10 August 1889. He also had a daughter. Ujamshi Mulji did not return to India. He made regular remittances to his family in Wadhwan for their expenses.

His wife Ladkibai stayed in India and looked after the three sons and the daughter. In the absence of her husband she single-handedly shouldered the responsibility of the family. She was a lady of religious disposition. She brought up the children very well. After Ujamshi's death, the eldest son, Chunilal, went to Natal with his wife and stayed there for a few years. Maneklal too had gone to Natal. Both of them, however, returned to India without augmenting the family's fortunes.

The three brothers came to Bombay during the first decade of this century. Jagjiwan Ujamshi joined the firm of Messrs. Currimbhoy Ibrahim, who were the largest textile mill owners in India at that time. After gaining experience in the textile line, Jagjiwan Ujamshi started his own business of selling textiles. He did so well in this trade that he established a textile mill of his own. His elder brothers, Chunilal Ujamshi and Maneklal Ujamshi, also joined his business. After a few years, Chunilal Ujamshi, who had a spiritual bent of mind, withdrew from business and engaged himself in religious pursuits.

Chunilal's son, Jagdish Chunilal Sheth, later became Acting

Chairman and Managing Director of the government-owned Shipping Corporation of India, which is the largest shipping company in India. His career in shipping began with his service in Great Eastern in 1952. After about 10 years service in Great Eastern he joined the Shipping Corporation of India.

In the early 1920s, Jagjiwan Ujamshi started importing sugar from Java in the firm name of Messers. Jagjiwan Ujamshi Mulji. It was at this time that he found that time chartering of ships for carriage of sugar from Java to India was commercially most beneficial because the freight cost was far lower than that based on the prevailing conference rate. Besides lower freight cost, Maharajas of the maritime states in India competed against each other to give duty concessions on sugar imports over those prevalent in British Indian ports.

The firm imported shiploads of sugar in chartered steamers, which unloaded their sugar cargoes at the ports of Okha, Jamnagar, Bhavnagar, Porbunder and Janjira, which belonged to the princely states. The firm made arrangements with the rulers of these states, who also benefited considerably because large import duty was collected on the imports by them. On only one such consignment of sugar the Maharaja of Porbunder collected Rs. 6 lakh as import duty, which was one-third of the annual revenue of Porbunder state!

Jagjiwan Ujamshi, imbued with the nationalist spirit, patronized the Indian line Scindia Company. M.A. Master, the doyen of Indian shipping, referred to the courage and patriotism of Jagjiwan Ujamshi Mulji in glowing terms:

"When the steamer OTTO SWERDIP was unloading sugar at Porbunder in 1922, the Rana of Porbunder was pacing the sands near the port in a state of excitement. The reason for this excitement was very simple. While the annual revenue of that state at that time amounted to only Rs.18 lakhs, the unloading of sugar from OTTO SWERDIP brought to this state a magnificent windfall of over Rs. 6 lakhs. I have no doubt that the future historian of Indian shipping will accord a place of honour to Shri Jagjiwan Ujamshi Mulji for the bold step he took and the courage and the spirit of patriotism he showed in serving cargo to an Indian shipping line, despite the wrath that he would thereby incur of the British shipping interests and thus provided new incentive and strength to Indian shipping in its struggles for survival."[1]

In 1923 the members of the Java-India Conference, all foreign shipping companies, were charging a freight rate of Rs. 27 per ton less rebate of Rs. 5 per ton for carriage of sugar from Java to India. Messrs. Jagjiwan Ujamshi Mulji, who were importing sugar from Java to India, chartered steamers for import of sugar and brought down not only their own freight cost but freight costs of the entire trade. The chartering activities of Messrs. Jagjiwan Ujamshi Mulji forced the Java-India Conference lines to drastically reduce the freight rate from Rs. 27 per ton to Rs. 10 per ton. Even this reduced rate of Rs. 10 per ton was quite remunerative for shipping companies at that time.

Jagjiwan Ujamshi went to Russia in 1931 in connection with import of Russian sugar. His companion in Russia was Michael Golodetz, whose firm is one of the top sugar trading firms in the world today. Jagjiwan Ujamshi stayed in Russia for a few weeks in very difficult conditions which prevailed in Russia at that time, and was successful in importing Russian sugar into India.

In the second half of the 1920s Jagjiwan Ujamshi sustained heavy losses in the share business, and the textile mill had to be closed. The Great Depression which commenced in 1929 and continued up to the early 1930s caused much anxiety to businessmen and industrialists in India and other countries. The two brothers Jagjiwan and Maneklal were, however, made of sterner stuff, and they approached a wealthy Parsi businessman, Dossabhoy Bhiwandiwalla (later knighted by the British Government). Jagjiwan Ujamshi is reported to have told Dossabhoy Bhiwandiwalla that he and his brother did not have money but with their business skill they would multiply Bhiwandiwalla's investment.

The Bhiwandiwalla family of legendary wealth owned a large number of properties in and around Bombay and across the harbour at Uran. They were engaged in the business of manufacturing salt from their own salt pans and manufacturing liquor in their distilleries. They were also engaged in the distribution of salt and liquor. Their firm was called Khan Bahadur H.M.D.H. Bhiwandiwalla & Co. There were four Bhiwandiwalla brothers—Dossabhoy, Keikhushru, Ardeshir and Behramgore. Bhiwandiwallas became the financing partners, and the partnership between them and Maneklal and Jagjiwan Ujamshi was formed under the name Ardeshir Hormusji Bhiwandiwalla and Company (A.H. Bhiwandiwalla & Co.). The firm was engaged in the import and sale of sugar.

Jayantilal, eldest son of Jagjiwan Ujamshi, was sent to Java in 1932-33 in connection with the import of sugar from Java, and an office of the firm was established at Surabaya in Java. Large quantities of sugar were imported from Java by their firm.

The firm established itself as the largest importers of sugar in India. Its engagement in the ship chartering business gave it experience and appetite for getting into the shipping business. However, the firm could not go into purchase of ships at that time as the Second World War broke out, and it was no longer possible to purchase ships at reasonable prices.

It was in the 1930s that the Government of India granted protection to the sugar industry in India. A large number of sugar factories came to be established in Uttar Pradesh and Bihar. Some sugar factories were established in other parts of India also, including Maharashtra and South India. A.H.Bhiwandiwalla and Company also engaged itself extensively in the sugar distribution business.

The westernized Sir Dossabhoy used to move about and mix with the Britishers and Europeans of that time. In the 1930s he imported an aeroplane for his personal use. Dossabhoy died at the early age of 39 in 1940.

Keikhushru Bhiwandiwalla was not keeping good health. Therefore Ardeshir Bhiwandiwalla, who personified old world courtesy and charm and whose name the firm bore, along with Behramgore Bhiwandiwalla, actively concerned themselves with the firm.

Jagjiwan Ujamshi had a fervently nationalistic bent of mind. He burnt all his foreign clothes in 1932 in one of the bonfires of foreign clothes which were organised as part of the Swadeshi Movement. Maneklal Ujamshi was a religious person and a visit to a temple was part of his daily routine.

Jagjiwan Ujamshi had three sons and two daughters. Maneklal Ujamshi had two sons and one daughter. Jagjiwan Ujamshi's eldest son, Jayantilal, looked after the sugar factories after they were acquired in the early 1940s. The second son, Kantilal, was a surgeon, who also took interest in the family business when the need arose. The youngest son, Vasant, looked after and managed The Great Eastern Shipping Company Ltd after its establishment. Maneklal's son, Sevantilal, looked after and managed trading and import-export activities of the firm, which had a network of branches all over India. After Jayantilal Mulji's death he managed the sugar factory (Bhopal Sugar Industries Ltd) until it was sold to Wadhwans. He was director of The Great Eastern Shipping Company Ltd for some time. However, his first love always has been trading in commodities and shares and participation in diverse business deals. Maneklal's second son, Kanaiyalal (known as Kanu), joined The Great Eastern Shipping Company. He initially assisted and then shared in the management of the company with Vasant.

During the Second World War an acute shortage of sugar developed in Bombay and elsewhere in India.[2] In the first sugar control period, from 1942 to 1947, the Sugar Merchants Association in Bombay, under the guidance of the Ujamshi brothers, opened several fair-price shops in Bombay and its suburbs, Pune and Konkan districts, for sugar distribution at prices fixed by the government. The entire distribution was very ably organised, with a small commission to the sugar trade. As President of the Bombay Sugar Merchants Association, Jagjiwan Ujamshi organised the opening of several shops and outlets by members of the Association in different localities for sugar distribution. In Chowpatty area he opened such a depot in his car garage from where 2 lb packets of sugar were given to consumers at a fair price. Vasant Sheth, who was then in his teens, was made to sit in this improvised shop in the garage and attend to sale of these sugar packets. Jagjiwan Ujamshi became popular and was known as "Sugar Bapa" in the locality. The sugar trade thus remained in the hands of sugar merchants. The Government of Bombay Province appreciated the system of distribution adopted by the sugar merchants. This was all due to the able guidance of Ujamshi brothers who conducted the affairs of the Association in a disciplined and organised manner.

On 14 April 1944, there was a big and disastrous explosion in the dock area of Bombay. Along with several wholesale markets in Masjid Bunder area, the sugar market in Bombay was also completely destroyed. The sugar merchants of Bombay were in great distress. Undaunted and unperturbed, the Ujamshi brothers faced this calamity with determination and courage. Maneklal (who was President of the Sugar Merchants Association) and Jagjiwan, in order to revive the sugar trade, purchased a plot of land of about 4,000 sq. yards at Frere Road and constructed a sugar market building on this plot of land. A company known as the Bombay Sugar Market Ltd was incorporated under the stewardship of the two brothers. Ardeshir Bhiwandiwalla was the chairman and Dr. Kantilal Sheth was the first Managing Director of this company. Godowns and offices, with the facility of a post office and a bank, were allotted to the sugar merchants and the trade was centralised at one place. The shattered sugar trade was revived and many small sugar merchants who were on the verge of extinction in their business earlier were able to continue their trade.

After sugar was decontrolled in December 1947, the Indian Sugar Syndicate, a semi-government monopoly body, which controlled the sale and distribution of sugar produced by sugar mills in Uttar Pradesh and Bihar, opened an office in Bombay. They brought the sugar consignments and effected their sale at a price fixed by their controlling office at Kanpur. The Syndicate did not recognize the sugar trade nor the Sugar Merchants Association. Their sale policy was extremely detrimental to the sugar traders. The sugar merchants assembled in a meeting and urged the Ujamshi brothers to save the trade. The Ujamshi brothers took the lead and formed a small committee of five persons in which all powers of sale and purchase were vested. Jagjiwan Ujamshi, who headed the committee, bought a good quantity of sugar from the sugar mills in Maharashtra and South India which were not under the Syndicate. This quantity was pooled by the sugar merchants. Under the brothers' stewardship, the sugar merchants in Bombay provided tough competition to the Syndicate. Unable to match the business acumen and trading skills of the Ujamshi brothers, the Indian Sugar Syndicate ultimately sustained losses.

Jagjiwan Ujamshi was the President of the All India Sugar Merchants Conference held in Kanpur. He strongly advocated the abolition of the Indian Sugar Syndicate. The Kanpur and the Calcutta Associations joined hands with the Bombay Association and demanded the abolition of the Syndicate, which was harming the interests of sugar traders in the country. As a member of the Sugar Control Advisory Committee and Sugar Development Council, Jagjiwan Ujamshi also exposed the Syndicate's monopolistic role at the meetings of these bodies. His presentation of the case was very eloquent and effective. It resulted in the Indian Sugar Syndicate becoming a defunct body. The Syndicate ultimately was wound up.

The two brothers' names had become almost synonymous with the sugar trade. They came to be popularly known in sugar industry circles as Khandwala brothers or, in view of the name of their firm, Bhiwandiwalla brothers.

The brothers not only did exceedingly well for themselves but also wholeheartedly assisted the fraternity of sugar traders. Both the brothers had business acumen and their specific skills were complementary to each other. Jagjiwan possessed vision and original ideas. Maneklal had the organising and implementing ability. Between them they conceived and implemented many interesting business projects.

By 1939, thanks to the brothers' trading skill, their good timing of sugar purchases, the reduction in the cost of imports by chartering ships, and savings in duty brought about by competition among some of the native states to secure import duty income, the firm of A.H.Bhiwandiwalla and Company became virtually the sole importers of sugar. European and British indenting houses had totally withdrawn from participating in India's sugar imports.

In the year 1940 the firm purchased the Shree Changdeo Sugar Mills near Puntamba in Maharashtra. In 1943 the Bhopal Sugar Mills, which was located at Sehore in Madhya Pradesh, was purchased from the Nawab of Bhopal. M/s A.H.Bhiwandiwalla and Co. (Bombay) Pvt. Ltd. became the Managing Agents of both the companies.

The sugar business of A.H. Bhiwandiwalla and Co. grew to such proportions not only in Bombay but also at other centres all over India that they were called "Sugar Kings." The firm also engaged itself in trading of commodities and exports of commodities in a big way and conducted its business at 15 branches all over India.

The ambition of the Ujmashi brothers to start a shipping company, which arose out of their ship chartering business for import of sugar, was realised in 1948 with the purchase of a ship called *SS Fort Elice*, renamed *Jag Vijay*, from the U.S. Maritime Commission (See Chapter 2).

Jagjiwan Ujamshi and Maneklal Ujamshi wanted to see that the companies floated by them were run well. Training for their sons was essential. Their method of training was unique and excellent. They believed that practical knowledge was more important than academic degrees. Every day in the morning at 8.00 o'clock there would be a meeting at Jagjiwan's residence. The meetings were attended by their sons, Jayantilal, Vasant and Sevantilal. Policy matters were decided at this meeting. Kanu, being the youngest and still studying in college, joined this 'practical college' later. The younger generation was guided by both the Ujamshi brothers. They received their training in trading skills and business strategy. Thus the new generation was groomed to take over various industries. Jayantilal took charge of running the sugar manufacturing companies—Shree Changdeo Sugar and Bhopal Sugar. Vasant and Kanu were selected for managing the affairs of Great Eastern Shipping. Sevantilal was given charge of A.H. Bhiwandiwalla and Co., the trading firm.

Shri Changdeo Sugar Mill was sold in the 1960s and the Bhopal Sugar Mill was sold in the 1980s. The Great Eastern Shipping Company has become the largest shipping company in the private sector in India and one of the best managed and profitable shipping companies in the world. It has been stated that credit for the birth of Indian shipping in India goes to Scindia Company and for giganticism of development to government-owned Shipping Corporation of India. To Great Eastern however goes the undisputed prize in that crucial area of business: Profits.[3]

It would perhaps be appropriate to give here a short account of the Ujamshi brothers' humanitarian activities and services to society. Jagjiwan Ujamshi purchased a plot of land at Worli in Bombay and built a hospital which was run by his son Dr. Kantilal who was an FRCS. The Worli General Hospital was inaugurated by Morarji Desai, the then Chief Minister of Bombay. Dr. Kantilal proffered free surgery and free treatment to the poor. He balanced the hospital budget by the income in the hospital's nursing home. In a very short time the Worli General Hospital became a very popular hospital in Bombay. Unfortunately, Dr. Kantilal who was also the Honorary Surgeon at St. George's Hospital, died at a very young age on 3 April 1965. The Worli General Hospital premises are now used for very valuable research work on leprosy. The research work is financed by the Charitable Trusts of Godrej and Vasant Sheth.

The Ujamshi borthers also formed a family trust named Sheth Maneklal and Jagjiwan Ujamshi Mulji Public Charitable Trust, and made handsome donations to worthy causes. The Trust, in collaboration with the government of Gujarat, planned the establishment of a well-equipped eye hospital institution in Ahmedabad known as Maneklal and Jagjiwan (M&J) Opthalmic Institute, with an initial donation of Rs. 4 lakh from the Trust. This Institute was formally opened by the late Prime Minister Mrs. Indira

Gandhi on 12 December 1966. Jagjiwan Ujamshi had great sympathy and love for the down-trodden and weaker sections of society. He was greatly impressed by the activities of Shradhanand Mahilashram, to which he gave an initial donation of Rs. 50,000/-. He took active interest in the activities of the Ashram through his son Jayantilal, who became Managing Trustee of this charitable organisation. Jayantilal, in memory of his mother, donated Rs. 3.18 lakh for constructing an auditorium at the new building of the Ashram.

REFERENCES

1. *Indian Shipping - Its Struggles and Achievements*, by M. A. Master, Forum of Free Enterprise, Bombay 1959 p. 9.

2. The information about the role played by Messrs. Maneklal Ujamshi and Jagjiwan Ujamshi in the sugar trade in Bombay in the 1940s has been largely based on a Note entitled 'Ujamshi Brothers—Sheth Maneklal, Sheth Jagjiwan' prepared by Mr. Gautamlal A Shah, who was associated with Ujamshi Brothers from 1942. He was Secretary of the Bombay Sugar Merchants Association and Bombay Sugar Market Ltd. for a number of years. Thereafter he was Secretary of Shri Changdeo Sugar Mills Ltd. and The Bhopal Sugar Industries Ltd. Mr. Gautamlal Shah is an authority on the sugar trade and the writer gratefully acknowledges his debt to him for the valuable information furnished in his Note.

3. The journal *Gentleman* - October 1981 issue. Mridula Sood's article entitled 'Thriving in Troubled Waters', based on her interviews with Mr. Vasant Sheth.

2

The Beginnings and First Decade 1948-1958

In January 1947, Vasant Sheth, who was then 19 years old, was sent to the U.K. and the U.S.A. for grooming in business. He embarked on a Troop Ship, *Empress of Australia,* bound for Liverpool. After training in the U.K. for about four months he sailed for New York on the passenger liner, *Queen Mary.* On board the luxury liner, he met I.S. Chopra of the Indian Foreign Service, who was being sent by the Indian Government to assist Asaf Ali, Ambassador-designate to the U.S.A., to establish the Indian Embassy in Washington as India was about to gain independence. Vasant Sheth mentioned to Chopra his firm's plans to acquire and operate ships. Chopra took a liking for the young boy and told him to look him up in Washington. In Washington Chopra introduced Vasant Sheth to a lawyer who suggested to Vasant Sheth to apply on behalf of his firm, M/s. A. H. Bhiwandiwalla and Co., for release and allotment of a moth-balled liberty ship which was built in war time and which was being sold by the U.S. Maritime Commission.

The United States, a rich country, was selling the war-built liberty ships to shipowners or aspiring shipowners in other countries at an attractive price of about $5,00,000 per ship. The market price of such ships was 50 per cent higher. Over 3000 liberty ships were built during the war and the Henry Kaiser mass production shipyards in California could complete one ship in 27 days from start to finish. Greek interests bought 100 liberty ships for $ 5,40,000 each on deferred payment terms with 25 per cent of the price as down payment and the balance price payable over 18 years. This deal was the foundation of the modern Greek fleet and was one of the best shipping deals ever concluded. The Greeks now own, under the Greek flag as well as other flags, the largest shipping fleet in the world, of over 85 million DWT. In terms of DWT the Greeks own about 14 per cent of the world shipping fleet. Liberty ships were the perfect work horses for the bulk cargo trades and could also cater to liner trades of those times. Many of these liberty ships continued to sail up to the 1970s, until they became obsolete and were overtaken by bulk carriers and container ships.[1]

Vasant Sheth made enquiries in the States and was told that buying one of these ships would be an excellent purchase. He referred to his elders in Bombay by cable and got clearance. The application was prepared in consultation with the lawyer and forwarded to U.S. Maritime Commission (USMC) by the lawyer, who was to get a fee of US $ 25,000 if the ship was released and allotted to A.H.Bhiwandiwalla and Co. The outcome of the application was to be known in two to three months' time. Vasant Sheth left the U.S.A. and when he returned to India was immersed in his trading activity in sugar, spices and other commodities; he had almost forgotten about his application for release of a ship. On 9 April 1948 a telegram came from the Indian External Affairs Ministry advising that a ship was released by USMC to A.H.Bhiwandiwalla and Co. and that the money was to be paid in three weeks time; delivery of the ship was to be taken by the end of April. The payment of the sale price was made and the ship was registered in the name of A.H.Bhiwandiwalla and Co on 3 May 1948. It was decided to name the ship *Vijay* and the prefix *Jag*, which was a part of Vasant Sheth's father's name, Jagjiwan, was added. All the Great Eastern ships have the prefix 'Jag', which also means 'the world'; Jag Vijay means 'world victory.'

Many businessmen believe that the first asset or unit bought by a business or enterprise determines the venture's success or failure. The liberty ship *Jag Vijay* proved to be an excellent acquisition, laying the foundation for the progress and prosperity of her owners.

The first voyage of *Jag Vijay* was from Baltimore to Civitavechia in Italy, with a cargo of coal. The ship was managed by the London agents of A.H.Bhiwandiwalla and Co, namely Eggar, Forrestor and Verner Ltd. They appointed Capt. E.W. Kent as Master and recruited British officers and ratings to man the ship. Capt. Kent had also recruited some US nationals to man the ship. From Civitavechia she proceeded to Aden, from where a cargo of salt was carried to Calcutta. From Calcutta the vessel carried coal to Okha and from Okha the vessel came to home port, Bombay.

These voyages had been eventful, to say the least! A number of

British crew, who were of poor calibre, had either fallen ill and left the ship or deserted the ship. Capt. Kent had to employ Italians and Arabs in their place. When the vessel came to Bombay the ship's crew consisted of men belonging to various nationalities, and Capt. Kent had a mutiny on hand. An observer well-versed in shipping personnel matters who went on board the ship remarked that the crew were lax and negligent in their work but good at eating caviar and drinking champagne! Capt. Kent mentioned in Bombay that it was almost impossible to manage the sub-standard crew and officers of the ship. Vasant Sheth told him that as captain it was part of his duties to manage the ship, and that if he could not control and manage the ship's officers and crew he would have to leave. He assured Capt. Kent of the co-operation of the management to replace the undesirable crew and officers. The management of the ship was then transferred from London to Bombay. Excepting Capt. Kent and some British officers, foreign officers and crew were repatriated and Indians were recruited in their place. This ensured the satisfactory manning and operation of the ship.

It was decided to incorporate a new company for the shipowning and ship operating business. M/s. A.H. Bhiwandiwalla and Co was a partnership firm in which the Bhiwandiwalla and Sheth families had a 50 per cent share each. A.H. Bhiwandiwalla and Company (Bombay) Pvt Ltd, the shares of which were held equally by the Bhiwandiwalla and Sheth family members, were to be Managing Agents of the shipping company. At that time the managing agency system was in vogue in India. Large companies were usually managed by Managing Agents. Vasant Sheth, as director of the Managing Agents A.H. Bhiwandiwalla and Co (Bombay) Pvt Ltd, was placed in sole charge of the management of the company.

Name of the Company

The new company was named The Great Eastern Shipping Company Limited, as suggested by H.T. Parekh. Parekh was very close to Jagjiwan Ujamashi, who regarded him as one of his sons. Parekh was working at that time with a firm of stockbrokers. Later, he joined Industrial Credit and Investment Corporation of India (ICICI), and after retiring from ICICI as its Chairman he started the Housing Development Finance Corporation, now a highly reputed organization. Parekh in the initial years assisted the Great Eastern management by advising on their issue of share capital, raising of further share capital, etc.

The name Great Eastern proved a harbinger of growth and prosperity not only to the company but also to its shareholders and employees. And yet, ironically, *Great Eastern* was a 19th century ship that had been associated with much misfortune. It was the third of the great shipbuilding masterpieces of Isambard Kingdom Brunel, the other two being *Great Western* and *Great Britain*. *Great Eastern* was a ship far in advance of her time. Laid down in 1854 and launched in 1858 at a time when the largest ships afloat were of under 5,000 tons, the *Great Eastern* had a designed tonnage of 18,914. She was the first ship to incorporate a steering engine and also the first to be fitted with a cellular double bottom. She had a top speed of 15 knots. Brunel designed her to carry 4,000 passengers (or 10,000 soldiers if used as a troop ship) as well as 6,000 tons of cargo to India or Australia without requiring to take coal bunkers at intermediate ports on the way to India or Australia.

The ship was, however, unfortunate from the outset. Construction difficulties and launching delays ruined Brunel's collaborator, John Scott Russell, in whose yard the ship was built, and caused a breakdown in Brunel's own health; he died before the *Great Eastern* was able to make her maiden trip. She was used for the trans-Atlantic run instead of the designed Australia or India run, where she proved a failure. She was later converted to a cable carrier and employed in laying four cables across the Atlantic and one from Aden to Bombay. She was finally beached at New Perry, Cheshire in 1888 for breaking up.[2]

Fortunately the promoters of The Great Eastern Shipping Company and H.T.Parekh were not aware of this background to the name. Otherwise they might have given a different name to the company. For Great Eastern Shipping Company, the name has brought fine luck and good fortune to all those associated with it.

Incorporation of the Company

The Great Eastern Shipping Company Ltd was incorporated on 3 August 1948 with a paid up share capital of Rs. 20 lakh. Vasant Sheth, who was to manage the company as a director of the Managing Agents, was also appointed as director of Great Eastern Shipping

Company. The Certificate of Commencement of Business was granted to the Company on 1 September 1948 by the Registrar of Companies.

The Company's office was initially situated at Sugar Market Building, Frere Road, opposite Princess and Victoria Docks. Besides Vasant Sheth, the entire office staff consisted of three persons: Amritlal V. Mehta, Company Secretary, S.N. Sanklecha, Assistant Company Secretary, and Sonu Bane, peon. Some months after the incorporation of the Company, the office was shifted to 32 Apollo Street, Fort.

M/s. A.H. Bhiwandiwalla and Co handed over the vessel to The Great Eastern Shipping Co Ltd at the cost price at which they had acquired the vessel from U.S. Maritime Commission. They also did not retain the pre-incorporation profits of about Rs.59,000 on the operation of the ship under their ownership and passed this on to the company. The Managing Agents also waived their office allowances (payable to them in terms of the Managing Agency Agreement) up to the end of December 1948, and drew the office allowance only after the establishment of the company on a stable footing. A.H.Bhiwandiwalla and Co also assisted the company by purchasing salt cargoes on their own account and giving them to the company for carriage from the west coast of India to Calcutta. Coal cargoes from Calcutta to the west coast and return cargoes of salt from the West coast to Calcutta formed a substantial part of the coastal shipping business at that time, and this assistance was therefore very helpful to the company. A.H. Bhiwandiwalla and Co also had a number of branches all over India and also at Karachi in Pakistan. The branches in a number of Indian ports were of great advantage to Great Eastern, saving it the expenditure of establishing and maintaining its own branches at these places.

It is interesting to note that Vasant Sheth was at the time drawing as little as Rs. 500 per month as salary from the Managing Agents and not from the company. When the company was doing well and Vasant Sheth asked for an increase in salary, he was told by his father that he should in fact pay for the valuable experience he was getting instead of asking for an increase in salary! There was an all-pervasive sense of managing the company with utmost economy of expenditure.

A.H. Bhiwandiwalla and Co in the initial years also helped the company by giving it loans for its working capital at very nominal rates of interest. The company opened a branch office in Calcutta, the most important port for Indian shipping, at that time, in November 1948.

Board of Directors

The Board of Directors listed in the First Annual Report of the company consisted of:

Ardeshir Hormusji Bhiwandiwalla
F.H.Mehta
Manmohandas Madhavdas Amersey
Navinchandra Mafatlal
Madanmohan Ramnarayan Ruia
Pratapsinh Mathuradas
Behramgore Hormusji Bhiwandiwalla
Dr. Jayantilal Nerbheram Parekh
Sukhlal Mansukhlal Mehta
Maneklal Ujamshi
Vasant Jagjiwan Sheth

Out of the 11 persons listed above, eight have passed away. Out of the three still living, Pratapsinh Mathurdas (Vissanji) was a director of the company for many years and retired as director some years ago. Dr. Jayantilal Narbheram Parekh and Sukhlal Mansukhlal Mehta were associated with the company as directors only for a very short while.

S. S. Haligonian Duke

In the very first year of the company's existence, an unfortunate episode occurred with a time-chartered ship, *Haligonian Duke,* which was detained at an Australian port for 4 months. It almost jeopardized the existence of the company before it had established itself on a stable footing. The company had time chartered *S.S. Haligonian Duke,* belonging to Canadian shipowners and manned with non-Canadian crew on sub-standard wages. Great Eastern employed the time-chartered ship to carry a cargo of coal from Calcutta to Melbourne on account of the Victorian government. Return cargo of wheat from Australia to India on account of the Indian government was also booked. However, a major dispute of international magnitude developed, with the Canadian Seamens'

Union insisting that all Canadian vessels be manned by Canadian crew, and the owners of the vessel equally adamant that they would not change the non-Canadian crew of the vessel. When the vessel reached Melbourne, she was declared "black' by the Australian Seamens' Union. They refused to handle and unload the ship. Great Eastern was in no way concerned with the manning and personnel of the ship, which was the responsibility of the owners.

It became an unfortunate victim of circumstances beyond its control. There would have been a further detention of the vessel because no settlement seemed to be in sight. However, because there was a coal miners' strike in Australia itself, and coal was very badly required in the country, the Victorian government used military personnel for unloading the vessel. The vessel did not get the return wheat cargo due to this long delay and was redelivered to the owners.

J. J. Mehta, who had joined the company in Bombay in August 1948, was deputed to Calcutta office as Assistant Manager and afterwards became Manager in Calcutta office. He had gone on board the vessel from Calcutta to Melbourne, and the communications sent by him from Australia were very useful to the company in the arbitration proceedings in London in respect of the claim for charter hire and losses. Sir Robert Aske K.C. was appointed as umpire in the arbitration proceedings. Dr. Kantilal Sheth, who managed the Worli General Hospital, was requested to assist the company in the arbitration proceedings. Sheth, a doctor turned lawyer, handled the case very competently on behalf of the company. As against the owners' claim for Pound Sterling 40,000 against the company for charter hire etc., they were awarded Pound Sterling 6,000. The Victorian government later paid a compensation of Pound Sterling 20,350 to Great Eastern in respect of the detention caused to the ship.

The arbitration award in respect of the company's dispute with the shipowners was given in 1952, and the government of Victoria agreed to pay the compensation claim to the company in 1955, that is, six years after the unfortunate episode which took place. These disturbing events had taken place in the very first year of the existence of Great Eastern, and at one time appeared to threaten the very existence of the infant company.

In view of the difficult situation caused by the prolonged detention of *S.S. Haligonian Duke* and the oft-repeated claim of the Scindia

Steam Navigation Company that as pioneers of modern Indian shipping and the premier Indian shipping company, they helped other Indian shipping companies, Vasant Sheth, accompanied by his father Jagjiwan Ujamshi, met a very senior manager of the Scindia Company. They hoped to discuss Great Eastern's serious problem and seek Scindias' co-operation in tackling and solving the problem. On the contrary, the Scindia manager was very rude. He told them that they had no business to enter the shipping line, which was a complex one and could be handled only by experienced shipping operators. He even asked them to leave his room. He appeared to have forgotten that by his argument, Scindia Company itself had no business to enter shipping, and should have left it in the hands of the experienced British shipping companies which operated in India's trades during British rule!

K. M. Sheth Joins Great Eastern

In 1951, K.M. Sheth (Kanu) was studying at the Sydenham College of Commerce and Economics. Great Eastern Shipping Company, founded by his father and uncle in 1948, was expanding its activities, and a family member was needed to assist Vasant Sheth and to share his increasing responsibilities to manage the company. So Kanu left his studies and joined the company. After his early training in Japan and in the office, he was appointed Manager in October 1952.

As soon as K.M. Sheth joined Great Eastern in 1951 (as a trainee without pay), his first major assignment was to fly to Japan and supervise the construction of m.v. *Jag Ganga* and m.v. *Jag Jamna* (2,008 DWT each for transporting general cargo along the Indian coast) which were being built by Mitsubishi shipyard in Kobe for Great Eastern. After the Second World War Great Eastern was the first Indian shipping company to place an order for construction of ships in Japan. K.M.Sheth left for Japan by a Constellation plane (in those days there were no jet planes) and reached Tokyo after almost 24 hours. He stayed in Japan for about two months, during which time he visited Mitsubishi shipyard almost every day and watched the construction of the two ships all day. Sometimes he would go from Kobe to Tokyo and visit various Japanese shipping companies. He developed an extremely close relationship with I. Kimura, the then Managing Director of Yamashita Steamship

Company, one of the largest Japanese shipping companies, who were at that time acting as Great Eastern's agents in Japan. Besides a strong business relationship, Kimura regarded the young boy as his son. K.M. Sheth succeeded in getting for Great Eastern the all-India agency of Yamashita Steamship Company.

The agency lasted even after all Japanese shipping companies ran into serious financial crisis and Yamashita Steamship Company and Shinnihon Steamship Company amalgamated into a new company, namely, Yamashita-Shinnihon Line. The Yamashita-Shinnihon Line continued Great Eastern as agents in India. This agency arrangement came to an end on 1 June 1989 after Yamashita-Shinnihon Line and Japan Line amalgamated and they appointed other agents in India.

Areas of Operation

The company's ships were plying mostly in the coastal trade of India, with occasional overseas tramp voyages in the initial years. When the government announced and decided to implement the policy of coastal reservation in 1950, the company's ships were treated as coastal ships. This jeopardized the company's overseas tramping activities. The company then began to charter ships for coastal trading in substitution of its own ships, and operated its own ships for overseas trading.

A substantial part of the coastal trade of India at that time consisted of coal cargoes from Calcutta for discharge at other Indian ports including the west coast ports. Due to draught restrictions in the Hooghly river the owned vessels of about 10,000 DWT could not load or discharge full cargoes at Calcutta, and about 25 to 30 per cent of the shipping space was wasted. It was possible to time charter smaller vessels which could be fully utilised for loading coal cargoes. The larger owned vessels could load to their full capacity and carry cargoes in the overseas trade from and to ports other than Calcutta. Coastal trading requirements could be served with vessels with speeds lower than the speed required for vessels in overseas trades.

It was also possible at this time to use coal burning ships in the Indian coastal trade. As vessels had increasingly switched to oil from coal for ship propulsion all over the world at that time, the demand for coal burning ships had gone down and they could be chartered for Indian coastal trades at much lower rates than oil-propelled ships. The smaller size and lower speed vessels required for coastal trading further reduced the time charter hire payable on coastal charters. The company's owned vessels could be advantageously used in the overseas trade. This policy therefore enabled the company to improve its earnings and the country to earn more foreign exchange.

The company was building up its fleet and acquiring, whenever possible, oil burning units which could be employed in the overseas trade. The company's first ship, *Jag Vijay*, which was a coal-burner, was converted to oil in 1952. In doing so the company had taken it for granted that such units would be allowed to go overseas freely whenever opportunities occurred, although initially they would be licensed only for coastal trades. The company had entered into contracts of affreightment for carriage of cargo in the overseas trades such as the carriage of wheat from Australia to India, and sugar from the U.K. to India. Indian shipping companies which had no interest or stake in the tramp trades were asking the government to ban chartered ships in the coastal trades regardless of the special circumstances in which it was advantageous to divert an owned ship to the overseas trade and substitute it by a chartered ship on the coast. The Indian Coastal Conference and Indian National Steamship Owners' Association were in favour of banning time charters on the coast. The government, swayed by their views, placed a ban on coastal charters in November 1954 and insisted that the company's own ships should ply in the coastal trade. Great Eastern had therefore to charter ships to fulfill the contracts of affreightment in the overseas trades at very much higher rates of charter hire, and in some cases even had to sustain losses.

The government was unable to appreciate that for every foreign flag ship employed in the coastal trade and that too under the management of an Indian company, an Indian ship was being utilised in overseas trade. The company's owned vessels were losing 25 to 30 per cent of their shipping space in the coastal trade. Confining these ships to the coast and chartering ships for carriage of cargoes in the overseas trade involved not only financial loss to the company but also loss of foreign exchange to the country.

The government had been importing large quantities of bulk cargo which were carried entirely in foreign flag ships chartered by the government even at a time when the charter market was unusually high. Since for coastal trade, ships which were required to be chartered could well be old and low speed vessels, and even coal-burners, they would be, in terms of their charter hire cost, appreciably cheaper than ships required to be chartered for overseas trading. It became desirable therefore to use Indian ships for the overseas carriage of bulk cargo and to charter less foreign-flag ships for the purpose. For coastal trading, foreign-flag ships, required to be chartered for substituting the owned vessels, were more economical and involved less outgo of foreign exchange.

The reserved coast had been acclaimed as a 'nursery' for Indian shipping, and rightly so. Yet the concept of nursery could be meaningful only when the coast was utilised, consciously and deliberately, to help our shipping grow in stature and vigour so that it might be better equipped to venture out of the sheltered waters and to face the hard competition on the high seas where alone it could win its biggest prize and carve out its future for itself. A wise shipping policy would give every possible inducement to the shipowners to build up fleets of deep sea vessels by using the coast as an initial support and to sail out of the coast whenever possible to meet bigger challenges on the high seas. The goverment, however, was pursuing a diametrically opposite policy and the company was denied permission to employ its larger vessels in the overseas trade. Its ships were tied down to the coast even when this entailed a serious waste of their carrying capacity. By pursuing such a policy the biggest single advantage of coastal reservation was thrown away and the growth of our deep sea tonnage instead of being helped was hindered. The infant shipping industry was thus being nursed into becoming a permanent weakling.

The company had no other alternative than to submit in desperation and as a mark of protest against the unrealistic policy, notices of resignation from the membership of the Indian Coastal Conference and the Indian National Steamship Owners Association, in June 1955. A compromise was however arrived at, in that the company's requirements as a tramp shipping company were conceded to a limited extent. It was allowed to take its own vessels out of the coast for overseas trade and substitute them temporarily by time chartered ships on the coast on the condition that it would acquire further ships within a period of two years and place these ships on the coast. The company then withdrew its resignations.

Bulk cargoes of coal and salt constituted more than 50 per cent of the total sea borne coastal trade, and the company's ships carried these bulk cargoes. After the acquisition in 1951 of m.v. *Jag Ganga* and m.v. *Jag Jamna*, which were of 2,008 DWT each and well suited for carriage of general cargo on the coast, the company participated actively in the carriage of general cargo on the coast. The company's general cargo service was popular with the shippers and the general cargo carried by the company on the coast exceeded 30 per cent of the total dry cargo liftings on the coast by the company in 1951-52 and in each of the subsequent years in the first decade.

In the initial years the company's ships plied mainly in the coastal trade and occasionally carried out overseas voyages, and were increasingly participating in the overseas tramp trades. Chairman A.H.Bhiwandiwalla at the 7th Annual General Meeting held on 16th October 1955, mentioned that the company's ships carried 1,10,000 tons of wheat from Australia to India and also entered into contracts to lift 70,000 tons of sugar from the U.K. to Indian ports. The company's ships also carried, on trip charter basis, other overseas cargoes such as oil-cakes and iron ores from India to Europe, miscellaneous cargoes to Indonesia, fertilizers from the Continent to China, and iron ores from China to the Continent.

K.M. Sheth Takes Charge of Shipping Operations

In those days there was neither telex nor fax facility and the only form of urgent communication was either trunk call booking or exchange of LT, ordinary and urgent telegrams. K.M. Sheth used to go through the telegrams, consult Vasant Sheth and then give suitable replies. Vasant Sheth, quite satisfied with K.M. Sheth's way of handling operations, decided that he should handle the actual fleet operation.

Capital Structure and Dividends

The initial paid capital of the company in 1948 was a modest figure of Rs. 20 lakh. Since then the company capitalised the reserves and issued bonus shares of Rs. 10 lakh each twice in the financial years 1951-52 and 1955-56. The company also issued further equity shares on rights basis to existing shareholders for Rs. 20 lakh and preference shares of Rs. 25 lakh in the financial year 1954-55.

The paid-up capital of the Company thus stood at Rs. 85 lakh on 30 June 1956, out of which Rs. 60 lakh was equity share capital and Rs. 25 lakh preference share capital. In 1956-57 the company issued further equity shares of Rs. 60 lakh (6 lakh shares of Rs. 10 each) as right shares to the existing shareholders. Rs. 5 out of Rs. 10 per share were called up and paid. The company's paid-up share capital therefore on 30 June 1958 was Rs. 115 lakh, out of which Rs. 90 lakh was equity share capital and Rs. 25 lakh preference share capital.

The company paid a dividend of 5 per cent on the equity share capital for the very first year, that is, 1948-49. Thereafter it maintained, up to the year 1953-54, dividend at 10 per cent each year on its equity capital. For the year 1954-55, in lieu of dividend, it was decided to issue bonus shares which were isued to the shareholders in the year 1955-56. For the years 1955-56 and 1956-57, dividend at 15 per cent on the enlarged equity was paid to the shareholders. For the year 1957-58, dividend at 18 per cent was paid to the equity shareholders.

Progress During the Decade

The company began operations in 1948 by owning one ship of 10,680 DWT. At the end of five years the company owned five ships of 25,446 DWT (total). The cargo lifted by the company's ships (owned as well as chartered) during the first year amounted to 1,52,763 tons and the total freight earnings were Rs. 39.82 lakh. During the year 1952-53 the company's ships lifted a total cargo of 4,40,128 tons and the freight earnings amounted to Rs. 170.28 lakh. The cost of the fleet (one ship) in the first year was about Rs. 22 lakh. At the end of 5 years the cost of the fleet was Rs. 162 lakh. At the end of 10 years the company owned 14 ships with a DWT of 1,20,973 and the cost of the fleet had risen to Rs. 6 crore. The cargo liftings by the company's ships had gone up to 843,278 tons and the freight earnings amounted to Rs. 3.60 crore. The gross profit for the year 1948-49 was Rs. 5,58,000, for the year 1952-53 it had risen to Rs. 25,06,000 and for the year 1957-58 it was still higher at Rs. 1.21 crore. The net profit for the year 1948-49 was Rs. 3,02,000. It increased to Rs. 12,71,000 in the year 1952-53 and Rs. 64,97,000 in the year 1957-58.

The company, which started its operations with one owned ship of 7125 GRT in 1948, in the course of a decade, built up a fleet of 14 ships of 78,792 GRT as on 30 June 1958. The total Indian shipping fleet as on 31 December 1958 consisted of 143 ships of 6,47,812 GRT. The company therefore had a share in the Indian fleet of almost 10 per cent in terms of number of ships and of 12 per cent in terms of GRT. The company's freight earnings for the year ended 30 June 1958 were Rs. 3.60 crore. The total freight earnings of Indian shipping companies for the year 1957-58 amounted to Rs. 33.75 crore. The company's ships therefore had a share of 11% in terms of the freight earnings of the entire Indian fleet. The number of persons employed by the company including those manning the ships increased from 79 in 1948-49 to 840 in 1957-58.

Pioneers of Tramp Shipping

The company played a pioneering role in the field of tramp shipping in India. India's overseas trade largely consisted of bulk cargoes. This cargo was carried almost entirely in foreign ships. These bulk cargoes at that time were mainly imports of foodgrains and fertilizers and exports of coal, iron ore etc, and were suitable for carriage by tramp ships. In the early post war years the international bulk cargo trades, both dry as well as wet, increased tremendously and shipowners from countries like Norway and Greece who participated in the tramp trades prospered. There was great scope for India's shipping development in the tramp sector for carriage of bulk cargoes. It was Great Eastern Shipping Company which started participating in the tramp trades on a regular basis. Vasant Sheth, with his trading experience and instincts, did very well in tramp shipping operations, which were characterized by keen international competition. Compared with other Indian shipping companies, the company fared far better financially and also made significant contributions to the development of shipping in the first decade.

Other Indian shipping companies, quite apart from their involvement in the Indian coastal trade, were interested in India's overseas liner trades. The Scindia Steam Navigation Company, the premier Indian shipping company at that time, was most impressed and influenced by British liner shipping of the 1920s and 1930s, and wanted to concentrate on development of liner shipping in disregard of the circumstances which prevailed in post-war years, and which were specially applicable to Indian conditions. The volume of liner cargo was far less than that of tramp cargo in India's overseas trade. In shipping it is the volume of cargo and not the value of cargo which is important for employment of ships. Moreover, India's liner trades were controlled by the Shipping Conferences which were fully dominated by British and other foreign shipping companies. They were reluctant to admit Indian lines into the Conferences and even where they admitted them to the Conferences they gave them a very small proportion of the trade for carriage. The prospects for growth in liner shipping for Indian shipping companies were thus very limited. The Indian shipping companies and the government, which had been swayed and influenced by the views of liner minded shipping companies, had no understanding of the requirements of tramp shipping. The regulatory requirements of the government, like licensing of ships for specified trades and routes, rigid control on chartering in and out of ships, etc., which did not pose problems for coastal shipping companies and liner shipping companies, constituted obstacles in the progress of tramp shipping. The company therefore had to educate the other shipping companies and the government about the requirements of tramp shipping; this was a very slow process. In spite of this handicap the company played a significant role in the growth of Indian shipping by its pioneering role in tramp shipping in India.

As an illustration of the ignorance of the role of tramp shipping in the Indian shipping circles which prevailed at that time, one may quote the words "tramps are a dying breed" uttered by a senior spokesman of the Scindia Company at a meeting of the Indian National Steamship Owners' Association (INSOA now INSA). Vasant Sheth who was present at the meeting contradicted the statement and challenged the Scindia Company's spokesman to justify by facts and figures the derogatory expression he had used about tramp shipping. Vasant Sheth also wrote a letter which was published in *Indian Shipping* (the official journal of INSOA). In this letter he pointed out that far from being a dying breed, tramp shipping played a very important role in international trade and therefore had a great future.

With bulk cargoes being dominant in India's dry cargo seaborne trade, adequate development of Indian shipping could take place only if ships were acquired by Indian shipping companies for this trade. It was Great Eastern which first opened the doors for operations and growth of this type of shipping and other Indian shipping companies also followed suit, leading to the growth of bulk cargo shipping in India. It was also Great Eastern's handsome financial results, which benefited its shareholders greatly, which acted as a spur and encouragement to entrepreneurs and businessmen to start shipping companies and acquire shipping tonnage.

Company "Firsts"

The company had many "firsts" to its credit. After the Second World War, when Japan was defeated and her economy shattered, shipping companies were reluctant to place orders for the construction of ships in Japan. The Japanese were however making all-out efforts to rehabilitate their economy. The Japanese ship-building industry was also making efforts to build ships for their own requirements and also for export. In fact the ship-building prices in Japan were much lower than those in traditional ship-building countries like U.K. Great Eastern was the first Indian company to place orders for construction of two ships, m.v. *Jag Ganga* and m.v. *Jag Jamna* in Japan at very favourable prices in 1950-51.

In the early 1950s, oil refineries were being established by foreign oil companies in India. At that time it was estimated that about 18 lakh tons of refined products would have to be distributed annually in tankers plying on the coast. This coastal oil cargo was almost equal to two thirds of the coastal dry cargo at that time and could support a substantial tonnage. The Indian fleet did not contain a single tanker at that time either for the overseas trade or the coastal trade. Great Eastern was the first Indian company to purchase a motor tanker, *Bianca* of 8283.87 GRT (13125 DWT) in March 1956, which was delivered to the company in April 1956 for operation in the coastal trade. The vessel was purchased at a cost of Rs. 89,13,000 and renamed *Jag Jyoti* and given on time charter to the Stanvac Oil Refinery.

It is interesting to recall that the government was hesitant to give approval to the acquisition of a tanker by Great Eastern in spite of the fact that it was the first and only company to have approached the government for their approval to the acquistion of a tanker.

The then Shipping and Transport Minister, the late Lal Bahadur Shastri, informed Vasant Sheth when he met him in Delhi that permission to acquire the tanker would be given to the company only if it agreed to the condition that the ownership of the tanker would be handed over to a public sector company if the government so decided later. Vasant Sheth replied that he would consult his elders on phone, and convey the outcome to the Minister later on the same day. He went back to the hotel where he was staying and after some time returned and told the Minister that the company would agree to the condition which was being laid down by the government.

Thereafter the government did not permit private sector shipping companies to acquire tankers for some time (until Dr. Jayanti Dharma Teja came on the scene with his Jayanti Shipping Company). Great Eastern therefore could not acquire more tankers during this decade.

India faced a difficult foreign exchange situation from 1957-58. The government stopped the release of foreign exchange for payment of the cost of ships to be acquired from abroad. Under these adverse circumstances, the company was the first to initiate the self financing scheme and acquire ships under it. The company purchased a secondhand ship, *Chepman*, for about Rs. 41 lakh. The ship was renamed *Jag Janani.* The ship was paid for by arranging a loan with a foreign bank and placing an equivalent rupee deposit as security with its Bombay office. The loan was to be repaid out of the net foreign exchange earnings of the ship herself. The company was not only the first to acquire a ship under the self-financing scheme but also to acquire the largest number of ships under the scheme at that time. It bought five ships in this way at that time.

The company was also the first to have a 12,970 DWT dry cargo ship m.v. *Jag Laxmi*, built to order which when delivered in February 1957 was the largest dry cargo ship on the Indian Registry at that time. A motor ship, *Jag Jiwan*, a still larger dry cargo ship of about 14,000 tons, was also ordered to be built at a German yard during the first decade of the company's existence and when delivered it was to be the largest ship on the Indian Registry.

Chartering of Ships

It is the business acumen and trading instincts, due to the commercial background which the Sheth family possessed, that led to the success of the company in the first decade of its existence. Time chartering of ships, which amounts to buying freight wholesale and then fixing them on voyage charters voyage by voyage, which amounts to selling freight in retail, was resorted to right from the inception of the company. In the first three years of its existence, the company employed more time chartered tonnage than own tonnage in its operations. Thereafter, as the company's own tonnage grew year by year, the chartered tonnage, although less than own tonnage, still formed a good part of the total tonnage employed by the company.

The authorities in India now recognise that timing of purchase and sale of ships in the cyclical shipping industry is of crucial importance in successful operation of shipping companies, and must be left to be decided by the commercial judgement of the shipowners. Ships purchased at low prices with their low capital costs greatly contribute to the profitable operation of the ships. Secondly, profits made on purchase and sale of ships constitute a very important avenue for augmenting the profitability of the shipping business.

In those early years, when there was no awareness in India of the importance of profits on purchase and sale of ships, the management of Great Eastern earned surpluses on purchase and sale of ships. For example, *Lake Geneva*, which was renamed *Jag Rani*, was purchased at a price of about Rs. 8,63,000 in the year 1949-50 and sold in the year 1950-51 at a price of Rs. 15,76,000.

The company also developed a very good agency business and acted as agents for many foreign shipping companies. By securing the agencies of the Yamashita Line of Japan and Hellenic Lines of Piraeus and New York, the company's agency business grew considerably. During the calendar year 1956 the company handled more than 100 ships as agents in Indian ports. The vessels of the Hellenic Lines, which were sailing from Indian ports to the U.S. ports, and the vessels of the Yamashita Lines and a number of tramp operators which called at Indian ports, brought agency revenue to the company. Agencies of foreign shipowners provided the company with very valuable exposure to the operations and strategies of shipowners like P. G. Callimanopolis of Hellenic Lines and J. Billmair of Stanhope Shipping Company, who possessed very interesting know-how and ideas in respect of shipping, and the company benefited by coming in contact with them.

The company would have earned far more and expanded its shipping fleet speedily, had it not been for the obstacles it encountered because of the rigid regulatory policies of the government. The proposals made by the company for time chartering out of its own ships were disapproved by the government. Referring to the company's proposal to time charter out its ship *Jag Laxmi* at very favourable rates prevailing in the first half of 1957, which was rejected by the government, Chairman A.H. Bhiwandiwalla, in his speech at the 9th Annual General Meeting of the company held on 28 November 1957, observed: "This vessel alone then would have earned net foreign exchange annually of the order of Sterling Pounds 375,000. Your company would have earned back the whole cost of the ship, viz. Rs. 1.20 crore, in about 2 years. The company's net earnings and country's net foreign exchange earnings in 2 years on this vessel would have been sufficient to purchase another ship costing as much as *Jag Laxmi.* The foreign exchange famine has jeopardized the success of the Five-year Plan itself and it saddens my heart that owing to the dogmatic approach on the part of the Government such splendid opportunities for earning foreign exchange were missed." Since the freight rates declined steeply from 1958 and continued to remain at low levels almost up to 1963, the time chartering out of the company's ships in 1957 would have ensured high and stable earnings for the company even in the shipping recession and would have accelerated the expansion of tramp shipping.

Contracts of affreightment form an important part of the tramp shipping business. The company, even during its infancy, entered into contracts of affreightment, such as a contract for carriage of 1,10,000 tons of Australian wheat to India and a contract for carriage of 70,000 tons of sugar from the U.K. to India. The company contracted for carriage of 52,000 tons of Australian wooden sleepers and 30,000 tons of fertilizers from Europe and about a similar quantity of fertilizers from Japan and China. The State Trading Corporation in 1956 contracted with Japanese steel mills for the sale of 7.2 million tons of iron ore without asking Indian shipping interests whether they would be interested in carrying part of the cargo. The sale was effected on f.o.b. basis and the control of the carriage of cargo was transferred to Japanese hands in spite of the State Trading Corporation's commitment to protect the interests of Indian shipping.

Great Eastern acted quickly and directly contacted the Japanese steel mills. Okura Trading Company (at that time known as Kishimoto Shoten), brokers of the Japanese steel mills, had floated a global tender for carriage of 60,000 tons of iron ore from India to Japan. Great Eastern won the tender and successfully carried out the contract for the carriage of iron ore. This was the beginning of a long relationship that the company developed with the Japanese steel mills. Thereafter the company has been carrying large quantities of iron ore from India to Japan for the Japanese steel mills.

In the initial years, as mentioned earlier, many times the promoters of the company, A.H.Bhiwandiwalla and Company, purchased salt in bulk on their account and provided the company's ships with salt cargo on their return voyage from Saurashtra ports to Calcutta. The company also floated a subsidiary company, Jagat Trading Company Private Limited, which could trade in commodities and goods with a view to providing cargoes for the company's ships in their coastal voyages.

Vasant Sheth's Dynamic Management

Vasant Sheth was not only responsible for getting the release and allotment of the first ship from the U.S. Maritime Commission, but also took charge of the new company's management as director as well as director of the Managing Agents who managed the company. He was a young man of 19 years when he began to manage the company's first ship, *SS Fort Elice*, renamed *Jag Vijay*. His father Jagjiwan Ujamshi and uncle Maneklal Ujamshi did not attend the company's office regularly. However, their guidance was always available.

Arthur S. Lall, who met Maneklal Ujamshi at a party soon after being appointed the first Director General of Shipping in 1949, asked him how they had placed such a young boy in charge of a shipping company, and said that they should have appointed a more mature and experienced person to manage the company. But at the end of his tenure, he took back his words. He had dealt with Vasant Sheth, and had come to believe that they could not have found a better person than him to manage the company.

With the company making good progress and impressed by the qualities of Vasant Sheth, Indian shipowners elected him as President of the Indian National Steamshipowners' Association (INSOA, now INSA) in 1956. At 29 he was the youngest President of the Association.

In an appraisal of the first decade of the Company's operation, it must be recorded that it was the vision, dynamism and leadership of Vasant Sheth which largely contributed to the laying of the solid foundation of the Company and in achieving growth and stability for the Company.

Great Eastern's Board of Directors decided to grant K.M. Sheth Power of Attorney on 2 May 1952 and appointed him as Manager effective from 1 October 1952.

K. M. Sheth ably assisted Vasant Sheth in the management of the company. The important role that he was to play of looking after the employment of the company's ships and the management of shipping operations took shape during this decade. He increasingly took over the responsibilities for fixing ships for their employment and for the day-to-day management of the company.

Several capable persons manned the company's decks. Dr. Sudhir Sen, economist (and amongst other things one-time Economic Adviser to Vijayalaxmi Pandit when she was the Indian Ambassador to Russia) joined the company as General Manager in 1954. He remained with the company for two years. He left the company to join the United Nations service. During his two years of service with the company he prepared a number of memoranda and representations on the role and requirements of tramp shipping, ably and eloquently setting out the company's case for development of tramp shipping.

T. M. Sanghavi, who joined the company on 7 November 1952, was a young engineer. He was put in charge of all technical matters including supervision of maintenance and repair of ships, floating personnel and technical aspects of new building projects (ships). He carried out his assignments competently. He was son-in-law of the late Maneklal Ujamshi who was the founder director of the Company.

S. N. Sanklecha became the Company Secretary in 1951. He was the company's draftsman who prepared various representations to the government and most of the Chairman's speeches during this decade, and assisted Vasant Sheth in educating the shipowners and the government on formulating policies which would not place hurdles in the development of tramp shipping.

B. N. Adappa joined the company in 1952 and competently handled ships operations and floating personnel. Recognising his ability for hard and conscientious work, the management gave him the onerous responsibilities of assisting K. M. Sheth in managing the employment and operations of ships.

Measures of Assistance which Brought about Growth of Indian Shipping

The Annual General Meeting of INSOA was to be held on 17 December 1957 and the then Transport Minister Lal Bahadur Shastri was invited to inaugurate the meeting. Vasant Sheth's Presidential speech dealing comprehensively with the problem of the shipping industry was prepared with great care. The speech was sent in advance to Lal Bahadur Shastri. Shastri, conscientious as he was, came fully prepared to respond to Vasant Sheth's speech. Shastri announced three epoch making measures of assistance, which have been responsible for the growth of the shipping industry in India. He announced the constitution of a non-lapsable Shipping Development Fund Committee (SDFC) to provide a perennial source of finance for acquisition of ships to the industry. A subsidised interest rate of 3 per cent per annum would be levied by the SDFC on loans advanced to shipping companies for purchase of coasta ships as well as overseas ships. He also announced the setting up of Shipping Co-ordination Committee for ensuring availability of government owned and controlled cargoes to Indian ships. He also conveyed the government's decision to raise the Development Rebate Allowance on acquisition of ships from 25 per cent to a higher figure. The Development Rebate Allowance, which was in addition to the 100 per cent depreciation and which could be claimed by a company for taxation purposes, enabled the shipping companies to build up reserves by securing exemption from tax which would otherwise have been payable, and thus assisted the shipping companies in expanding their fleets. Sir Ramaswamy Mudaliar in his vote of thanks at the meeting stated that Lal Bahadur Shastri's speech was a historic speech as the concessions announced by the Minister were not merely hopes for the shipping companies but pointed to a very optimistic future. The announcements marked a turn in the tide for the shipping industry, which could now equip itself with more tonnage to meet the demands of shippers in India as well as overseas.

Prophecy about Mr. Shashtri becoming Prime Minister

There was an interesting anecdote. Vasant Sheth arranged a dinner party in honour of Lal Bahadur Shastri at his residence. Leading shipowners and industrialists were invited to the party. Naval Tata who had a hobby of reading palms of men and predicting their future read Lal Bahadur Shashtri's palm and said : "Sir, you will become the Prime Minister of India". This prophecy did come true. After Jawaharlal Nehru's death Lal Bahadur Shashtri became the Prime Minister of India.

Constraints on the Growth of the Company

In the post-war years up to 1957, international shipping enjoyed much prosperity. Since 1948, there was tremendous expansion in world trade. The world's sea-borne trade increased from 490 million metric tons in 1948 to 960 million metric tons in 1957, a 96 per cent rise. The world's sea-borne trade in dry cargo, which was 280 million metric tons in 1948, increased to 540 million metric tons in 1957. The dry cargo trade rose by 93 per cent. The oil trade increased from 210 million metric tons in 1948 to 420 million metric tons in 1957, that is by 100 per cent over the 1948 level. Shipping as a consequence entered into prosperous times. During 1948-57 world dry cargo tonnage expanded by 23 per cent whilst world tanker tonnage recorded an increase of 100 per cent.

During this period two events enhanced demand for shipping tonnage. The Korean war in 1951 enhanced demand for shipping tonnage for stock piling and military requirements. The Suez Canal crisis in 1956 led to the closure of the canal, and increased demand for shipping—actual as well as anticipated—with the lenghtening of sea routes. There was optimism all round in shipping circles. Indian shipping companies, however, with the exception of Great Eastern Shipping Company, could not participate in the general prosperity because their activities were restricted to coastal shipping and liner shipping in India's overseas trade.

Great Eastern could benefit because of its participation in the tramp trades. However, the company was not exclusively a tramp shipping company. It also had other interests such as a sizeable share in the coastal and adjacent trades and also a tanker in the coastal trade on a long term time charter with an oil refining company. The company's fortunes were tied to the conditions in these trades. Moreover, the government's regulatory procedures, framed as they were without understanding or appreciation of the requirements of tramp trades, hindered the growth of the company.

Licensing Procedure for Ships

The major obstacle faced by tramp operators was the procedure for licensing of ships followed by the government. During war time, control on movement and employment of ships was ensured by utilising the system of licences. This control was continued in peace time under the Control of Shipping Act 1947. Licences issued by the Directorate General of Shipping to ships made them eligible for operations in the coastal trade or specified overseas liner trades. A specified voyage licence had to be obtained from the Directorate General of Shipping for each voyage of an owned ship operating in the international tramp trades.

Ships trading on the Indian coast and those plying in fixed liner trades had no difficulty in following the licensing procedure, since the companies knew the areas of operation in advance. However, tramp ships traded on a world-wide basis according to availability of full shiploads of cargo. A tramp ship might be fixed to carry a cargo of coal from America to Europe, from Europe a cargo of fertilizers might be available to an Indian destination. After discharge of fertilizers at an Indian port the ship could load a cargo of ore, say for Japan. The licence could be applied for only after the vessel was fixed for particular employment. However, paradoxically, the employment itself could not be fixed without obtaining the government's prior approval. Since there was an international tramp market where a large number of tramp operators tendered for carriage of particular cargoes, business had often to be fixed on telephone or by cable. Delay meant in many cases loss of business, which was secured by a tramp operator in another country who could be more prompt.

Time Chartering of Foreign Flag Ships

Similarly, sometimes foreign ships were required to be chartered by a tramp operator who had to maintain flexibility of operation. He might be able to locate a particular ship which was free at or near the port where the tramp operator wanted to employ her for carriage of cargo. The ship might be available at a very advantageous rate of charter hire. However, the tramp operator in India could not fix the charter immediately because he had to obtain the approval of the Directorate General of Shipping and Reserve Bank of India to these charters. Meanwhile the foreign vessel might have been fixed for another employment and would not be available to the Indian operator. These procedural difficulties made efficient tramp operation very difficult.

Ban on Time Chartering to Foreign Parties

Further, there was opposition to and a ban on time chartering out of Indian ships to foreign parties. The purpose of government loans, it was stated, was to augment Indian tonnage so that cargo in India's own trades could be increasingly carried by Indian ships, whereas hiring out of ships to other parties would defeat this purpose. This was a misconceived view of the shipping industry and ran counter to important business considerations. Two way time chartering was an integral part of shipping, especially tramp shipping. At times it was particularly useful in covering business risks.

The advantages in time chartering out of ships were many. A charter executed in a period of profitable rates remained profitable even when voyage charter rates fell. The employment of the vessel being secured, managerial capacity was free to attend to other vessels, thus increasing the tonnage that one management could handle. Time charters, once executed, involved few risks for the shipowner and provided a cushion for earnings in bad periods. A judicious mixture of ships on voyage charter and time charter enabled a tramp operator to enjoy greater stability of earnings than if all the ships were on voyage charter. He could then borrow with impunity as a more highly geared capital could be used than was safe for a company engaged only in operation in the voyage charter market. Time chartering out of ships was therefore a very important device for bringing about expansion of the fleet at a faster rate. Proposals made by the company for time chartering out its own ships were, however, disapproved by the government.

In sum, the freedom and flexibility of operation, which is the very *sine qua non* of efficient tramp operations and is fully permitted and encouraged in all established maritime countries, was denied to Great Eastern. Issue of global licences to ships operating in tramp trades or coastal-cum-tramp trades could have solved the problem faced by Great Eastern, which was operating in tramp trades and coastal-cum-tramp trades. The government however did not agree to issue of global licences at that time. In respect of chartering in of foreign ships and chartering out of Indian ships also, the government policy was most unhelpful.

Company's Participation in the Coastal Trade

As a substantial part of the operations of the company's ships was in the coastal trade, the fortunes of the company were influenced by the conditions of the coastal trade. Since the reservation of coastal trade for Indian shipping companies in 1950, coastal trading did give satisfactory returns for a period of about four years, up to 1954. However, there was stagnation in coal shipments, which formed almost 40 per cent of the total coastal trade. The increased costs of operation could not be met by increase in coastal freight rates, which were controlled by the government.

As these factors were adversely affecting the fortunes of Indian coastal shipping, the government appointed the Rail-Sea Co-ordination Committee in June 1955. The Committee submitted its report in April 1957. It had come to the conclusion that the rates were uneconomic for coastal shipping and therefore recommended a general increase of 15 per cent in the freight fates over those in force prior to 15 October 1955, an increase in sea-borne coal movement by 6 lakh tons, diversion of cargoes like foodgrains, cement, fertilizers, iron and steel from rail to sea etc. Subject to certain reservations, the government accepted the recommendations regarding increase in freight rates. However, other recommendations for improving the sea-borne movement of coastal cargo were not implemented. The quantum of 15 per cent increase in coastal freight rates allowed to coastal shipping was soon found inadequate due to mounting costs of operating vessels, and serious delays and detention to ships at coastal ports.

The coastal tanker acquired by Great Eastern and given on time charter to Stanvac Oil Refinery was earning satisfactorily for the company. However, the government did not allow the company to acquire more tankers. It was a public sector shipping company which alone was permitted to acquire tankers for coastal trade. Had things been different, Great Eastern would have acquired more tankers at this time, which would have further strengthened its financial position and contributed to the expansion of its shipping tonnage.

Failure to Build the Tramp Fleet Responsible for slow Growth of Indian Shipping and Inability to share in International Shipping Boom

So while shipping companies practically all over the world were making large profits and paying good dividends to their shareholders, Indian shipping companies, with the exception of Great Eastern, could not prosper. Their annual accounts did not make encouraging reading; their shareholders received very small amounts by way of dividends. No wonder therefore that the shares of almost all Indian shipping companies, with the exception of Great Eastern, were quoted below par and the investing public shied away from these companies. Confined to the sheltered coastal trade where their fleets could not be operated at maximum efficiency, and to a few liner trades where they perforce had to play a subservient role, the only way shipping companies could make rapid progress in the development of Indian mercantile marine was through the growth of tramp fleets. Despite the various fetters outlined earlier, Great Eastern played a pioneering role by undertaking tramp operations and building up a nucleus tramp fleet, and by trying to educate shipping interests as well as authorities about the requirements and importance of tramp shipping.

OWNED VESSELS IN THE FIRST DECADE

S.No.	Vessel Name	Built	DWT	GRT	Period during which owned and operated by the company
1.	S.S. JAG VIJAY	1942	10670	7125	1948-60
*2.	S.S. JAG RANI (1)	1928	8010	4410	1949-51
3.	M.V. JAG GANGA	1951	2008	1527	1951-
4.	M.V. JAG JAMNA	1951	2008	1527	1951-66
5.	S.S. JAG RANI (II)	1952	8010	5103	1952-65
*6.	S.S. JAG BINDU	1942	2740	1791	1953-55
7.	M.V. JAG LAADKI	1942	10200	7268	1953-65
8.	S.S. JAG SHANTI	1942	9395	6331	1954-61
9.	S.S. JAG TARA	1954	7000	3982	1955-65
10.	M.T. JAG JYOTI	1948	13125	8284	1956-66
11.	S.S. JAG JANANI	1944	8960	6140	1957-60
12.	M.V. JAG LAXMI	1957	12970	8798	1957-76
13.	S.S. JAG SEVAK	1940	8970	4843	1958-65
14.	S.S. JAG MATA	1940	8910	4904	1958-63
15.	JAG DEVI	1943	8710	5988	1958-63
16.	JAG DOOT	1948	10037	6972	1958-66

* S.S. JAG RANI (I) and S.S. JAG BINDU were sold in 1951 and 1955 respectively and therfore did not form part of the fleet which consisted of 14 vessels as on 30 June 1958. The total GRT and DWT of these 14 vessels amounted to 78,792 GRT and 1,20,973 DWT respectively.

REFERENCES

1. 100A1 Lloyds Register April 1988 issue. Article entitled 'Greek Shipping- Top of the League.'

2. *The Oxford Companion to Ships and the Sea* Edited by Peter Kemp, Oxford University Press, 1988, pp. 352, 353.

3

The Second Decade
1958-1968

The world shipping recession which prevailed from 1958 to 1963 together with the dismally uneconomic trading conditions on the Indian coast affected the fortunes of shipping companies in India badly.

Shipping Recession

The year 1957 signalled a reversal of fortunes for international shipping, which had been enjoying an era of prosperity. With the reopening of the Suez Canal, the demand for shipping tonnage tapered off, especially because a good deal of stockpiling had been resorted to during the Suez crisis. Also an unusually mild winter in Europe meant that the requirements of fuel in Europe were less than anticipated. The supply of shipping tonnage had increased more than indicated by its volume because faster and more superior vessels had been built. In 1958, the dry cargo trade, which had been continuously increasing since 1948, for the first time decreased by 9 per cent. The oil trade, which had been increasing since 1948 at an average annual rate of over 11 per cent, increased only by 5 per cent in 1958. The total world seaborne trade, which had been growing at an average annual rate exceeding 10 per cent since 1948, registered a decline of 3 per cent over its 1957 level. Since there is always a considerable time-lag between the adjustment of tonnage supply to the demand, as ships ordered with the shipyards are delivered after some time, the supply of total shipping tonnage increased by 7 per cent in 1958 and 6 per cent in 1959 as compared with the immediately preceding years. The tanker tonnage increases were 13 per cent in 1958 and 12 per cent in 1959. The non-tanker tonnage increased by 5 per cent in 1958 over the 1957 level and by 4 per cent in 1959 over the 1958 level. The world sea-borne trade resumed its upward trend from 1959 onwards. There was, however, also expansion of the world shipping fleet. The shipping industry continued to be in the doldrums almost until the end of the third quarter of 1963.

In view of a steep fall in the freight rates, a large number of ships, especially old ships, were laid up because shipping companies owning them would sustain higher losses by operating these ships at the prevailing freight rates than by laying them up. A.H. Bhiwandiwalla, the then Chairman of the company, in his speech at the company's Annual General Meeting held on 12 December 1958 said that out of the total estimated world tramp tonnage of about 20 million GRT, 5.2 million GRT, that is, over one fourth of the total dry cargo tramp tonnage, was laid up.

Coastal Trade

The coastal freight rates were controlled by the government. The increase in the freight rates granted by the Rail-Sea Co-ordination Committee fell short of the rise in operating costs, which continued to increase. Indian shipping companies were finding it most uneconomic to carry coastal cargoes at the prevailing freight rates. The paucity of the cargo on the coast and uneconomic freight rates had created conditions bordering on a crisis for coastal shipping. Chairman A.H.Bhiwandiwalla at the 13th Annual General Meeting of the company held on 12 December 1961 summed up the situation: "I think we must now all face the fact that the coastal trade is on the verge of collapse. Shipping companies that have operated predominantly on the coast have lost heavily; their resources are wiped out and many of them are fast using up the capital." As only a part of the company's fleet was engaged in coastal trading, and one of them was a coastal tanker earning a satisfactory rate on time charter, the impact was much less severe for the company.

In 1961 and subsequent years, the government appointed successively Commissions/persons to go into the coastal freight structure and make recommendations for increase in freight rates. On the recommendation of the one-man R.G. Abbhi Commission, the government decided in May 1962 to increase the freight rates by 15 per cent, with the exception for coal from Calcutta to ports up to and including Cochin, for which 10 per cent increase was made applicable. Thereafter, on the recommendation of T.S. Parasuraman for a 5 per cent increase in the freight rates, the government decided in July 1965 to grant an increase of 10 per cent. In 1966 and 1967 the Maritime Freight Commission conducted a freight rates inquiry and made their recommendations, the contents of which were not disclosed to shipping companies. The government in July 1967 decided to grant an increase of 10 per cent in freight rates.

The procedures adopted by the government to sanction the increase in rates involved inordinate delay and by the time the government sanctioned the increases, the costs of operation had escalated further, rendering the revised rates obsolete and uneconomical and subjecting coastal operations to continuing losses. A number of Indian shipping companies, mostly plying their ships on the coast, either closed down their business or went into liquidation during this or the next decade. These included the following companies: Ambica Steam Navigation Company Ltd, Ashok Lines Ltd, Ambassador Steamship Company Ltd, Bharat Lines Ltd, Chandbali Steam Navigation Company Ltd, Hindustan Steamship Company Ltd, Gill Amin & Company Ltd, Meridian Steamship Co Ltd, Merchant Steam Navigation Co Ltd, P.C. Ray & Co (Bengal Line).

It was therefore a prudent policy which Great Eastern followed in progressively decreasing its participation in coastal shipping.

Public Sector - Private Sector

Another great handicap which the company suffered was the discrimination shown by the government in favour of the public sector shipping corporations in the allotment of government owned and controlled cargoes, in the discriminatory rates of freight, entry to Conferences, grant of control and management to the public sector corporations where both the corporations and the company had contracted for the carriage of cargo, etc. The Eastern Shipping Corporation, which was established in 1950 in the joint sector, became a public sector company, with Scindias relinquishing the managing agency in 1957 as a result of some provisions of the new Companies Act 1956. Another public sector Corporation, Western Shipping Corporation, was established in 1956. The two corporations merged into the Shipping Corporation of India in 1961.

Chairman A.H. Bhiwandiwalla, in his speeches at the Annual General Meetings of the company pointed out several instances of discriminatory treatment in favour of the public sector corporations, and the harm this had done to the company. A look at some of the specific instances: Indian railways' cargo of wheel sets from Japan for which the company had first offered its owned ship which was ready to load the cargo was not allotted to the company's ship. The cargo was allotted by the Indian Embassy in Japan to a foreign ship chartered by the Shipping Corporation. The country lost precious foreign exchange, and the company's owned ship lay idle for a long time. The company had to utilise this time for carrying out special survey repairs about three months in advance. A part cargo of 3,000 tons was loaded by the company's ship after an inordinate delay because its original full cargo was wrongfully allotted to the chartered vessel of the Corporation and the company's vessel had to wait for a month to get this further cargo which was beyond the capacity of the Corporation's chartered vessel to take. The Corporation being essentially a liner company at that time was not entitled to carriage of these tramp cargoes when ships of a tramp shipping company were available; moreover, it was beyond its capacity to cater to any large scale movement of tramp cargoes.

In another instance, the government Shipping Corporation and the company had jointly contracted in the proportion of 70 per cent and 30 per cent respectively for the carriage of about 175,000 tons of wooden sleepers cargo from Australia to India for the Railways. The berthing of ships was to be co-ordinated by mutual consultation between the Corporation and the company. However, the Corporation kept booking cargoes out of this quantity and lifting them from Australia in two or three of their ships without prior reference to the company. Thereafter the company too booked a full shipload of cargo and ballasted s. s. *Jag Vijay* from Calcutta to Australia. But when the vessel was about to reach Australia, the government Corporation made the Railway Ministry issue instructions to the Australian shippers that the cargo that was booked for *Jag Vijay* should be held back for a ship of the Corporation which was calling at the Australian ports at a later date. s. s. *Jag Vijay* idled in Australia for a few days, and the company was compelled to send the vessel away from Australia without any cargo for another employment.

Instead of the previously agreed joint control of both the

government Shipping Corporation and Great Eastern, the Railway Ministry had left the entire control over the contracted cargo, including that to be carried by the company's ships, in the hands of the Corporation.

Great Eastern's ships had become the regular carriers of iron ore to Japan. The company was also endeavouring to get return cargoes from Japan to India. Shipping Corporation of India was a member of the Bay of Bengal/Japan/Bay of Bengal Conference in which the foreign lines dominated. For government owned or controlled cargoes the government gave higher rates of freight to the Shipping Corporation and other foreign members of the Conference and lower freight rates to Great Eastern. An unfair discrimination, because the company provided the government and the shippers with exactly the same service provided by the Shipping Corporation. The company gave them as many sailings as regularly as any conference line did.

If the company had not provided its ships to carry the cargo at the reduced freight rates, the government would have been compelled to pay the higher freight rates to foreign shipping companies who were members of the conference and also would lose that much foreign exchange.

The company was serving the India-Japan-India trade regularly for a number of years. The company had established itself in these trades after six years of hard work and effort. It was therefore shocking to find that the company's application for membership of the Conference was rejected. The company's interests were not taken into account nor was it consulted before an arrangement in regard to the Japan-India trade was arrived at under the auspices of the government.

Chairman A.H.Bhiwandiwalla at the 14th Annual General Meeting of the Company held on 20 December 1962 put it succinctly : "The Estimates Committee of the Parliament in their Report declared that the Government-owned Eastern Shipping Corporation Ltd., which is now the Shipping Corporation of India Ltd., would support our membership of the Conference catering to the trade between Japan and India. In view of this pronouncement we were trying for the last two years to secure membership of the Conference. Pending our admission to the membership of the Conference, our ships were only given overflow of the Government cargo moving from Japan to India after the ships of The Shipping Corporation of India Ltd., were filled up. Since we were likely to secure admission to the Conference, we refrained from encroaching on Conference cargoes which we could have, by quoting lower rates of freight. We confined ourselves to the 'overflow' and carriage of full load cargoes which could be carried economically by tramp ships. Not only has our application been rejected but also the present trend of Government thinking appears to be towards offering the overflow cargoes to foreign conference members and not to us which is contrary to what was done in the interim period. The Members of the Conference, with the exception of the Shipping Corporation of India Ltd., which is the only Indian Company, are foreign shipping companies. If this arrangement remains unchanged we shall be wiped out of existence from the Japan-India trade." The company had to withdraw from the Japan-India trade.

The government gave the government-owned cargoes for carriage to members of the Conferences of which a few Indian lines or the Shipping Corporation were members but with a very limited stake. In such cases the government many times gave the cargoes for carriage to foreign members of the Conferences in preference to Indian lines which were not members of the Conference. However the government disregarded this criterion in the Near Trades Conference of which all the members were Indian lines. They allowed the ships of Shipping Corporation which was not a member of this Conference to lift Burma rice on their way from Far East to India.

The government was guilty of double standards in regard to the shipment of government cargoes by Indian ships. If the ship belonged to Shipping Corporation which was not a member of the Conference the government was not worried about the niceties of the Conference trade even if the members of the Conference were all Indian shipping companies. However, if the ship belonged to an Indian company participating in tramp trades, like Great Eastern, the government gave the cargo to a foreign ship belonging to a Conference member, in preference to an Indian ship.

The government partiality towards and discrimination in favour of the public sector corporation assumed such serious proportions that the Chairman A.H.Bhiwandiwalla commented at the 13th Annual General Meeting of the Company held on 21 December 1961 that "All Government cargoes are offered first to the Shipping Corporation of India, and, if there is any overflow, it is offered to the Great Eastern Shipping Co. or any other line. Frequently, this policy is inconvenient to the consignees of cargo as it has to wait for the Shipping Corporation's vessels before it is shipped. Besides the Government today is perhaps the largest single importer in this country. If, therefore, they follow a policy of preferring the Shipping Corporation of India to other Indian Companies . . . there will come a stage when the only company that can expand with any degree of confidence will be the Shipping Corporation of India. Although we welcome any expansion in the public sector, we believe that there is room for expansion for the private sector as well, provided the government encourages both equally.

"Besides it would be a most unfortunate policy for any Government to follow to discriminate in favour of independent public sector units in a mixed economy. If public sector steel mills use public sector banks and Government Ministries use public sector shipping Companies, regardless of all commercial considerations then there seems to be no point in setting up independent public sector corporations; they may as well become a supply depot to the Government."

Profitability Comparison

In spite of all the government patronage to The Shipping Corporation in respect of cargoes and partiality and discrimination in their favour in other respects, the profitability achieved by Great Eastern as indicated by the rate of return on capital employed was not only higher than the two largest shipping companies of that time in the private sector, namely, Scindias and India Steamships, but also higher than that of Shipping Corporation of India.

The Committee on Public Undertakings (1971-72) of Parliament in their 20th Report[1], which was on the Shipping Corporation of India, have given a comparative statement for 10 years from 1961-62 (from the inception of the Shipping Corporation of India) to 1970-71, giving the figures for year-wise capital employed, return thereon, and the latter expressed as a percentage of the former for each of the 10 years. They have also summarised the comparative position of the average return as shown below:

Name of the Company	Percentage of Average Return on Capital Employed from 1961-62 to 1970-71
The Shipping Corporation of India	8.17%
The Scindia Steam Navigation Co. Ltd.	6.22%
The India Steamship Co. Ltd.	4.49%
The Great Eastern Shipping Co. Ltd.	9.28%

Company's Office

It was in the beginning of this decade, in August 1958, that the company shifted its head office in Bombay from Royal Insurance Building at Jamshedji Tata Road to Mercantile Bank Building (now renamed Honkong Bank Building) at 60, Mahatma Gandhi Road, Flora Fountain, in the Fort area, which was the most prominent business locality in Bombay. For over three decades this continued to be the company's headquarters.

Residential Accommodation for Executives and Senior Officers

The company purchased a plot of land on Mount Napean Road for about Rs. 30 lakh for constructing two buildings to provide accommodation to its executives and senior officers.

The two buildings were constructed and after keeping the flats for housing the executives and senior officers, the remaining flats were sold to outsiders. Later a housing co-operative society was formed for the two buildings. These two buildings, named Manek and Jiwan, are among the best residential buildings in Bombay. The company used its own funds for the construction of these two buildings and did not utilise even a rupee from the loans given by the Shipping Development Fund Committee (SDFC) for acquisition of ships. The sale of the flats not required by the company more than met the entire cost of land and buildings, and the company got the flats for its requirements free. This excellent housing facility for the key personnel of the company helped to ensure the continuity of their service with the company.

Death of Founders

It was in the first half of this decade, when the going was not good for shipping companies, that the founders of Great Eastern, Maneklal Ujamshi and Jagjiwan Ujamshi Mulji, passed away. Maneklal Ujamshi, who was born on 24 July 1884, died on 22 April 1959; Jagjiwan Ujamshi Mulji, who was born on 10 August 1889, died on 5 July 1959. Maneklal Ujamshi was director of the company since its inception and also director of the Managing Agents of the company. Both brothers besides being founders, had made a significant contribution to the growth of the company. After their deaths, the company was deprived of their valuable guidance based upon their keen business acumen and mature judgement.

Entry Into Overseas Liner Trades

In India's most important liner trade at that time, the India-UK Continent Liner trade, which was controlled by the UK-India Continent Liner Conference, there were two Indian lines who were members of the Conference, and were participating in these trades—The Scindia Steam Navigation Company and India Steamships. There was scope as well as necessity for another Indian participant in this liner trade. Great Eastern therefore applied for membership of this Conference and hoped that the two Indian lines which were members of the Conference would support its application. It was learnt that the company's proposal for membership was opposed by the foreign lines who were members of the Conference. Surprisingly, the Indian members of the Conference too did not support the company's application. The company therefore could not participate in the India-UK Continent liner trade. Later, the government-owned Shipping Corporation of India applied for membership and with the support of the Government of India and the two Indian lines became a member of this Conference.

Great Eastern decided to operate a liner cargo service on a regular basis from the West Coast of U.S.A and Canada to India. It inaugurated this service in November 1962. The service became very popular with the shippers and consignees. The company's ships, which were carrying iron ore from India to Japan, after discharge of iron ore cargo, proceeded to the West Coast of U.S.A and Canada to lift general cargo from U.S.A and Canadian ports to India. The company made very satisfactory earnings from these services.

The company was the first Indian line to start a liner cargo service from the West Coast of U.S.A. and Canada to India. Thereafter Jayanti Shipping Company entered this trade and the two Indian lines between them were catering to 65 per cent of the trade on this route. However, later the Scindia Company began to berth its ships on this route in competition with the two Indian lines, leading to overtonnaging on the route. The government was consistently following a policy of not permitting overtonnaging in any liner trade of India. In this case the government after hearing the concerned parties decided to restrict the operations of the Scindia Company in this trade, but later withdrew this restriction.

Capital Structure, Profits and Dividends

The paid-up share capital of the company on 30 June 1959 was Rs. 115 lakh, consisting of Rs. 90 lakh equity share capital and Rs. 25 lakh preference share capital. On 30 June 1961, the preference share capital of Rs. 25 lakh was redeemed and returned to the shareholders. The paid up share capital on 30 June 1961 was therefore Rs. 90 lakh in equity shares and continued to remain at the same level on 30 June 1963.

Although the tonnage under actual operations increased by 25 per cent in 1958-59, the freight and charter hire earnings due to a fall in the freight market dwindled sharply from Rs. 3.6 crore in 1957-58 to Rs. 2.75 crore in 1958-59. The net profit, which was Rs. 65 lakh in 1957-58, fell to Rs. 32 lakh in 1958-59. The dividend on equity shares was lowered from 18 per cent in 1957-58 to 15 per cent in 1958-59. In 1959-60 there was increase in tonnage under operation of about 11 per cent. The freight and charter hire earnings amounted to Rs. 3.30 crore and the net profit about Rs. 20 lakh in 1959-60. The dividend on equity shares was lower at 10 per cent in 1959-60. In 1960-61 the deadweight tonnage under operation decreased from 132,265 tons in 1959-60 to 115,294. The freight and charter hire earnings in 1960-61 amounted to Rs. 2.84 crore. The company sustained a net loss of about Rs. 3.18 lakh before taking into account the estimated Burma Income Tax refund of Rs. 5.35 lakh which had not been received by then. An amount of Rs. 8.81 lakh was transferred from Reserves to the Profit and Loss

Account to enable the company to pay the dividend on preference and equity shares. The dividend on equity shares was 7.8 per cent. The freight and charter hire earnings in 1961-62 amounted to Rs. 3.24 crore. The net profit was Rs. 12.32 lakh and a dividend of 10 per cent was paid on equity shares. In 1962-63 the freight and charter hire earnings amounted to Rs. 4.51 crore. The net profit however amounted to only Rs. 57.24 lakh. A dividend of 10 per cent was paid to the shareholders. Fairly good earnings made by the company in the cargo liner service from the West Coast of U.S.A. and Canada to India started during the year 1962-63 partly accounted for the improvement in its financial results.

Shipping in the Doldrums

Indian shipping was in the midst of shipping recession and faced dismal trading conditions on the coast. There were foreign exchange difficulties for acquisition of ships. Adding to this was a poor provision of Rs. 55 crore made for shipping in the Third Five Year Plan as against the recommendation made by the National Shipping Board for a provision of Rs. 104 crore. As a result, there was all round pessimism in Indian shipping circles.

In 1960 the Government of India entered into an agreement with the government of U.S.A. for import, over a period of four years, of 7 million tonnes of foodgrains consisting of 6 million tonnes of wheat and 1 million tonnes of rice. When the agreement for import of foodgrains was signed, great hopes were raised about the participation of Indian ships in the carriage of foodgrains as control over the shipping arrangements rested with the Indian government. Under P.L. 480 governing the despatch of these foodgrains, 50 per cent of the quantity was to be transported in US flag ships and 50 per cent in ships of the government of India's choice.

However, Indian participation in this trade did not materialize because of very low tramp freight rates which were prevailing on account of the continued international shipping recession and inadequacy of outward cargo from India to U.S.A. The effective freight rates received by the US flag ships were much higher than international tramp rates paid by the Indian government since US flag ships were subsidised by the U.S. government. The Indian government was liable to pay the same rates to US flag ships which were paid to non-US flag ships. Therefore the government was not in a position to agree to higher freight rates for Indian ships as its liability for freight payment to US flag ships would have increased. Tankers (converted for carriage of foodgrains) and dry cargo bulk carriers which were larger in size than tramps of traditional sizes, because of the economics of large scale transportation, could carry foodgrains from U.S.A. to India at low freight rates. There was a trend in the post-war years, especially from 1954 onwards, for building ships of larger sizes, especially tramps, bulk carriers and tankers, to lower the operating cost per unit of cargo carried. Indian shipping companies kept asking for higher freight rates without success, but they did not give serious thought to the matter of building or acquiring large sized ships for catering to the bulk cargo trades of iron ore exports and foodgrain imports. Thus a gloomy spell was cast over Indian shipping. It appeared as if there were no bright days ahead and no speedy expansion possible.

Jayanti Shipping Adds New Dimensions to Growth of Indian Shipping

It was Jayanti Shipping Company which first placed orders for building bulk carriers. Other Indian shipping companies then followed suit. The formation of Jayanti Shipping Co Pvt Ltd in February 1961 can be considered as an important landmark in the development of Indian shipping.

Jayanti Shipping Company placed a bold and unconventional tonnage acquisition scheme before the government. The scheme envisaged the addition of 13 ships (bulk carriers and tramps) of about 185,000 GRT before the end of 1964 at a cost of Rs. 22.50 crore.

Jayanti Shipping Company was able to place orders for the construction of ships in a Japanese shipyard on deferred payment basis under which no payment was to be made to the yard till the ships were delivered. On delivery, 10 per cent of the price became payable. The balance 90 per cent was to be paid subsequent to delivery of the ships in seven equal annual instalments.

Thus, with a negligible expenditure during the Third Five Year Plan and without any expenditure of foreign exchange before the delivery of the ships, a sizeable expansion of 185,000 GRT was attained before the end of 1964. The only foreign exchange expenditure before the ships started earning foreign exchange was of the 10 per cent of the cost that was to be paid on delivery.

Another unorthodox way of financing the purchase of a ship in India to some extent followed the pattern of the financing methods adopted by the Greeks and Norwegians, who had achieved a spectacular growth of tanker tonnage in the post war years. Jayanti Shipping acquired a tanker for overseas trade by paying instalments to the seller out of the charter hire earnings of the tanker placed on long-term time charter with an oil company.

The government made a number of relaxations in their rules and regulations, set procedures, loan terms etc. to enable Jayanti Shipping to finalise its loan arrangement and put through its expansion plans. The ban on shipping companies in the private sector on purchase of tankers was also withdrawn to accommodate Jayanti Shipping. If there had been no ban, Great Eastern, which was the first to acquire a tanker in India, and other companies in the private sector would have acquired more tankers even during the Second Plan period.

In the initial stages there was a lot of opposition and prejudice against the expansion undertaken by Jayanti Shipping, but as it emerged, Jayanti Shipping acquired ships which were very suitable for India's participation in the bulk cargo trades at favourable prices and credit terms. The big expansion undertaken by Jayanti Shipping not only added a sizeable tonnage on the Indian Register but also spurred other Indian shipping companies to undertake expansion schemes. The mood of gloom and pessimism among Indian shipping companies was dispelled. The dynamic expansion, for which shipping companies and the government share equal credit, took Indian shipping tonnage at the end of the Third Plan on 31 March 1966 to about 15.40 lakh GRT, as against the Third Plan target of 13.25 lakh GRT.

The Man Behind Jayanti

Dr. Jayanti Dharma Teja, founder of Jayanti Shipping Company, was a very remarkable person. He was an excellent showman and salesman with a lot of derring-do. He so impressed Prime Minister Nehru that government rules, regulations and procedures were set aside to accommodate his projects; Nehru even gave him letters of introduction, which could be justified by saying that they were required for national shipping development, to the Japanese shipyard and to the head of an international oil company having its interests in India. Teja got very favourable prices and credit terms from the Japanese shipyard for building his ships. The head of the international oil company who asked Teja at first to meet the chief of his tanker divison to discuss time-charter of Jayanti Shipping Company's tanker was reportedly told by Teja that he would on his return to India tell the Prime Minister that the oil company chief should have as a matter of courtesy to the Prime Minister's letter met Teja himself which he refused to do. The head of the oil company which had large business interests in India did not want to take the risk of offending the Prime Minister of India. He therefore met Teja and in the bargain Teja was able to get a satisfactory employment for his tanker at a favourable rate of charter hire which was somewhat higher than the market rate for the tanker. At this time a tanker of Ratnakar Shipping Company owned by the Birla Group was also fixed on time-charter to another international oil company at the market rate of charter hire. Teja, it is reported, told the Prime Minister and others that he had better business acumen than Birlas and that is why he could get a higher rate for his tanker.

It is interesting to cite an anecdote about the company's contact with Teja. When Jayanti Shipping Company's expansion plans were announced in the newspapers, Vasant Sheth wrote to Teja saying that since Teja would be occupied with policy and finance aspects of his ambitious expansion scheme, Great Eastern with its shipping experience would be able to attend to the management of Jayanti's ships for mutual benefit. Teja replied to Vasant Sheth that he was very happy that Great Eastern was looking upon Jayanti Shipping not as a competitor but as a partner in the development of Indian shipping. He would be very happy to co-operate with Great Eastern. He had studied Great Eastern's annual report and accounts and found that Great Eastern enjoyed strong liquidity and had about Rs. 5 crore in cash, bank balances and short term investments. Since Teja did not have enough rupee resources he would like Great Eastern to contribute 16 per cent of Jayanti Shipping Company's share capital of Rs. 5 crore. This would come to about Rs. 80 lakh, and that posed no problem for Great Eastern. Thereafter Teja pursued this matter with Vasant Sheth. Great Eastern decided to discuss the matter with Teja, and arrangements were made for a day-long discussion between the representatives of Jayanti Company and Great Eastern in Great Eastern's office.

The meeting was held in Great Eastern's Board Room. Teja was accompanied by an impressive array of foreign brokers which included freight brokers, insurance brokers P & I Club brokers, etc. But Great Eastern did not see their presence as necessary, and they were sent away! True to style, Teja had brought them along to impress the Great Eastern management with the wide contacts he had in shipping!

Two issues were discussed. First, the proposed collaboration between Great Eastern and Jayanti Shipping Company, and the terms. Second, some of the ships ordered by Jayanti Shipping Company were too large to be handled at Indian ports at that time, and their employment in international cross trades was a topic for discussion.

As the discussion on the employment of ships in cross trades began, Teja mentioned a few names like Jack (Jack Kennedy) who, he claimed, would be helpful in getting his ships employed for carriage of U.S. grain cargoes to China. In fact when the discussion was about to develop, telephone calls for Teja claimed to be from Delhi interrupted the discussion. Teja informed the meeting that Prime Minister Jawaharlal Nehru wanted Teja to go immediately to Delhi to meet him, and that since he could not get the tickets by airline, he would charter a plane and go to Delhi. The meeting then adjourned for lunch hosted by Great Eastern at the Willingdon Club. After the lunch also the discussions continued in the same way as in the morning with Dr. Teja getting calls supposedly from high dignitaries in the U.S.A. and France. In spite of the day-long deliberations the meeting remained inconclusive.

Later Great Eastern learnt that Jayanti's cash requirements were escalating, and heard of the rumoured mismanagement of funds. Dr. Nagendra Singh, the then Shipping and Transport Secretary, cautioned the Great Eastern management not to get involved, in view of the impending investigations to be launched by the government for recovery of their loan funds with Jayanti Shipping. Fortunately for Great Eastern, therefore, the proposed collaboration with Jayanti did not materialise.

Teja undoubtedly made a significant contribution to the development of Indian shipping. It is however unfortunate that due to financial mismanagement and unethical practices by the management of Jayanti Shipping, the company incurred huge liabilities and came to grief. Serious allegations were made against the company and its chairman, Teja. There was strong pressure from the creditors. The company's management was taken over by the Shipping Corporation of India by an Ordinance on 10 June 1966. The Ordinance was replaced by an Act of Parliament, The Jayanti Shipping Company (Taking over of Management) Act 1966, which came into force on 3 September 1966. The Shipping Corporation of India were appointed the Managing Agents of the company. At this time the Jayanti fleet consisted of 21 ships of 3.21 lakh GRT. The company became a subsidiary of the Shipping Corporation of India on 17 October 1971. On 1 January 1973 the company was amalgmated with the Shipping Corporation of India, which acquired a very valuable tramp fleet. In 1966 itself civil and criminal proceedings were started against Teja and his associates. Teja stayed out of India for a number of years and it was a sad and forlorn Teja who returned and passed his years in comparative oblivion in Hyderabad. He died abroad on 25 December 1985.

More Ships for the Company

Great Eastern made an excellent start in the second half of the second decade. Its fleet on 30 June 1963 consisted of 15 ships with GRT of 95,872 and DWT of 1,38,255. Before the close of the financial year 1962-63, the company decided to add five to seven ships to the company's fleet. In the year 1963-64, five ships were purchased at a cost of Rs. 1.70 crore. After taking the scrapping of one ship into account, the company's fleet as on 30 June 1964 consisted of 19 ships with a GRT of 127,924 and DWT of 183,942. This expansion was achieved at favourable prices, which were low as a result of the prolonged shipping recession, and happily coincided with the lifting of the shipping recession at the end of 1963.

The company also placed an order for the construction of two bulk carriers in 1963 with a Japanese shipyard. Initially the designed size of each of the two bulk carriers was 36,000 DWT, which was later increased to 38,500 DWT. The price of the two bulk carriers was approximately Rs. 4.12 crore, with shipyard credit facility; they were expected to be delivered in early 1966. The bulk carriers were being acquired for carriage of bulk cargoes like iron ore and foodgrains. This was in accordance with the world trend in shipping. The war-built standard ships and tramps were being replaced by modern bulk carriers. In 1960 bulk carriers carried only 16 per cent of the 5 major bulk commodities (7 per cent of total dry cargo). In 1969 bulk carriers transported 74 per cent of the total seaborne cargo in respect of the 5 major bulk commodities. Their share in the carriage of all the dry seaborne cargoes was 36 per cent.

Capital Structure, Profits and Dividend in the Second Half of the Second Decade

In the second half of the second decade the paid up share capital of the company on 30 June 1963 was Rs. 90 lakh in equity shares. In the year 1963-64 Rs. 5/- per share was called up on 6 lakh partly paid equity shares of Rs. 10/- each, on which Rs. 5/- per share was paid up. These shares became fully paid, resulting in the addition of Rs. 30 lakh in paid up capital. During the same year further 3 lakh shares of Rs. 10/- each were issued as bonus shares by capitalising reserves, resulting in a further increase of Rs. 30 lakh in the paid up capital. Thus the paid up share capital went up from Rs. 90 lakh in 1962-63 to Rs. 150 lakh in 1963-64.

In 1965-66 there was further capitalisation of reserves of Rs. 29,91,430 and the paid up share capital went up to Rs. 1,79,91,430. In the year 1967-68 bonus shares were issued by capitalising reserves of Rs. 59,88,284 and the paid up share capital went up to Rs. 2,39,53,130.

In the year 1963-64 freight and charter hire earnings were Rs. 5.26 crore and the net profit Rs. 44.46 lakh. A dividend of 10.8 per cent was paid to the shareholders. In the year 1964-65 freight and charter hire earnings amounted to Rs. 5.25 crore. The net profit was Rs. 31.99 lakh and a dividend of 11 per cent was paid to the shareholders. In the year 1965-66 the freight and charter hire earnings amounted to Rs. 6.28 crore and the net profit Rs. 1.34 crore. A dividend of 16 per cent was paid to the shareholders. In the year 1966-67 the freight and charter hire earnings amounted to Rs. 8.25 crore and net profit to Rs. 1.77 crore. A dividend of 20 per cent which was tax free in the hands of the shareholders was paid. In the year 1967-68 freight and charter hire earnings were Rs. 8.82 crore, the net profit Rs. 2.18 crore. A dividend of 20 per cent which was tax free in the hands of the shareholders was paid.

In the year 1964-65, with the discarding of old ships there was decrease in the tonnage under operation and the company's investment in the fleet at original cost decreased from Rs. 11.85 crore to Rs. 11.25 crore. The freight and charter hire earnings therefore did not go up. There was also increase in operating cost, so the net profit declined. From the year 1965-66 onwards there was increase in the tonnage under operation each year. There was full employment of dry cargo shipping in 1965 and on an average tramp rates were maintained at the highest levels as compared with those ruling in the previous eight years since the Suez crisis in 1956-57, although the rates were lower than those attained during the Suez crisis. There was therefore improvement in the freight and charter hire earnings and the net profit in the year 1965-66.

The financial results of the company improved considerably in the year 1966-67 because the rupee was devalued in 1966 and this led to higher freight and charter hire earnings of the company in terms of rupees. There was also improvement in the freight market as a result of the closure of the Suez Canal in 1966-67. It was mentioned in the Directors Report of 1966-67 that due to the closure of the Suez Canal the tanker freight markets improved almost 200 per cent over the pre- Suez closure and the tramp freight rates rose by about 30 to 40 per cent over the pre-Suez closure. There was considerable strengthening of the financial position of the company. The net profit in the years 1965-66, 1966-67 and 1967-68 amounted to 74 per cent, 98 per cent and 91 per cent of the paid up capital during the respective years.

It is remarkable that even during the prosperous times through which the company was passing, the Chairman A.H. Bhiwandiwalla, at the 20th Annual General Meeting held on 23 December 1968 referred to the increased profitability and the considerable augumentation of the company's reserves and uttered the following prophetic words: "The strong reserves position thus built up, I hope, will stand us in good stead to face an uncertain and an unpredictable future, which is fraught with serious possibilities due to the crisis in international currencies and the overwhelmingly large world shipbuilding capacity which may set up an imbalance in supply and demand for ships." These words were to come true a few years later. Subsequent to the OPEC crisis at the end of 1973, the imbalance in supply of and demand for ships led to a prolonged shipping depression.

Progress During the Decade

On 30 June 1958 the company's fleet consisted of 14 vessels with a total GRT of 78,792 and total DWT of 120,973. On 30 September 1968 the Company owned 16 ships with a GRT of 1,79,376 and DWT of 2,84,119. The increase in tonnage was much more than the increase in the number of ships because ships acquired during the decade, in accordance with the world trend, were by and large of larger sizes.

In the year 1958-59, the company's ships carried cargo of 877,157 tons and earned freight and charter hire of Rs. 2.75 crore. In the year 1967-68 the cargo carried by the company's ship amounted to 13,76,818 tons and freight and charter hire earnings were much higher at Rs. 8.82 crore. There was considerable increase in the overseas operations and decrease in coastal operations. The cargo carried by the company's ships in the overseas trade increased from 363,148 tons in the year 1958-59 to 11,20,811 tons in the year 1967-68. The cargo carried by the company's ships in the coastal trade excluding mineral oil in bulk decreased from 364,108 tons in 1958-59 to 91,147 tons in 1967-68.

The company's equity capital went up from Rs. 90 lakh in 1958-59 to Rs. 2.40 crore in 1967-68. In the year 1958-59 the company earned a net profit of Rs. 29.80 lakh. In 1967-68 the net profit was much higher at Rs. 217.74 lakh. The reserves and surplus amounted to Rs. 1.92 crore on 30 June 1958. The reserves and surplus increased to Rs. 6.54 crore on 30 June 1968.

The company's fleet as on 30 September 1968 was 1.79 lakh GRT. The GRT of the total Indian fleet as on 1 April 1968 was 19.37 lakh GRT. The company's tonnage (in GRT terms) constituted about 9 per cent of Indian tonnage. In the year 1967-68 the company's ships carried cargoes totalling 11.2 lakh tonnes in the overseas trade. The cargo liftings of the Indian ships in the overseas trade amounted to 7.7 million tonnes in 1967-68. Great Eastern's share therefore in the carriage of cargoes by Indian ships in the overseas trade was over 14 per cent. The company's freight and charter hire earnings in the year 1967-68 amounted to Rs. 8.82 crore, which was 7 per cent of Rs. 121.30 crore, which was the total freight and charter hire earnings of Indian shipping companies in the year 1967-68. It may be stated that the freight earnings of a tramp ship are much less than those of a traditional liner ship. The freight of a liner ship has to be higher since the shipowner has to pay out of the freight substantial stevedoring expenses both at the loading and discharging ports. Great Eastern being a tramp shipping company, its percentage share of India's freight earnings was lower than its percentage share of the Indian tonnage.

Dr. Nagendra Singh

The story of Indian shipping, or for that matter any Indian shipping company which was established in the post-Independence period and grew in the 1950s and 1960s, would be incomplete if it did not record the worthy role played by the late Dr. Nagendra Singh in the development of Indian shipping. Nagendra Singh was Director General of Shipping from 1956 to 1966. He was simultaneously Joint Secretary in the Ministry of Transport and Communications from 1956 to 1962 and Additional Secretary from 1962 to 1964, and Special Secretary in 1964 in the same Ministry. He was Secretary to the Ministry of Transport and Communications in 1965 and 1966. He played an active part in getting and implementing for Indian shipping three epoch-making measures of assistance which ensured the subsequent growth of the Indian shipping industry. These were announced by Lal Bahadur Shastri, the Minister for Shipping and Transport, at the Annual General Meeting of Indian National Steamship Owners Association in 1957. The setting up of the Shipping Development Fund Committee for grant of soft loans to Indian Shipping Companies for acquisition of ships, the establishment of Shipping Coordination Committee and a central Chartering Organisation (Transchart) for giving government owned and controlled cargoes, on a preferential basis, for carriage to Indian ships, and the enhancement of the tax incentive of development rebate from 25 per cent to 40 per cent for the shipping industry were the three measures of assistance.

Dr. Singh was actively associated with the setting up of the Transchart and Shipping Development Fund Committee and administered their working. His learning, dynamism, administrative abilities and above all his dedication and zeal for development of Indian shipping made a great contribution to the development of Indian shipping. It was he who saw that tramp shipping had a great role to play in the growth of Indian shipping. He changed or modified many shipping policies which had their origin in the narrow self-interest and prejudices of liner shipping companies and which were stifling the growth of tramp shipping. He issued global licences to tramp ships. During Nagendra Singh's stewardship of more than a decade in the Shipping and Transport Ministry, Indian shipping tonnage grew from 4,79,880 GRT on 1 April 1956 to 18,67,220 GRT on 28 February 1967. It was during Nagendra Singh's tenure that a firm foundation for the future growth of shipping was laid.

Nagendra Singh's brilliant career discloses the very rare feature of a unique combination of great administrative experience and academic excellence. He was born on 18 March 1914 and was a son of His Highness the Maharaja of Dungarpur in Rajasthan. At the Indian Civil Service examination held in London Nagendra Singh was awarded the Cama Prize by St. John's College, Cambridge, for high distinction in the examination.

Nagendra Singh's academic degrees could be summarised as under:

M.A., LL.D. (Cantab), D.Sc., (Law; Moscow), D.C.L. (Delhi), M.A., B. Litt., LL.d. (Dublin), D.Phil. (Calcutta), D. Litt (Pol. Sc.) (Bihar), Bar-at-law. He submitted learned theses to the various universities and secured Doctorates from them.

He has written a number of learned books and papers on topics in various branches of international law. His two books entitled *International Conventions of Merchant Shipping* and *Shipowners* have been published as volume 8 and volume 13 in the well-known British Shipping Law Series published by Stevens & Sons London.

From 1938 onwards he held various important posts. The following are some of these posts :

* Director General of Shipping (1956-66)
* Secretary - Ministry of Transport (1965-66)
* Secretary to President of India and thereafter Chief Election Commissioner of the Government of India.
* On the international scene he represented India at many international conferences as Head of the Indian Delegation and he was President of the International Maritime Organisation from 1963 to 1965.
* Nagendra Singh was Vice President of the Comite Maritime International (CMI) since 1974.

* He was elected Judge of the International Court of Justice for 9 years from 6 February 1973 and was re-elected for further 9 years from 6 February 1982.
* He was Vice President of the International Court of Justice from 1976 to 1979 and President from 1985 to 1988.
* He had the distinction of being the Nehru Professor of International Law and Co-operation at the Graduate Institute of International Studies, University of Geneva, Switzerland and many other Universities. Nagendra Singh delivered endowment or memorial lectures in several universities both in India and abroad. These included the Universities of Cambridge, Bombay, Belgrade, Cairo, Baghdad and Tribhuvan in Nepal, the Hague Academy of International Law. His learned books and articles have received great appreciation and some of them have been acclaimed by experts in the respective fields as being outstanding.

He died on 11 December 1988.

From 1956 to 1966 when he was concerned with shipping he worked with dedication and devotion for development of Indian shipping.

Two anecdotes demonstrate how sincerely he worked for the expansion of Indian shipping. Although the anecdotes given here relate to Great Eastern, it may be stated that he assisted all Indian shipping companies in the same way.

Great Eastern purchased a ship, subject to government sanction, in 1960s. As release of foreign exchange was involved the file had to be cleared by, besides the Transport Ministry, the Finance Ministry, Company Affairs Department, Planning Commission etc. By oversight the Ministry of Transport, which secured clearances from other Ministries, did not approach the Planning Commission for their clearance. The date by which government approval had to be conveyed by Great Eastern to the sellers was fast approaching. In the mean time prices of ships had gone up. Vasant Sheth therefore proceeded to Delhi and met Nagendra Singh, who found that by oversight no reference had been made to the Planning Commission and it would take at least a week or ten days to obtain their clearance. Since the last date for conveying the government's approval to the sellers was about to expire, the purchase would have fallen through. Nagendra Singh then telephoned Tarlok Singh, Secretary to the Planning Commission (who was his colleague in the Indian Civil Service), and told him that he would like to meet him over a cup of tea. He also told Tarlok Singh that a young friend of his from Bombay would accompany him. In the afternoon Nagendra Singh took the file, and accompanied by Vasant Sheth, went to see Tarlok Singh. When he met Tarlok Singh he profusely apologised to him for his oversight in not making a reference to him and told him that if the approval was not given immediately the country would lose a good bargain. The prices of ships had gone up in the meantime and the seller would cancel the sale. Tarlok Singh immediately cleared the file by putting his signature and gave it back to Nagendra Singh. Great Eastern was thus able to convey government approval to the sellers in time and take delivery of the ship.

In the early 1960s Great Eastern had to pay an instalment of about Rs.2 crore to a Japanese shipyard which was building a ship for Great Eastern. The company did not have enough liquidity at that time and Rs.2 crore was a formidable amount at that time. Vasant Sheth therefore told the writer that he should go to Delhi and meet Nagendra Singh and try to get the amount of Rs. 2 crore from Shipping Development Fund Committee (SDFC) in a matter of three or four days. The writer was deputed to Delhi because he had free access to Nagendra Singh in view of his academic pursuits. When he met Nagendra Singh and explained to him the grêat urgency of the company's requirement for a loan from SDFC and stated that he would like to have the SDFC cheque in 3 or 4 days time. Nagendra Singh laughed and remarked : " Sanklecha, you do not seem to know how the Government departments work and that is why you are expecting the cheque in a matter of days". Nagendra Singh however added that he would see what best he could do to assist the Company. After three or four days the writer again called on Nagendra Singh and asked him whether he would get the cheque that day. Nagendra Singh smiled and said "You do not seem to have the realisation of what I am doing to assist you. In the Government, one works on the principle that involve as many necks as possible so that your neck will not go". He had arranged for SDFC to approve the matter by a circular resolution. The signatures of the members from the various ministries had to be obtained. As soon as their procedure was completed SDFC would hand over the cheque. The next day, the cheque was ready. The Secretary of the SDFC however would not hand over the cheque in person to the writer and told him that he would send it by registered post to Bombay. The writer felt that it was not worthwhile to take up the matter again with Nagendra Singh and get his instructions to the SDFC Secretary for delivery of the cheque. So he returned to Bombay and the company received the cheque by registered post and the company was thus able to make payment of the instalment to the Japanese shipyard in good time.

Better Appreciation of Requirements of Tramp Shipping

A. H. Bhiwandiwalla, the company's Chairman, at the 11th Annual General Meeting of the company held on 10 December 1959 stated that there was now a better understanding and appreciation in government quarters of the special problems of tramp shipping. He however stated that it was essential for the government to enunciate and announce their policy in order that operators of tramp shipping were certain about the government policy, and a proper climate for the expansion of tramp shipping was created.

With the establishment of Jayanti Shipping Company, which was the second tramp shipping company in India, the government bent or short-circuited their regulations and procedures. This was however due to the political influence of its Chairman Teja and his close contact with Prime Minister Nehru.

In 1964 Nagendra Singh happened to be the examiner of the doctoral thesis on tramp shipping in India submitted by the Company's Secretary S. N. Sanklecha to the Bombay University. He was greatly impressed by Sanklecha's analysis and comprehensive treatment of the problems and requirements of tramp shipping and recommended to the Bombay University to publish the thesis for its educative value for those concerned with or interested in shipping. When the book was published in 1966 by the Bombay University, Nagendra Singh wrote a Foreword to the book in spite of the strong criticism of the Government policies contained in the book. After leaving the Shipping and Transport Ministry, Nagendra Singh, in his letter, complimented Sanklecha for the great contribution he had made to the literature on tramping.

Although the government policies ceased to be hostile to the growth of tramp shipping, government regulations and restrictions on shipping persisted. Freedom of operation was the basis and pre-condition for success in tramp shipping, which had to operate and grow under conditions of international competition. Although licensing of Indian ships for tramp trades ceased to be a problem once global licences were issued, the restrictions on time chartering in of foreign ships and time chartering out of Indian ships and on sale and purchase of ships continued to be in force. In this connection it is interesting to quote Erling D. Naess, a renowned shipowner and Chairman of the American Committee for Flags of Necessity from 1958 to 1961. He first proposed the idea of the Norwegian International Register. He was asked a question whether he agreed with the statement of Onassis, the well-known Greek shipowner in the BBC Television interview that one of the great advantages of having ships registered under the Flags of Convenience was that the decisions as regards buying, selling or chartering of ships could be made promptly without reference to Government departments. Naess answered "Of course the more interference with shipping and the more restrictions and regulations they introduce, the greater the brake on enterprise and the slower international trade becomes."[2] Naess in his book on the subject, referring to freedom from bureaucratic controls and oppressive taxation, observed: "In order to provide cheap and efficient tranportation for oil, ore, coal, bauxite and other raw materials and the seaman with the highest possible degree of welfare including wages, it may not be possible to sustain any thick layer of bureaucratic fat or excessive meat for the tax collector to carve. As long as some countries look upon international shipping as a milking cow to sustain bureaucratic fat and the tax collector's knife, the fleets of the free flags will continue to grow."[3] Although the Government policies in India were no more hostile to its growth, they failed to provide adequate nourishment to tramp shipping in India.

Reduction in Calcutta Office Staff and Expenditure

When the Company started its operations, Calcutta was the most important port for sea-borne traffic in India. Coastal coal cargo which was loaded at Calcutta and coastal salt cargo which was discharged at Calcutta formed 50 per cent of the total coastal cargo. Calcutta was an important port for overseas cargo also. However, stagnation or decline in the sea-borne cargoes loaded or discharged at Calcutta due to fall in the draughts of the Hooghly river and the progressive increase in the sizes of ships built in post-war years, led to the decline in the importance of Calcutta port.

Great Eastern had its major interest in co·.stal shipping in the early years after its incorporation, and Calcutta was the most important port for the company's ships. The company therefore had a large office and establishment in Calcutta. Due to decline in the company's coastal operations and no hope of improvement in its business at Calcutta, it decided on retrenchment of part of the staff at Calcutta for reducing expenditure there. The company discussed this matter with the Calcutta employees' union and arrived at a mutual agreement for reduction in the number of staff members at Calcutta on an agreed basis. The problem was solved to the satisfaction of staff members as well as the company in the year 1966-67.

Management

Vasant Sheth continued to be in overall charge and management of the Company. His business vision, excellent rapport with the Ministers and top officials of the Ministry of Shipping and Transport and the qualities of leadership which was a source of inspiration for the excellent teamwork of the officers and staff members of the Company made a great contribution to the efficient working and growth of the Company. K. M. Sheth during this decade fully assumed the responsibilities for management and administration of the company. He fixed the employment of ships most advantageously and made a substantial contribution to the success of the company. The Company's competitive strength and potential for growth lay in the combined dynamic management of Vasant Sheth and K.M.Sheth. In 1960, Sudhir Mulji, a brilliant economics graduate of the Oxford University, son of Jayantilal Mulji, a director of the company as well as of the Managing Agents of the company, and nephew of Vasant Sheth, who had been educated in the U.K., joined the company as a senior officer. He ably assisted both Vasant Sheth and K. M. Sheth, and at the end of the decade assumed management responsibilities.

S.N. Sanklecha prepared the company's applications for ship acquisitions, loan applications to Shipping Development Fund Committee and banks. He was the company's draftsman who prepared the representations and memoranda to the government and Chairman's speeches at the company's Annual General Meetings which dealt with government policies in respect of the shipping industry in general and its tramp sector in particular. He not only wrote his widely acclaimed book on *Tramp Shipping in India* but also contributed papers on various aspects of shipping which were published in reputed journals. These had a great educative value and were of assistance in altering the unfavourable environment for tramp shipping and securing government approvals to the company's proposals.

B.N. Adappa, who had his early training with K.M. Sheth, looked after fixing of employment and operations of the company's ships. Hard working and most conscientious, he believed in the philosophy of 'karma' — "Do a day's work well and tomorrow will take care of itself." He has played a worthy role in the successful operation and growth of the company.

T. M. Sanghvi, who had joined the company in the early 1950s and left the company in November 1969, as Technical Manager of the company looked after the maintenance and repairs of the ships. He was also in charge of the floating personnel. He looked after this work very well. He was also consulted on ships specifications and technical suitability when orders for building of ships were placed or when second hand ships were purchased by the company, and the company benefited by his advice. He played a very useful role in keeping the management informed about the changing technology in marine engineering such as use of cheap heavy fuel in place of costly diesel oil, use of turbo-charging diesel engine, etc. and their impact in commercial terms.

After Sanghvi left, D.C.H. Storey took over Sanghvi's responsibilities. Storey had previously served as Chief Engineer on the company's ships and later was stationed in the company's Calcutta office for looking after maintenance and repairs of the company's ships. Calcutta was a very important port for repairs of the company's ships in the early years. In fact in 1956, when m.v. *Jag Tara* had grounded near Bassein in Burma, Storey proceeded to the grounded ship. It was due to Storey's skill and courage that the vessel was able to refloat with the assistance of a salvage tug and was able with tug assistance to reach Calcutta port.

A.R. Balsubramaniam, who joined the company in 1958 as Assistant Accountant, took charge later as Chief Accountant. He efficiently handled the accounts and finances of the company.

K.J. Vesuna, who was a rank holder in the CA examination,

joined the company as an Assistant Accountant in 1961. Later he joined the Operations Department and along with B.N. Adappa very competently handled the shipping operations which were entrusted to him.

N.E. Pardiwala, Chartered Accountant, joined the Accounts Department in 1962. Later he took charge of the machine accounting in the Accounts Department. Thereafter he was placed in charge of the company's floating personnel, that is, the ships' officers and crew. After Utam Singh, Personnel Manager, left the services of the company, Pardiwala took full charge as Personnel Manager of the staff ashore as well as the staff afloat. Fond of discipline and meticulous attention to details, Pardiwala endeared himself to the management and discharged his work efficiently.

J. J. Mehta joined the company immediately after its incorporation in August 1948 and after a few months in Bombay office was, on the opening of Calcutta office, posted as Assistant Manager in Calcutta. He was promoted as manager in Calcutta office in July 1959. Calcutta, as we have seen earlier, was at that time a very important port for the company's ships which loaded coal and discharged salt at Calcutta, and also in respect of the company's coastal general cargo service which was very popular with the shippers and consignees. Mehta rendered meritorious service in Calcutta.

Composition of Staff Members

One of the most admirable and outstanding features was the composition of the staff members of the company. The Management in their recruitment and promotion policies showed no bias and made no discrimination on the basis of religion, caste, state or locality to which the intended employees or persons already employed belonged. The Management's outlook was and is to treat the entire country as one in disregard of caste, religion or provincial considerations in making appointments and giving promotions. The composition of the company's staff members provides an ideal illustration of national integration.

The other feature was the young average age of the employees in the first two decades, especially of those in the management and executive cadres, many of whom joined the company whilst starting their careers and grew up with the growth of the company.

REFERENCES

1. 20th Report of Committee on Public Undertakings (1971-72) (Fifth Lok Sabha) on Shipping Corporation of India Ltd. Lok Sabha Secretariat, New Delhi, April 1972, pp. 94, 124.

2. Erling D. Naess, *The Great PanLibHon Controversy - The Fight over the Flags of Shipping*, Gower Press, 1972, Epping Essex, p.37.

3. *Ibid.*

4

The Third Decade 1968-1978

This decade was marked by far reaching and dramatic developments in world shipping. International sea borne trade greatly increased from 2,060 million tonnes in 1968 to 3,210 million tonnes in 1973. The average annual rate of increase in international sea-borne trade was 9 per cent. In terms of ton-miles, which provide a better measurement of the demand for shipping services, the average annual rate of increase was over 15 per cent. In fact even before 1968, in the post-war years (except during the shipping recession from 1958 to 1963), international shipowners by and large saw good times — the Korean war in the early 1950s, the Suez Canal closure in 1956 and then again the closure of the Suez Canal in 1967 gave further boosts to the rising freight markets and enhanced the good times through which international shipping was passing.

Most of the time in the five years from 1968 to 1973, shipowners all over the world were making excellent profits, and there was optimism all round. The world shipping fleet grew at the average annual rate of 8.3 per cent in this period. The year 1973 up to October 1973 was an exceptionally excellent year for shipowners, before the Arab-Israel war, which led to an oil crisis. A record volume of shipbuilding orders of 73.60 million GRT were placed in 1973 due to the continued boom in shipping.

As the shipyards were fully booked by shipbuilding orders there was a considerable time lag consisting of the waiting period for the commencement of shipbuilding and the further period of 1 to 2 years required for ship construction. Therefore, in spite of the turning point provided by the oil crisis at the end of 1973 in the fortunes of shipping, the shipbuilding output was at its highest in 1974, 1975 and 1976 at 33.54 million GRT, 34.20 million GRT and 33.20 million GRT respectively notwithstanding the dwindling volume of annual shipbuilding orders of 28.37 million GRT in 1974, 13.70 million GRT in 1975 and 12.94 million GRT in 1976. In 1977 and 1978 the annual volume of shipbuilding orders placed by shipowners dwindled further to 11.09 million GRT and 8.03 million GRT respectively. However, the shipbuilding output in these years was much higher, at 28.53 million GRT and 18.19 million GRT.

As a result, the world shipping fleet, which was 194 million GRT in mid 1968, in a decade more than doubled itself and was 406 million GRT in mid 1978. One can better appreciate this tremendous growth in world shipping during this decade if one looks at the mid-1990 world shipping fleet figure of 424 million GRT. An increase of only 18 million GRT over a period of 12 years from 1978 to 1990, which amounted to less than 0.4 per cent average annual increase.

In India also, in accordance with this world trend, the Indian shipping fleet, which was 1.9 million GRT in mid 1968, grew three times to 5.8 million GRT in mid 1978. During the next 12 years from mid 1978 to mid 1990, the Indian fleet increased to 6.5 million GRT only. Great Eastern's fleet, which was 1.79 lakh GRT on 30 September 1968, increased to 4.05 lakh GRT on 9 November 1978. In 10 years it increased 2.25 times the 1968 tonnage. Despite the great handicap at which the company was placed in regard to receipt of financial assistance from the government in this decade as compared with Shipping Corporation of India and other major Indian companies (which is discussed later in this chapter), aggravated by the denial of even the committed loan assistance for acquisition of ships, the company achieved creditable growth.

Another notable feature which marked this decade was the phenomenal increase in the sizes of tankers and bulk carriers. Although progressive increase in sizes of ships was a post-war phenomenon and continued in the 1950s and 1960s, the development during the decade attained ship sizes which will not be materially exceeded up to the year 2000 A.D. The era of VLCCs (Very Large Crude Carriers) and ULCCs (Ultra Large Crude Carriers) in tanker shipping was ushered in. The first generation of 200,000 DWT tankers came into service in 1968 and 1969. The largest tankers which were delivered included the following:

Year	Name	DWT	Owners
1968	TT Universe Ireland	326,585	Bantry Transport
1971	TT Nisseki Maru	372,648	Tokyo Tanker
1973	TT Globtik Tokyo	483,664	Globtik Tanker
1975	TT Batillus	550,001	Shell Francaise

The average size of the dry bulk carriers at the end of 1978 was 36,900 DWT. The average size of the combination carriers (Ore Oil carriers, OBO carriers) at the end of 1978 was 117,100 DWT. However, in the composite category of combination carriers and dry bulk carriers, in mid-1978 there was one ship of 282,000 DWT. In the same category there were ships above 200,000 DWT per ship and below 275,000 DWT per ship whose total tonnage was 78,72,000 DWT. In accordance with the world trend, set by technological advance and economies of scale for large-sized ships, Great Eastern ordered building of there OBO carriers before or by 1973. One of the OBO carriers was of 101,500 DWT and each of the other two was 122,500 DWT.

Another important feature of this decade was the container revolution in world liner shipping. The first container ship service in the international sea-borne trade was started in 1966 by SEA-Land Service Inc in the North Atlantic. It was in the decade 1968 to 1978 that it progressively and on a large and increasing scale replaced traditional break-bulk liner shipping in the important liner trades of the world. Great Eastern as a bulk cargo shipping company was not directly interested in this development. However, other major Indian companies, the Shipping Corporation of India, Scindia Steam Navigation Company and the India Steamship Company, who were participating in India's liner trades and who were carrying almost 40 to 45 per cent of India's liner trade, did not acquire and operate any cellular container ship in this decade or even in the next decade. They continued operations with the break-bulk liner ships, with the result that Indian shipping's share in the carriage of its liner trade went down steeply. It is the foreign container shipowners and operators who took over the bulk of India's containerized liner trade.

Mode of Management Change

The Managing Agents A.H.Bhiwandiwalla & Co had made a

great contribution to the growth of Great Eastern from a one-ship company with assets of about Rs. 25 lakh in 1948 to a 15-ship company with assets of about Rs. 33 crore in 1970. However the institution of Managing Agents, which had evolved in India under British rule, was abolished by the Government of India with effect from 3 April 1970 by passing of the Companies (Amendment) Act 1969. A.H. Bhiwandiwalla and Company (Bombay) Private Ltd therefore ceased to be Managing Agents of Great Eastern with effect from 3 April 1970. The company was however fortunate that A.H. Bhiwandiwalla, Vasant Sheth and K.M. Sheth continued to manage the company. Under the new arrangement, A.H.Bhiwandiwalla was appointed as Executive Chairman and Whole-time Director, Vasant Sheth as Deputy Chairman and Managing Director and K.M. Sheth as Managing Director for a period of five years with effect from 3 April 1970. A.H. Bhiwandiwalla in his speech to the shareholders of the company at the Extra-Ordinary General Meeting held on 20 March 1970 convened to seek their approval to the change in the management and new appointments stated: "You are very fortunate in as much as that although the Managing Agents who have done so well for you for the last 21 years will cease to operate, the same persons will now manage the affairs at about half the commission that the Company would have to pay to retain the services of the Managing Agents."

Proposal for Acquisition of 40 per cent share in South India Shipping Corporation

Pratapsinh Mathuradas, who was director of Great Eastern from its inception and was Chairman of Bombay Burmah Trading Corporation Ltd, purchased 40 per cent of the shareholding of the South India Shipping Corporation held by non-Indians, that is, P & O and Anglo-Norness, for the account of Bombay Burmah Trading Corporation, Great Eastern Shipping Company, Pratapsinh Mathuradas, A.H. Bhiwandiwalla, Vasant Sheth and their friends, by which they would have acquired a controlling interest in South India Shipping Corporation. The purchase of shares from P & O and Anglo-Norness was subject to the approval of the Reserve Bank of India. This deal would have been in the interest of Great Eastern, who would have managed a fleet of bulk carriers. It would have benefited South India Shipping Corporation too, who would have achieved substantial growth by its association with Great Eastern.

However, people managing South India Shipping raised some sort of bogey about a South Indian company being taken over by businessmen in North India. By political lobbying and manoeuvring in New Delhi, they brought about the cancellation of the share acquisition proposal.

Passing Away of the Company's Solicitor N.H. Pandia

N. H. Pandia, who had prepared the company's Memorandum and Articles of Association and attended to the legal procedures for the incorporation of the company and had been the senior partner of the company's solicitors N. H. Pandia and Co, died on 4 September 1970. N. H. Pandia provided very competent legal guidance to the company on various legal matters and issues and also attended as solicitor in respect of the litigations in which the company was involved. He had also founded a society for free legal aid to the poor. He was the embodiment of simple living and high thinking. The company's link with the Solicitors Pandia and Company finally ceased when N. N. Pandia, son of N. H. Pandia, died at the end of 1977 and the firm ceased to exist.

Capital Structure, Profits and Dividends in the First Half of the Third Decade

The paid up share capital of the company as on 30 June 1969 was Rs.2,39,83,488, consisting of 23,95,313 equity shares of Rs.10/- each (Rs. 2,39,53,130) plus Rs.30,358 on account of forfeited shares. The financial year 1969-70 was altered to end on 31 March 1970 (a period of 9 months). During the year 1969-70 bonus shares were issued by capitalising reserves of Rs. 2,39,53,130 and issuing bonus shares to the shareholders in the proportion of one bonus share for one share already held by them. The paid up share capital on 31 March 1970 therefore amounted to Rs. 4,79,36,618 consisting of 47,90,626 equity shares of Rs. 10/- each (Rs. 4,79,06260/-) plus Rs. 30,358/- on account of forfeited shares. The paid-up share capital of the company remained the same up to 31 March 1973.

In the year 1968-69 the freight and charter hire earnings amounted to Rs. 10.10 crore and the net profit was Rs. 2.33 crore. A dividend of 25 per cent was paid on the paid up share capital of the company.

In the year 1969-70, which covered a period of 9 months, the freight and charter hire earnings were Rs.7.90 crore, the net profit was Rs. 1.59 crore. A dividend of 12 per cent was paid on the enlarged paid up share capital of the company, which was double that of 1968-69.

In the year 1970-71 the freight and charter hire earnings amounted to Rs. 12.53 crore, the net profit was Rs. 3.57 crore and a dividend of 22.5 per cent was paid on the paid up share capital of the Company.

In the year 1971-72 the freight and charter hire earnings amounted to Rs. 14.29 crore, the net profit, Rs. 3.15 crore. A dividend of 22.5 per cent was paid on the paid up share capital of the company.

The freight and charter hire earnings in the year 1972-73 amounted to Rs. 14.64 crore, the net profit was Rs. 4.29 crore. A dividend of 25 per cent was paid on the paid up share capital of the company.

Profitability Comparison

The returns on capital employed in respect of Great Eastern and the three other major Indian shipping companies for the years 1968-69 to 1972-73 are set out below.

Percentage Return on Capital Employed

Name of the Company	1968-69	1969-70	1970-71	1971-72	1972-73	Average for 5 years
Great Eastern	11.6	8.5	13.3	12.5	12.3	11.6
Shipping Corp.	7.4	6.7	6.5	6.4	4.5	6.3
Scindia Steam	8.0	6.4	7.7	8.7	8.7	7.9
India Steamship	11.8	6.7	1.1	9.6	12.9	8.4

Source: Various issues of *Indian Shipping*

The return has been calculated on capital employed, which is the sum total of paid-up capital, reserves, surplus and loans. Profit or total return has been calculated before providing for interest on loans, development rebate, Managing Agent's commission and taxation.

It may be observed from the above data that Great Eastern was the most profitable Indian shipping company amongst the four major Indian shipping companies.

Coastal Trade

The company's participation in the coastal dry bulk trade during the years 1968-69 and 1969-70 was negligible. In the year 1970-71 the company's ships did not carry any dry bulk cargo on the coast at all. However, in the year 1971-72 the export of iron ore from the east coast of India to Japan was considerably hampered by difficulties faced by the Minerals and Metals Trading Corporation Ltd. There was also a strike by the dock labour on the West Coast of the U.S.A and the company's ships were therefore unable to berth at those ports for carriage of cargo from American ports to India. In view of these difficulties in availability of cargo, the company placed some of its ships in the coastal and near trades. The company's ships carried out 19 coastal voyages during the year 1971-72 and carried over 1 lakh tons of coal and 33,000 tons of salt on the coast.

In the year 1972-73 the company's vessels carried out 10 coastal voyages and lifted coal and salt cargo which was less than 50 per cent of the coastal cargo carried by the ships in 1971-72.

This participation in the coastal trade in the year 1971-72 and 1972-73 came about not because the coastal trade was remunerative but because there was a fall in the outward cargo of iron ore from India to Japan for ships becoming free in India. Since there was paucity of bulk cargoes other than iron ore moving outwards from India, alternative employment for the company's ships becoming free at Indian ports had to be found. There was also pressure from the government on Indian shipowners to berth their ships for coastal trade.

The Indian Coastal Conference had made a representation to the government in June 1969 for a 23 per cent increase in the coastal freight rates, and had been granted an increase of 20 per cent. In May 1972 the Coastal Conference, in view of the heavy losses sustained by Indian shipowners in the carriage of coastal trades, asked for a 50.32 per cent rise in freight rate. The government granted in December 1972 an increase of 15 per cent in the freight rates on general cargo and salt and 5 per cent on coal.

The increases sanctioned were inadequate. The total coastal dry cargo shipments also declined from 20.74 lakh tonnes in 1969 to 16.49 lakh tonnes in 1973. The Indian coastal shipping fleet had progressively declined from 90 ships of 3.42 lakh GRT in February 1968 to 59 ships of 2.01 lakh GRT in 1973.

A. H. Bhiwandiwalla Resigns

A.H. Bhiwandiwalla, who along with Maneklal Ujamshi and Jagjiwan Ujamshi Mulji had founded the company and who was Chairman and Director of the company for 25 years since its inception and Executive Chairman since the abolition of the Managing Agency on 3 April 1970, resigned as Chairman and Director of the company with effect from 18 October 1973. The Board made strenuous efforts over more than six months to persuade A.H. Bhiwandiwalla to withdraw his resignation. As he could not be persuaded to continue, the Board of Directors at their meeting on 27 June 1974 reluctantly accepted his resignation with effect from 18 October 1973. Vasant Sheth was unanimously appointed at the same meeting by the Board of Directors as Chairman in place of A. H. Bhiwandiwalla.

A. H. Bhiwandiwalla's cordial, balanced temperament and vast experience in industrial and business matters enabled him to play a most fruitful role in the Board meetings of Great Eastern. At the Annual and Extra-Ordinary General Meetings of the company he was extremely popular and immensely liked by the shareholders. The house flag of Great Eastern displayed by all its ships when they are in port and on festive occasions, and the funnel markings of each of the Great Eastern vessels, bear his initials, 'AHB'. They will always bear eloquent testimony to his most creditable role as a founder and Chairman of the company during its early formative period. A. H. Bhiwandiwalla died on 20 April 1991.

Death of Jayantilal J. Mulji

Jayantilal J. Mulji, who was founder director of the company, died on 16 April 1974. He had been a director on the Board of Great Eastern till the time of his death. His guidance, particularly in the formative and crucial years of the company, had been invaluable. Many times, his guidance was sought on problems faced by the company and his mature advice always benefited the company.

Sudhir J. Mulji Becomes Joint Managing Director

Sudhir J. Mulji, who was already looking after the affairs of the company along with Vasant Sheth and K.M.Sheth, was appointed as an Additional Director on the Board on 27 June 1974. He was appointed as Joint Managing Director with effect from 14 August 1974 for a period of five years.

Induction of New Directors

Sanat P. Mehta, an eminent income tax lawyer, and Rusi N. Sethna, Solicitor and Partner of Romer Dadachanji Sethna and Company, a well-known firm of solicitors, were appointed as additional directors with effect from 27 June 1974 by the Board of Directors and elected as directors by shareholders at the Annual General Meeting held on 26 September 1974.

Sanat Mehta's association with the company as the company's tax counsel dated back to the early 1950s. His advice and guidance was very useful to the company in tax planning. He also successfully appeared for the company before various legal forums in a number of tax cases. A very learned lawyer and gentleman to the core, Sanat Mehta made a very useful contribution to the deliberations of the Board.

Rusi N. Sethna, a brilliant solicitor with a very practical bent of mind, was very useful to the company in the various legal matters, problems and cases. In the deliberations of the Board, his thorough grasp of legal aspects and a knack of finding solutions to vexed problems enabled him to play a most active and useful role. Whenever thorny problems arose, the Chairman, the Deputy Chairman and the Company Secretary always consulted him and received valuable and practical advice from him.

Sevantilal M. Sheth, director in charge of A. H. Bhiwandiwalla and Company (Bombay) Private Ltd was appointed as an Additional Director by the Board on 27 June 1974 in the casual vacancy caused by the demise of Jayantilal Mulji, and elected as director by the shareholders at the AGM held on 26 September 1974. He was a very dynamic and experienced businessman who managed and handled the business of Bhiwandiwallas after the death of his father Maneklal Ujamshi and uncle Jagjiwan Ujamshi. In view of his other business commitments, he resigned from the Board of Great Eastern effective from 22 December 1976.

S. Jagannathan, I.C.S. (Retired) was appointed as Additional Director by the Board on 30 June 1977 and elected as Director by the shareholders at the AGM of the company held on 29 December 1977. S. Jagannathan was Director General of Shipping in 1950 and thereafter held many important financial positions in government. He was Financial Commissioner, Railway Board, Economic Secretary, Ministry of Finance, Governor, Reserve Bank of India; Executive Director, World Bank; Executive Director, International Monetary Fund; and also had held the post of Ambassador for Economic Affairs, Indian Embassy, Washington. His vast and varied experience and his profound knowledge of economic and financial matters was very useful to the company. He played a very active and useful role in the deliberations of the Board and made significant contributions in the discussion of economic and financial aspects of all important problems and issues placed before the Board.

Hindustan Shipyard hikes price

In February 1971, the company had voluntarily, without any pressure from the government, placed an order for building of four ships of about 21,610 DWT each with Hindustan Shipyard. It may be stated that there was no compulsion on the company at that time of any *pari-passu* obligation, which was introduced by the government later for placing orders for building of ships at Indian shipyards against ships purchased or built abroad by Indian shipowners. The contract with Hindustan Shipyard was for a fixed price of Rs. 5.50 crore per ship, that is, Rs. 22 crore for all the four ships. The ships were to be delivered by Hindustan Shipyard to the company on specified dates. However, the delivery of the ships was considerably delayed, as can be seen from the table below:

	Schedule of Delivery Dates as per contract	Actual Delivery Dates
1st ship	31.12.1973	23.3.1975
2nd ship	31.3.1974	20.3.1976
3rd ship	30.6.1974	6.9.1976
4th ship	30.9.1974	12.3.1977

The average delay in delivery of the ships was more than two years. During this time the company had to unproductively lock up building price instalments paid to Hindustan Shipyard. Worse, these ships could not take advantage of the excellent dry cargo freight market which prevailed in 1974 and 1975, losing substantial profits and consequent cash in-flows. The ships were delivered when the recession in the dry cargo freight markets set in!

Due to the delay in completing construction, the building costs went up. The company had a fixed price contract with the shipyard. However, taking undue advantage of the Emergency, which was declared by the then Prime Minister Indira Gandhi in the country on 26 June 1975, the government pressurised the company in 1975 and 1976 to agree to an escalation of price of the ships in spite of the clear contractual provision of a fixed price. The government even threatened the company that its ships would not get government-owned and controlled cargoes fixed by Transchart, and that the company's proposals for purchase and sale of ships would not be approved. The company was thus forced to pay Rs 8.75 crore as escalation over and above the price of Rs. 22 crore, which was a 38 per cent hike in the price. The additional burden in annual interest of Rs. 39 lakh and annual depreciation of Rs. 44 lakh on the additional price totalled to Rs. 83 lakh per annum. The company was also precluded from claiming any compensation for delayed delivery of the ships from Hindustan Shipyard.

The other very adverse consequence of the price escalation was the unnecessary and unwarranted cash outgo on repayment of instalments of a 95 per cent loan which was sanctioned to meet the escalation in price, interest instalments on this loan, and the balance 5 per cent of the escalation cost paid out of the company's cash resources.

Proposed Collaboration with Swires

John Swire and Sons is a very reputed business house with large business interests in the U.K., Australia and the Far East. Their major business interests include shipping, aviation, and banking.

Sudhir Mulji had a very good relationship with Sir Adrian Swire, who later became President of the British Shipowners' Association, namely The General Council of British Shipping. It was at Sudhir Mulji's initiative that Swires were appointed as agents for looking after Great Eastern's ships in Japan. On the initiative taken by Sudhir Mulji, Swires agreed in 1975 to have a joint venture shipping company in collaboration with Great Eastern in Singapore.

It was proposed to start the company with a paid-up capital of about U.S. $ 4 million. The 51 per cent holding in the company was to be that of Swires and 49 per cent of Great Eastern. The company was to purchase from Great Eastern a Pioneer Class ship, which was being constructed on account of Great Eastern at Visakhapatnam by Hindustan Shipyard, at a price of Rs. 10 crore.

The joint venture could have bought more Indian built ships in the future. Export of Indian-built ships would therefore have received an impetus. The company would have been able to achieve fast expansion because of easy availability of foreign credit for acquisition of ships under the Singapore flag. Threre was full freedom and flexiblity of shipping operations in Singapore and it was therefore easy to get foreign loans for acquisition of ships. The joint venture shipping company with the participation of the well known and influential Swire group would have considerably enhanced Great Eastern's own image internationally as a multinational company, which would have resulted in the company getting foreign exchange loans more readily and on better terms from foreign bankers and financiers.

The freedom of operation under the Singapore flag, absence of taxes on shipping income in Singapore and efficient management of foreign exchange earnings and disbursements in the absence of restrictions on foreign exchange in respect of shipping companies in Singapore would have helped the joint venture to operate efficiently and earn comparatively higher profits than was possible on the same investment under the Indian flag. But this was not to be.

Strenuous efforts were made by Great Eastern to secure the

Government of India's approval. In fact, when the company was compelled to pay a price escalation for the four ships it had ordered, government officials had assured the company that they would clear the proposal for the formation of the joint venture company in Singapore. The company could thus sell 1 of the 4 ships to the joint venture company. Swires, in view of their close business relationship with Great Eastern, waited for more than a year for the Indian government's clearance to Great Eastern to float the joint venture company. Permission, however, was not forthcoming, and the joint venture proposal could not become a reality.

Denial of Committed SDFC Loans

The company on 31 July 1973 owned a fleet of 4,29,144 DWT. The cost of the fleet as on 30 June 1973 was Rs.45 crore. The company decided to undertake a bold fleet expansion programme, which on implementation would have trebled the investment in the fleet. The expansion programme was to be on these lines:

Particulars of ships to be built or acquired	Deadweight tonnage of ships to be added	Estimated cost of acquisition Rs. in crore
2 OBO Carriers of 122350 DWT each	244,700	57.35
1 Product Carrier of 32,360 DWT	32,360	13.16
2 Bulk Carriers of 26645 DWT each	53,290	18.40
Total	330,350	88.91

This expansion programme could be implemented if adequate loan assistance from Shipping Development Fund Committee (SDFC) was assured. The company therefore held discussions with the then Secretary to the Ministry of Shipping and Transport who was also Chairman of SDFC. On the basis of the assurance of loan assistance from SDFC, the company decided to implement the expansion programme. The entire expansion programme was completed in November 1976 and cost due to currency fluctuations had gone up to Rs. 100 crore.

The year 1973 had been a boom year in shipping. Shipping companies were enjoying excellent profitability and cash-flow. In the discussions with M.G.Pimputkar, the then Transport Secretary to the Government of India and Chairman of SDFC, Great Eastern's representatives were told that although the company was eligible for loans of up to 90 per cent of the price of the product carrier and the 2 OBO carriers, grant of 40 per cent loan on the product carrier, that is, Rs. 5.26 crore, and 30 per cent on the two OBO carriers, that is, Rs. 17.2 crore, would ensure successful implementation of the expansion undertaken by the company. However, if difficulties arose, SDFC would consider stepping up of the loans as it appreciated that the Rs. 100-crore expansion needed adequate funds.

SDFC decided in meetings held in October and December 1973 to grant loan assistance on these lines. In 1974, however, the company was told that the delay in processing the approved loans in respect of the product carrier and the two OBO carriers was due to inadequacy of funds with SDFC. Subsequently, SDFC went back on its commitments. After a great deal of follow-up by the company, SDFC sanctioned in 1976 a meagre loan of Rs. 188.67 lakh for the product carrier. Meanwhile, the prevailing international shipping depression had very adversly affected the cash-flow position of the company. After strenuous efforts by the company, SDFC in 1977 approved a loan of about Rs. 3.75 crore on terms analogous to those under the new foreign exchange financing scheme (SAFAUNS Scheme) to enable the company to meet part of its foreign exchange repayment obligations in the year 1977-78. But even this loan, approved by SDFC in June 1977, was not disbursed and was not made available to the company.

From 1974 onwards, tanker shipping, and from 1976 onwards, dry cargo shipping, plunged into an acute and prolonged depression. The company therefore needed far increased loan assistance than what was approved by SDFC. The tragic irony of the situation is that even the modest loan assistance of 40 per cent of the price of the product carrier and 30 per cent of the cost of the two OBO carriers, for which SDFC stood committed, was not given.

Any less efficient shipping company implementing a Rs. 100-crore fleet expansion, suddenly divested of promised loan assistance on which the expansion was largely based, and then faced with an acute and continuing shipping depression, would have gone into bankruptcy. Great Eastern, however, survived through various measures taken at great cost to the company, such as sale of ships at low prices in depressed times to augment the cash-flow, arrangement of Euro-currency loans and moratoria from foreign lenders at greatly increased interest cost, etc. The company also could not seize the opportunity like Greek and Hongkong shipowners at that time to purchase ships at throwaway prices which were prevalent in 1977 and 1978 and achieve tonnage expansion at minimum cost in the interest of the company as well as the country.

The whimsical way in which SDFC dealt with this matter was in sharp contrast with the foreign lenders and financial institutions who, aware of the company's cash-flow difficulties but also aware of its inherently sound financial position, waived their contractual provisions of repayment and granted moratoria to the company. What the company had required from SDFC was nothing more than the loan funds assured by it, on the basis of which the company had embarked upon its Rs. 100-crore expansion programme. The company did not want any "rescue" loans which most other shipping companies required over and above the normal loans already received by them from SDFC. A national development financing institution going back on its commitment and withdrawing support is an unbelievable phenomenon.

The main reason cited by SDFC for non-disbursement of the committed loans was the company's declaration of dividend of 36 per cent on its equity share capital for the financial year 1974-75. The amount of Rs. 3.45 crore distributed to the shareholders was only 32 per cent of the net profit of Rs. 10.89 crore earned during the year. The balance 68 per cent was ploughed back into the business. The amount distributed as dividend gave a return of 11 per cent to the shareholders on their total equity (paid-up share capital plus reserves) of over Rs. 31 crore in the company. At that time there was no clause containing any restriction on payment of dividends in the loan agreement with SDFC nor did SDFC give any directive that dividends beyond a specified percentage should not be declared. In fact the government and SDFC Director A. K. Srivastava (who was later designated Executive Director of SDFC) was present at the Board Meeting which recommended this dividend. He not only did not oppose the idea but spoke at the meeting, joining in the consenus of recommending a 36 per cent dividend.

This dividend was declared before the depression in the dry cargo freight market set in, and adversely affected the profitability and cash-flows of the company. The company did not pay any dividend to the shareholders for the financial years 1977-78 and 1978-79 when the company's financial position was adversely affected by the acute shipping depression. It is therefore most surprising that payment of 36 per cent dividend in respect of a very good financial year for the company should have been made an excuse for non-disbursement of committed loans.

It was also contended that SDFC did not disburse the loans because it had not got government sanction to the payment of the loan. The fact was, that it was SDFC which did not pursue the matter of obtaining government approval and went back on its own commitments.

The distortion in SDFC's loan assistance policies which commenced and gathered full force in the decade not only adversely affected shipping development in India but placed government funds in jeopardy and ultimately resulted in the winding up of SDFC in the next decade.

Great Eastern Shipping Company was not only adversely affected by distorted SDFC loan assistance policies but also became a victim of unjustified denials of promised and committed SDFC loans in respect of its Rupee 100 crore expansion. The onset of shipping depression in the dry cargo sector from 1976 onwards further aggravated the serious situation for the Company. The adverse consequences can be summarised as under :

1) As SDFC loan funds at the interest rate of 4 per cent per annum were not available, the company had to resort to reschedulement of foreign exchange loans in respect of two OBO carriers and the interest cost was London Inter-bank Offered Rate (LIBOR) + ∫ per cent spread on Euro-currency loans. The loss due to higher interest payments was estimated at Rs. 10.58 crore.
2) The reschedulement of foreign exchange loans in respect of OBO carriers involved paying repayment instalments in later years at unfavourable rates of exchange, resulting in an estimated loss of Rs. 2 crore.

3) The cash flow position of the company compelled it to sell some of its ships at almost throw-away prices in the shipping depression.

4) In 1978, for raising cash resources, the company had to transfer office accommodation of about 43,000 sq.ft. at World Trade Centre, Cuffe Parade, Bombay, which it had booked in 1974, to Computer Maintenance Corporation Ltd and the State Bank of India. The company had acquired these office premises on a very long term lease at Rs. 250 per sq. ft., and this was transferred to the buyers at Rs. 300 per sq. ft. Later, it acquired office accommodation in 1989 of about 8,000 sq. ft. at World Trade Centre, and had to purchase in 1991 a building at Palton Road near Victoria Terminus Station. The average cost of acquiring these two permises exceeded Rs. 4,000 per square foot. The total area of these permises taken together is only about 30,000 sq. feet, and is therefore not full replacement of the office area of about 43,000 sq. feet which the company had to dispose of in 1978.

5) Another fall out of the loans not materializing was that the company could not acquire ships at throw-away prices during the depression and lost the opportunity of achieving sizeable expansion during the depression years of the decade.

Capital Structure, Profits and Dividends in the Second Half of the Third Decade

In the year 1973-74 reserves of Rs. 4,79,06,260 were capitalised and bonus shares were issued in the proportion of one bonus share for one share held by the shareholders. The paid-up share capital therefore went up from Rs. 4,79,36,618 (inclusive of forfeited shares of Rs. 30,358) on 31 March 1973 to Rs. 9,58,42,878 (inclusive of forfeited shares of Rs. 30,358) on 31 March 1974. In the year 1976-77 reserves of Rs. 5,74,87,520 were capitalised and bonus shares were issued in the proportion of three bonus shares for five shares held by the shareholders. The paid-up share capital therefore went up from Rs. 9,58,42,878 on 30 June 1976 to Rs. 15,33,30,368 on 30 June 1977. The paid-up share capital remained the same on 30 June 1978.

The freight and charter hire earnings rose from Rs. 14.64 crore in 1972-73 to Rs. 19.33 crore in the year 1973-74. The net profit was Rs. 3.59 crore. A dividend of 12 per cent was paid on the paid-up share capital of the company. The dividend was restricted to 12 per cent in view of the provisions of the Companies (Temporary Restrictions on Dividends) Ordinance 1974 under which the company could declare or pay dividends not exceeding distributable profits which were defined as one third of the net profit for the financial year or an amount required to pay 12 per cent, whichever was lower.

In the year 1974-75, the freight and charter hire earnings amounted to Rs. 38.79 crore. The net profit amounted to Rs. 10.89 crore. A dividend of 36 per cent was paid on the paid-up share capital of the company. In accordance with the amendment to the Companies (Temporary Restrictions on Dividends) Act 1974 and the Companies (Temporary Restrictions on Dividends) Act 1975 the declared dividend was paid thus: 12 per cent was paid immediately and the balance 24 per cent was deferred, out of which 12 per cent was paid on 5 July 1976 and 12 per cent was paid on 5 July 1977.

The freight and charter hire earnings in the year 1975-76 (15 month period) amounted to Rs. 44.33 crore. The net profit was Rs. 11.71 crore. A dividend of 20 per cent was paid for the 15 month period (1 April 1975 to 30th June 1976) on the paid-up share capital of the company.

In the year 1976-77 the freight and charter hire earnings amounted to Rs. 42.03 crore. The net profit was Rs. 8.79 crore out of which the profit on sale of ships was Rs. 7.35 crore. In the previous year 1975-76 (15 month period) the net profit of Rs. 11.71 crore included an amount of Rs. 5.30 crore on sale of ships. The decline in the operating net profit was due to the shipping depression which prevailed at that time. A dividend of 15 per cent was paid on the paid-up share capital of the company.

In the year 1977-78, which was a period of acute depression, the freight and charter hire earnings amounted to Rs. 30.89 crore. The company sustained a loss of Rs. 8.82 crore. In view of the loss sustained by the company, no dividend was paid for the year 1977-78.

Profitability Comparison

The returns on capital employed in respect of Great Eastern and the other three major Indain shipping companies for the years

1973-74 to 1977-78 are given below:

Percentage Return on Capital Employed

Name of the Company	1973-74	1974-75	1975-76	1976-77	1977-78
Great Eastern	8.1	16.2	11.1	9.1	-1.6
Shipping Corporation	5.6	10.2	4.8	4.8	2.0
Scindia Steam	10.6	14.5	7.3	4.2	-2.5
India Steamship	11.4	19.3	9.9	4.9	3.8

India Steamship was entirely a liner company, Scindias were predominantly a liner company and the Shipping Corporation also had substantial liner operations. Liner shipping, as far as freight rates were concerned, were not adversely affected to the same extent as tramp shipping (bulk cargo shipping) was affected. The capacity utilisation of liner ships was reduced. Indian liner shipping companies also had the advantage of remunerative bilateral arrangements with the shipping companies of the Communist Bloc in Europe (Russia and the East European countries) in regard to the carriage of trade between India and the communist bloc in Europe.

In addition to the depression, Great Eastern was subjected to the handicap of the heavy additional interest burden, exchange losses etc. due to denial of SDFC loans. There was also additional interest and depreciation burden imposed on the company due to the escalation of prices of the four Hindustan Shipyard built ships in spite of the fixed price contracts. However, the performance of Great Eastern in spite of these severe handicaps was very satisfactory.

London Office Opened

London has been the most important maritime centre in the world. For purchase and sale of ships, London brokers have been very active. For chartering of ships, for fixtures of ships with cargoes etc., the Baltic Exchange and London brokers play a very important role. There are banks and financial institutions in London which specialise in shipping finance. Lloyds underwriters and company underwriters in the U.K. provide the most important marine insurance market. Lloyds Classification Society, Salvage Association and other maritime services, such as protection and indemnity insurance, provided in London, add to the value of London as the most important maritime centre. Therefore opening an office in London provides direct access to very valuable maritime services required by shipping. It also enables the shipowner with an office in London to keep abreast of the important developments in shipping, judge the market trends and increase his efficiency.

It became an urgent necessity for the company to open a London office. With the onset of the depression, the tanker and the OBO carrier freight market was most adversely affected, and Great Eastern had a problem finding employment for its tankers and OBO carriers. The supply of these ships far exceeded the demand for them. The offers of oil cargoes from the shippers or charterers were few and far between, and they dictated their terms to shipowners. Shipowners had to accept the offers promptly if they did not want their ships to idle. London was the centre where these offers were made, and it was therefore most essential for the company to have an office in London. With Reserve Bank of India's approval, the company's Board of Directors approved the lease of office premises for its London office on 27 June 1974.

The opening of a branch office in London resulted in better employment of the company's OBO carriers and tankers during the difficult depression years. Sudhir Mulji, who already had excellent contacts in London, looked after the London office. The fixtures which he arranged for the company's OBO carriers and the guidance he gave to the company in respect of various aspects of shipping, including shipping finance, was of great value to the company. London office provided a window on international technological, operational and financial developments in shipping. It was therefore a very important event in the history of the company.

Closure of Calcutta Office

In 1966-67, in view of the decline in the importance of the port of Calcutta, and consequent decline in the company's operations there, staff had been reduced (see Chapter 3). The position had worsened since then. The cost of maintaining and running the Calcutta office was disproportionate to the reduced operations and activities of the company's ships in the port of Calcutta. Work at Calcutta could be carried on at a lesser cost by appointment of an agent, and the Board of Directors, on 30 October 1976, decided to close down the Branch office at Calcutta and appoint an agent to look after the company's business there. Some employees retired on payment of compensation and some members of the staff were transferred to Bombay. The Calcutta office premises were transferred to a business house. Not only did the office rental expenses cease, the company also got a fee for the transfer of office premises. The closure of the Calcutta office was one of the self-help measures adopted by the company to economise during the shipping depression.

House Journal

In August 1974 it was decided to start a House Journal so that floating staff on board the company's ships, the company's office staff, important business houses with which the company had business relationships, the government offices with which the company had dealings etc. could be kept posted about developments in the company. The Board authorised Mrs. Jyotsna K. Sheth to declare herself as editor, printer and publisher of the house magazine. Jyotsna Sheth, wife of K.M. Sheth—Deputy Chairman and Managing Director of the company—was a journalist even before her marriage and had been associated with the *Times of India* for some time. After her marriage she became a free-lance journalist and her contributions and articles appeared in leading newspapers and journals from time to time. The house magazine was named *Gesco News*, and under Jyotsna Sheth's editorship performed a useful function of keeping the employees and others having dealings with the company or interested in the company posted with the latest events in the company.

Sale of a Ship to Tata Chemicals

It was in April 1977 that the Board of Directors approved the sale of the company's ship, *Jag Dev*, to Tata Chemicals for Rs. 4.87

crore. Tata Chemicals, after becoming owners of the ship, entrusted the management of the ship to the company. Vasant Sheth joined the Board of Directors of Tata Chemicals and Darbari Sheth of Tata Chemicals joined the Great Eastern Board as a Director. It was hoped that this collaboration between the company and the house of Tatas would be mutually beneficial. However, unfortunately, the time that Tata Chemicals entered shipping turned out to be unfavourable. In the continuing depression Tata Chemicals did not earn money from this project.

Cadet Academy

Great Eastern always believed that its best asset was well-trained, able, reliable and loyal manpower. It was felt that the company should start its own institution for training, whereby young cadets taken directly should be trained ashore and afloat so that the company could have competent and loyal deck officers. A residential Cadet Academy was therefore started on board *Jawahar*, the sea cadet training ship at Pilot Bunder, Colaba, Bombay on 31 March 1975. The venue is ideally suited for training young men for a sea career.

The foundation stone of the Academy was laid by Mrs. Asha Sheth, wife of Vasant Sheth, who was keenly interested in the development of well-trained manpower for shipping. Great Eastern was the first Indian shipping company to start such an academy for selection and training of navigating officers. Commodore R.S. Malia, who had retired from the Indian Navy, was placed as Administrator in charge of this Academy. Commodore Malia has made a very worthy contribution to the efficient running and development of the Academy. The Academy has been conducting courses for pre-sea training (duration 3 months) and mid-sea training (duration 4 months).

Its rigid selection procedure for candidates is as follows:

Selection is on an all-India competitive basis. The candidates are subjected to written test, followed by psychological test/screening with a view to test the candidates' aptitude and motivation for a sea-going career, and finally interviewed by the Administrator of the Academy and Selection Board. Only those who make the merit list are inducted finally.

A broad syllabus of 3 months duration has been drawn,

incorporating practical seamanship including boatwork, ship organisation and some cargo work, navigation theory and practical and signals in depth. Academics consisting of higher nautical physics and mathematics, algebra etc. are taught to provide firm grounding. Parade training is a part of the syllabus.

All this is augmented by frequent, organised tour visits to the ships of the company in harbour and naval and commercial shipping yards.

The young cadets are given a defence orientation through visits to Indian naval ships and training establishments like National Defence Academy, Khadakwasla etc. Training visits to merchant navy ships, *T.S. Rajendra*, Nehru Planetarium, Colaba Meteorological observatory etc., are regular features of the course.

In addition to professional subjects, equal emphasis is laid on developing officer-like qualities. Instructors help cadets in imbibing a sense of discipline, initiative, integrity, teamwork, resourcefulness and loyalty to the organisation in which they serve. Cadets are helped on parade, off parade to achieve this through special lectures and personal guidance.

The academy has conducted 37 courses of 'pre-sea' and 'mid-sea' training since its inception. In addition to meeting the requirement of Great Eastern, the Academy has trained cadets drawn from 17 other Indian and international shipping companies.

The cadets trained here during the last 17 years have been appointed as Captains, Chief Officers and Second Mates on ships. Almost all officers passed Second Mate (F.G.), Mates and Command Examinations in their first attempt.

The cadets selected and trained at the Cadet Academy have proved to be very good and competent navigating officers. A number of them are in command of the Great Eastern's ships. The Academy has also conducted courses for other Indian and foreign shipping companies. The Academy has already established its reputation as a leading Merchant Navy officers training institution owned by a shipping company in the private sector with Government of India recognition.

Recognition by the Government

In January 1979, the Ministry of Shipping and Transport accorded approval to the Academy's pre-sea training syllabus for direct entry cadets who were selected and trained at the Academy. This approval entitles the cadets to remission of sea time for the period they were under training ashore after selection.

In August 1982, the Director General of Shipping gave approval for full remission of sea time for the advanced mid-sea training courses being conducted at the Academy.

This is considered a notable achievement as the Academy stands recognised by the government as a residential institution authorised for imparting professional training up to Second Mate Examination level to cadets during apprenticeship period.

Shipping Depression

The Director's Annual Report to the shareholders dated 31 August 1973 for the year ended 31 March 1973, prepared in boom times before the oil crisis at the end of 1973, when the company made excellent profits, showed awareness of the cyclical nature of the shipping industry. The report stated: "The oceans have been a bountiful provider to all those who have ventured but equally the perils of the sea should not be forgotten. The high-tide of today's freight market will, if and when it crashes, hit a low ebb and it is during that period that the sternest test of the Management and Shareholders of the company will come. Your Directors will do their best to safeguard against these heavy swings in fortune. It will require a determined and courageous effort to move into modern tonnage, to take decisions to sell older ships and to judge the market with some skill. We trust that we shall have your support in all these decisions in the hope that the strength of the company remains undiminished in future years."

As already mentioned earlier in this chapter, in the post-war years there was tremendous growth in world sea-borne trade which provided demand for shipping services. The world shipping fleet which supplied the shipping services, also therefore recorded commensurate growth. The Arab-Israeli conflict and subsequent oil crisis at the end of 1973, during which the prices of oil were quadrupled, brought about a slowing down of the increase in world sea-borne trade and even decrease in some of the years subsequent to the oil crisis. The growth in supply of ships however did not adjust itself to the slackening growth and even decrease in demand up to the year 1975-76. This was because of the progressive increase in the world shipbuilding capacity due to expectation of a continued rise in demand of ships represented by the world sea-borne trade and the assistance given by the governments to their shipbuilding industries because of their strategic and employment value. There could not be a sudden curtailment of the output of ships because there is normally a time-lag of 1 to 2 years between the ordering of ships and their delivery. The table below gives the year-wise details of annual shipbuilding orders placed and annual completion of ships from 1968 to 1978.

It will be observed from the following table that 1968 shipbuilding output of 16.84 million GRT doubled itself in each of the years 1973, 1974, 1975 and 1976. The shipbuilding output underwent adjustment from the year 1977 onwards. It declined to 18.19 million GRT in 1978, which was about the level reached in 1969.

Shipbuilding volume of orders and completions from 1968 to 1978

Year	Annual volume of order placed (Million tons gross)	Annual completions (Million tons gross)
1968	26.14	16.84
1969	30.05	18.74
1970	41.03	20.98
1971	29.64	24.39
1972	30.36	26.75
1973	73.60	30.41
1974	28.37	33.54
1975	13.79	34.20
1976	12.94	33.92
1977	11.09	27.53
1978	8.03	18.19

Source: Lloyds Register of Shipping Annual Report 1979 Section entitled 'World Shipbuilding Report.'

As a result of great surplus of shipping tonnage in the context of the demand for it, ships were laid-up for want of employment. Slow steaming of ships at lower speeds which reduced the fuel consumption in the context of the greatly rising fuel cost, also absorbed a part of this surplus tonnage. Laid-up tonnage is regarded as a sort of barometer for recording the intensity of the shipping depression. The figures in respect of the laid-up tonnage from 1974 to 1978 are given below :

World Laid-up Tonnage in the Shipping Depression 1974-78
(In million GRT and percentage of the then existing fleet)

July 1	Million GRT	Percentage
1974	0.6	0.2
1975	17.2	5.4
1976	25.2	7.5
1977	20.0	5.6
1978	29.7	8.0

Source: Dr. A. Stromme Svendsen's paper entitled 'The Impact of the present crisis in Shipping on Liner Activities', in *Liner Shipping in Eighties* published by Institute of Shipping Economics, Bremen, 1979.

As a result of the imbalance between supply and demand the freight rates declined from 1974 to 1978. The following table containing freight rate indices shows the extent of the fall from the year 1973 to 1978 in respect of the three sectors of shipping namely dry cargo tramps, liners and tankers (crude carriers).

Freight Rate Indices

Year	Dry cargo tramp trip charter July 1965 to June 1966=100	Liner 1965=100	Tanker Worldscale = 100 as effective in each year — Crude Carriers
1973	162	140	192
1974	218	186	98
1975	142	204	52
1976	134	215	50
1977	133	229	50
1978	140	241	66

Source: *Norwegian Shipping News* for dry cargo tramp trip charter index, Bundeaministerium fur verkehr, Hamburg for liner index, and tanker index.

It will be observed that there was a steep decline in the tanker freight rates from 1974 onwards. However, dry cargo trip charter rates almost recorded a rise in freight rates in 1974, and even up to the end of 1975 the decline was not substantial. It was a very interesting phenomenon that the dry cargo boom coincided with the tanker slump in 1974 and 1975. However, the massive influx of tankers and combination carriers due to very low tanker freight rates into the dry bulk trades later adversely affected the dry bulk cargo freight rates also.

It may also be mentioned that from 1974 onwards the costs of operation, especially due to quadrupling of fuel prices and also due to inflation, went up, which is not reflected in the freight rate indices. This factor must be taken into account in considering the rise in liner freight rate indices. Moreover, the capacity utilisation of liner ships went down as a result of the depression.

Indian shipping companies therefore in view of their predominant interest in dry cargo trade (bulk dry cargo as well as liner trade) fared well in the years 1974-75 and 1975-76 and made good profits.

As regards Great Eastern, the company had one OBO carrier and two small tankers which were susceptible to the decline in the tanker freight market. The Directors' Report for the year ended 31 March 1975 stated that the vulnerable part of the fleet, namely the one lakh ton OBO carrier and two tankers, were fixed profitably right through March 1977. The Japanese steel mills with whom the company had a long term relationship maintained the quantum of iron ore cargo to be carried but reduced the freight rates by 10 per cent. This therefore ensured that approximately 50 per cent of the company's fleet would remain employed profitably. The barometer for the rest of the fleet continued to indicate rough weather. However, the company was fortunate in that it was left with a residue of fleet on which adverse effects on revenue could be avoided. However, it could not avoid the effects of the shipping depression in the years 1976-77 and 1977-78. The Directors' Report for the year ended 30 June 1976 very aptly described the prospects which were to be encountered in subsequent years as follows:

"The last few years have been ones of unprecedented growth and high profits; the tide has now turned and we can expect to face adverse conditions. It is hoped that it will not be for too long. We trust that we shall be able to ride the storm and when the fair weather comes we shall be ready. Your company has a fleet of new ships sturdily built with an average residual life of 15 more years. If recovery in the world trade gathers sufficient momentum we shall soon see light in the tunnel of recession. Till then we shall be constantly reminded of the high stake in the game."

Management and Executives

This decade could be characterised as one in which the company was managed by the trio Vasant Sheth, K.M. Sheth and Sudhir Mulji.

Vasant Sheth, with his business acumen, vision and his qualities to inspire and lead, K.M. Sheth with his great organising ability, to fix efficiently the employment of ships and meticulously look after the operation of ships, and Sudhir Mulji's expertise in economic and financial matters and his brilliance as a negotiator made a great contribution to the progress of the company. It also enabled the company to withstand the onslaught of the shipping depression from end 1975 to mid 1979, the first phase of the prolonged shipping depression.

K.M. Sheth was also looking after the management of the company's personnel, both afloat and ashore, and office administration. The efficiency, productivity and discipline of the office staff is evidence of the meticulous attention he paid over the years to this important area of management.

Sudhir Mulji, being an economist as well as a practical businessman, had developed excellent relationships with the high officials in the Ministry of Shipping and Transport and other Ministries who sought his advice on many matters. He therefore used to spend a lot of time in Delhi.

With the onset of the shipping depression and delivery of two OBO carriers the employment of these ships became a difficult problem. Mulji therefore took charge of the London office which was opened and took over the management and employment of the OBO carriers in this difficult period. With his good contacts in London and with his experience in arranging shipping fixtures, the OBO carriers were well employed during those difficult days. He kept the company posted with the latest international developments in regard to shipping technology, shipping operations and shipping finance, which enabled the company to plan and take timely action in these matters.

D.H.C. Storey, who took over as Technical Manager from T.M. Sanghavi, was designated Technical Director. He headed the Personnel and Maintenance Department and efficiently looked after the maintenance repairs and special surveys of the ships. The ships were maintained in a first class condition and operated smoothly with minimum of breakdowns and off-hire days.

S.N. Sanklecha, the Company Secretary, wrote and published about 50 papers on various aspects of shipping in various journals. The working group set up by the government for recommending the target and growth of the shipping industry in the Fifth Plan quoted from his paper in their Report. In view of the rapport established and strengthened by his writings on shipping, he had excellent contacts with the government officials dealing with shipping, which were very useful to the company. In the strictly regulatory regime for shipping, with controls and licences in respect of acquisition, licensing and operation of ships and provisions of Monopolies and Restrictive Trade Practices Act which applied to shipping at that time, Sanklecha's knowledge of various aspects of shipping and various laws placed the company in a more favourable position as compared with its Indian competitors in these matters.

B.N. Adappa, who headed the dry cargo division of the Operations Department, with his mastery in the subject of dry cargo operations, fixed the employment of the dry cargo fleet most advantageously and the company fared better than its competitors even during depression years. Conscientious and hard working, his capacity for putting in hard work of the best quality was unsurpassed.

A.R. Balasubramaniam, the Chief Accountant, looked after his ever-increasing accounts work, taxation matters and the recoveries of debts and liablities very efficiently.

K.J. Vesuna headed the wet cargo division and meticulously managed the company's OBO carriers and tankers. He also looked after the purchase/building of ships for the company. His expertise in financial and accounting aspects besides his knowledge of shipping operation were very valuable to the company.

N. E. Pardiwala as Personnel Manager looked after the shore personnel as well as the floating personnel of the company. He proved very useful whenever the management wanted to carry out tough and prolonged negotiations.

N.G. Kirpalani, who was transferred in August 1975 to the

company's London office, and N.L. Narasimhan, very ably assisted Storey in looking after the maintenance, repairs and special surveys of the company's fleet and ensured the smooth running and operation of the ships.

J. J. Mehta, who was Manager of Calcutta office and had managed the Calcutta office well, joined the Operations Department in Bombay on closure of Calcutta office.

K.S. Ramchandran, who had managed the New Delhi office right from its opening in the early 1950s, retired from the company on 1 November 1977. With his quiet and balanced temperament and his knack of getting along well with all, he had carried out liaison work in Delhi effectively. He had developed contacts and excellent relationships with officials in the government Ministries and Departments and successfully pursued the company's applications, representations and other matters.

Progress During the Decade

On 30 September 1968 the company's fleet consisted of 16 ships with a GRT of 179,376 and DWT of 284,119. On 9 November 1978 the company owned 19 ships of 405,015 GRT or 689,417 DWT. The ships acquired during the decade were by and large of larger sizes in accordance with the world trend, which accounted predominantly for the large increase in tonnage. The increase in the number of ships during the decade was only 3.

The fleet at cost on 30 June 1968 was Rs. 22.20 crore. The fleet at cost on 30 June 1978 was Rs. 186.33 crore and was more than 8 times the 1968 figure. The paid-up capital on 30 June 1968 was Rs. 2.40 crore. On 30 June 1978 the paid-up capital increased to more than 6 times to Rs. 15.33 crore. The entire increase in the paid-up capital was accounted for by the capitalisation of reserves and issue of bonus shares by the company. The reserves and surplus on 30 June 1968 amounted to Rs. 6.54 crore. On 30 June 1978 the reserves and surplus were three times higher at Rs. 19.85 crore.

The freight and charter hire earnings of Rs. 10.10 crore druing the year 1968-69 rose to Rs. 44.33 crore in the year 1975-76. Due to the shipping depression the freight and charter hire earnings were lower at Rs. 36.89 crore in 1977-78. In 1968-69 the company's ships carried 15.21 lakh tonnes of cargo. In 1977-78 the cargo carried by the company's ships increased more than three times to 50.69 lakh tonnes.

The net profit in the year 1968-69 amounted to Rs. 2.33 crore. In the years 1974-75, 1975-76 and 1976-77 the net profit was higher at Rs. 10.89 crore, Rs. 11.71 crore and Rs. 8.79 crore respectively. However, in the year 1977-78, due to acute depression, the company sustained a loss of Rs. 8.82 crore.

The company's shipping fleet of 4.05 lakh GRT on 9.11.1978 amounted to 7.6 per cent of the total Indian shipping fleet of 55.87 lakh GRT on 30 November 1978. The share of the company's tonnage fell from 9 per cent on 30 September 1968 to 7.6 per cent on 9 November 1978. The company's fleet at cost on 30 June 1978 of about Rs. 186 crore was about 10 per cent of the total Indian fleet at cost estimated at Rs. 1,850 crore on 30 June 1978.

The progress made by the company can be better appreciated if one takes into account that the SDFC backed out of its commitment of loan assistance on which the company's Rs.100-crore expansion was based and the shipping depression which prevailed in the closing years of this decade. In the year 1977-78 the company was losing almost a crore of rupees every month.

The Government of India had appointed a high level committee on Indian shipping (Honavar Committee) for examining the question of assistance to Indian shipping and to recommend long-term measures for the management of the shipping crisis that is, shipping depression and other related matters. The committee submitted its final report in June 1980. The committee gave financial data of eight companies. The capital employed by each company was calculated by them on the basis of net block plus investments plus working capital. Among the three major Indian shipping companies in the private sector, Great Eastern had the highest capital employed for the years 1976-77 and 1977-78. The capital employed by Shipping Corporation of India was of course much higher.

Capital Employed by Four Major Shipping Companies

(Rs. in crore)

	1976-77	1977-78
Great Eastern	163.92	151.57
Scindia	115.66	109.51
India Steamship	72.92	75.15
Shipping Corporation	341.36	580.14

The committee had also made an inter-firm comparison of efficiency of operation based on the results of the companies for the year 1978-79 which perhaps falls in the year outside the decade covered by this chapter. However, in view of its relevance as one of the years of the depression we quote the findings:

	Profit before Interest (Rs. in lakhs)	Profit per DWT (Rs.)
Great Eastern	1001.21	144
Scindia	124.64	14
India Steamship	478.70	138
Shipping Corporation	- 8.60	- 0.2

Note: Profit excludes gains and losses not relating to normal shipping activities

The inter-firm comparison made by the high level committee on shipping showed that Great Eastern stood first in efficiency of operation among four major Indian shipping companies.

It may also be mentioned that in the *Economic Times* dated 25 May 1981, which gave the ranking of the top 101 companies in the private sector in India on the basis of their 1978-79 assets, Great Eastern, with assets of Rs. 172.35 crore, was assigned fourth rank after (1) Tata Iron & Steel Co. Ltd. (2) Tata Engineering & Locomotive Co. Ltd. and (3) Scindia Steam Navigation Co. Ltd.

5

The Fourth Decade
1978-1988

During this decade, almost up to the beginning of 1987, barring the period between mid 1979 and mid 1981, the world shipping industry went through an acute depression. The industry was in a perilous state, suffering from overcapacity in all markets. Traditional fleets of well-established shipping companies were decimated and large shipping companies went bankrupt. Many of the shipping companies which survived were not able to repay the principal and interest instalments in respect of their loans and became sick units.

The factors which brought about this situation may be enumerated. The slowing down of growth in the world economy led to stagnation and decline in the world sea-borne trade. As outlined earlier, the supply of ships had gone up because of the boom in shipping in the early 1970s, when large shipbuilding orders were placed with the shipbuilding yards. The world shipping fleet went up from 290 million GRT in 1973 to 406 million GRT in 1978. A ship once constructed has an operating life of about 20 years or more. The world sea-borne trade, which was 3,250 million metric tons in 1973, went up to 3,551 million metric tons in 1978 and 3,769 million metric tons in 1979, which in itself was not a substantial increase; it registered a decline thereafter up to 1985. The year-wise figures are given below :

World Sea-Borne Trade 1978-88

Year	Million Metric Tons	Per cent Increase/ Decrease over Previous year
1978	3551	-
1979	3769	+6
1980	3704	-2
1981	3559	-4
1982	3273	-8
1983	3231	-1
1984	3410	+6
1985	3382	-1
1986	3459	+2
1987	3505	+1
1988	3735	+7

Source: *Maritime Transport 1990*, OECD, Paris.

World Shipping Fleet 1978-88

(as at mid-year)

Year	Million GRT	Per cent Increase/Decrease over Previous year
1978	406.0	-
1979	413.0	+1.7
1980	419.9	+1.7
1981	420.8	+0.2
1982	424.7	+0.9
1983	422.6	-0.5
1984	418.7	-0.9
1985	416.3	-0.6
1986	404.9	-2.7
1987	403.5	-0.3
1988	403.4	-0.0

Source: *Maritime Transport 1990*, OECD, Paris.

Thus 4.2 per cent of the world shipping tonnage in 1978 was surplus having regard to the demand for shipping services as given in the Table on tonnage oversupply later in this chapter. If the surplus tonnage is assessed taking into account not only the tonnage of ships laid up or lying idle for other reasons or tonnage not fully utilised due to slow steaming but also after taking account of factors such as delays awaiting shipments, part cargo shipments, floating storage employment for tankers etc., the surplus tonnage was at a higher level. The laying-up of ships brought about by the very low freight rates due to imbalance in demand for and supply of ships provides a temporary and costly corrective (for shipping companies) to absorb the surplus tonnage. The imbalance can only be corrected in the long run by demolition of ships and reduced shipbuilding output. The year-wise world shipping fleet figures from 1978 are given in a table on the previous page.

The world surplus tonnage which is not fully utilised due to slow steaming, lay up status or because it is lying idle for other reasons in terms of DWT as a percentage of the world merchant fleet's deadweight tonnage was :

Year	Total World Fleet (as at mid year) DWT	Surplus Tonnage DWT	Percentage share of Surplus Tonnage in World Fleet
1979	673.7	86.0	12.5
1980	682.2	97.1	14.2
1981	688.8	149.1	21.6
1982	693.5	184.1	26.5
1983	686.6	195.8	28.5
1984	674.5	171.2	25.4
1985	664.8	161.5	23.4
1986	639.1	108.0	16.9
1987	632.3	101.1	16.0
1988	627.9	83.4	13.3

Source: "Review of Maritime Transport 1989", United Nations. New York.

Consequent to these developments, freight rates declined to very low levels. The shipping companies were therefore making losses and had no cash resources left for meeting principal and interest instalments in respect of the loans which they had taken earlier for meeting purchase price of ships.

Laid-up tonnage is a barometer of the state of the shipping market. In good times laid-up tonnage is minimal. However, as imbalance represented by excess supply having regard to the demand increases and the freight rates decline, shipping companies find that they would be sustaining less losses by laying up their ships rather than by operating them. The greater the decline in the freight rates the larger is the tonnage that goes in lay-up. Lay-up is not cost-free idleness of ships. The shipping company has to incur expenditure for such items as interest on loans taken for acquisition of ship, reduced insurance premium charges, charges for the wages of the skeleton crew and watchmen, charges for transporting the ship to the lay-up location, cost of reactivating the ship when the ship is to be operated again. When the demand increases in relation to the supply of the ships, there is improvement in the freight rates and the laid-up ships are again progressively reactivated. The figures for laid-up tonnage from 1978 to 1988 are given below:

Year	Million DWT
1978	28.9
1979	9.8
1980	8.3
1981	21.0
1982	80.2
1983	74.7
1984	59.9
1985	48.0
1986	23.7
1987	16.3
1988	6.7

Source: "Review 1990", Fearnleys, Oslo

The laid-up tonnage will be high when the intensity of the depression is high. With the continuing recovery in the freight markets the ships will progressively come out of lay-up and will be operated.

Due to the prolonged shipping depression a very large number of shipping companies the world over were unable to meet their financial obligations to their creditors. Internationally known shipping companies like Reksten, Hansa Lines, Waage, Colocotronis, Maritime Fruit Carriers, Fearnley and Egar, Cast, Carrian, Hellenic, Salen, Sanko and a large number of other less known companies went bankrupt or became sick units.

Indian shipping companies were also overwhelmed by the shipping depression. Some of the Indian shipping companies went bankrupt. A majority of surviving shipping companies defaulted in respect of their loan obligations to the Shipping Development Fund Committee and financial institutions and became sick units. Some of these companies were not taken into liquidation by their creditors because by foreclosing mortgages and selling the ships at the prevailing low prices the creditors would have lost very large amounts. The creditors therefore waited for improvement in the freight markets in the hope that the return of viability would enable the borrower shipping companies to repay the loans in the long run.

The losses sustained by most of the shipping companies from the year 1981-82 onwards wiped out their reserves and eroded their equity. The Shipping Development Fund Committee initiated legal action for foreclosing the mortgages with a view to selling the mortgaged ships in respect of some of the companies which were in utter financial distress and for whom there was no hope of restoration of viability in the future. These companies included Nilhat Shipping Co. Ltd., R.A.J.Lines Ltd., Sujwala Shipping Co. Ltd. Some of the companies such as Thakur Shipping Co. Ltd., Damodar Bulk Carriers Ltd., Seven Seas Transportation Ltd., Indo Oceanic Shipping Co. Ltd. and Dempo Steamships Ltd., in view of their critical financial position, did not have prospects of revival and most of these companies were taken into liquidation.

The net worth position, debts, debt-equity ratios of some of the important Indian shipping companies are set out in the table that follows.

(Rs. in lakhs)

Name of company	Position as per Balance Sheet as on	Net Worth	Debts	Debt Equity Ratio
Public Sector:				
Mogul Lines	31/3/85	(-)6071.16	12257.31	Nil
Shipping Corporation	31/3/85	10259.67	96498.52	9.41:1
Private Sector:				
Scindia	30/6/85	(-)1612.44	10914.39	Nil
India Steamship	31/3/85	(-)3319.42	9107.67	Nil
Ratnakar	30/6/85	(-)1993.90	7424.64	Nil
Essar Shipping	31/12/84	4193.33	13271.20	3.16:1
Great Eastern	30/6/85	4984.41	12725.21	2.55:1
South India Shipping	30/9/85	930.99	6255.11	6.72:1

Capital Structure, Freight and Charter Hire Earnings, Profits and Dividends in the First Half of the Fourth Decade

The paid-up capital of Rs. 15,33,30,368 remained the same up to 30 June 1981. In the year 1981-82 bonus shares were issued to the shareholders in the proportion of two fully paid shares for every three shares held. The paid-up capital therefore went up and on 30 June 1982 amounted to Rs. 25,55,30,408. The paid-up capital remained the same on 30 June 1983.

The freight and charter hire earnings in the year 1978-79 amounted to Rs. 37.90 crore as compared with Rs. 30.89 crore in the previous year. The loss sustained in the year 1978-79 was Rs. 1.27 crore as compared with a much larger loss of Rs. 8.82 crore sustained in the previous year. The earnings were enough to cover interest charges and about 86 per cent of the depreciation. There was a marginal loss for the uncovered depreciation. In view of the loss, no dividend was paid for the year 1978-79. The freight earnings went up from Rs. 37.90 crore in 1978-79 to Rs. 52.45 crore in 1979-80. The net profit amounted to Rs. 15.80 crore, which included a profit of Rs. 4.30 crore on sale of a ship. A tax-free dividend of 25 per cent was paid on the paid-up share capital of the company.

In the year 1980-81 the freight and charter hire earnings were

Rs. 56.75 crore. The profit was Rs. 17.7 crore inclusive of a profit of Rs. 4.67 crore on sale of ships. A dividend of 20 per cent was paid to the shareholders.

In the year 1981-82 the freight and charter hire earnings were Rs. 67 crore. The net profit amounted to Rs. 4.46 crore. A dividend of 10 per cent was paid on the enlarged share capital of about Rs. 25.55 crore.

The freight and charter hire earnings in the year 1982-83 amounted to Rs. 55.90 crore. The company sustained a loss of Rs. 5.42 crore. The loss would have been much higher but was reduced by the profit of Rs. 7.09 crore on the sale of ships. In view of the loss, no dividend was paid for the year 1982-83.

Profitability Comparison

The returns on capital employed in respect of Great Eastern and four other major Indian shipping companies for the years 1978-79 to 1982-83 are set out below:

The following data have been taken from the various issues of the journal *Indian Shipping*. The return has been calculated on capital employed which is the sum total of paid-up capital, reserves, surplus and loans. Profit or total return has been calculated before providing for interest on loans and taxation.

Percentage Return on Capital Employed

Name of the Company	1978-79	1979-80	1980-81	1981-82	1982-83	Average for 5 years
Public Sector:						
Shipping Corporation	-5.2	4.7	7.1	6.4	1.8	2.96
Mogul Lines	-1.2	3.8	4.8	4.7	-8.6	0.7
Private Sector:						
Great Eastern	3.2	16.1	17.2	7.8	1.7	9.2
Scindia Steam	-2.9	6.8	7.9	-4.9	-5.3	2.16
India Steamship	2.1	5.4	8.3	2.0	-9.0	1.76

It may be observed from the above data that Great Eastern was the most profitable Indian shipping company amongst the major Indian shipping companies during this period.

Shipping Development Fund Committee

During the prolonged shipping depression, most of the companies which had received SDFC loans on the basis of the need-based concept defaulted in payment of their interest and repayment instalments to SDFC. Questions were raised as to why SDFC gave loans so freely to companies which did not have the financial strength or operating efficiency and why SDFC withheld funds from financially and operationally sound companies like Great Eastern.

Faced with such criticism, the SDFC Executive Director's office, on whose recommendations SDFC loans were disbursed, instead of rectifying matters or taking corrective steps, became hostile to the company. The company therefore continuously faced problems due to SDFC's hostile interference in regard to the remunerative investment of funds, diversification of activities and numerous other issues including the controversy regarding having Suvibha Investment Company Ltd as a subsidiary of the company.

SDFC's interference affected the smooth running of the company. The company's management and officers were unproductively occupied in dealing with matters relating to or raised by SDFC. Things got so bad that in the 80s the company was seriously considering repaying the remaining SDFC loans in order to be free from this interference. Opposition to SDFC in government circles and elsewhere grew as loss of substantial government funds disbursed as loans was feared. Finally, SDFC was wound up on 5 April 1987. On that day the company's problems with SDFC also ended.

The government took the decision to abolish the SDFC in 1986 and simultaneously advised the Industrial Credit and Investment Corporation of India Ltd (ICICI) to take over ship financing. As a result ICICI promoted and incorporated The Shipping Credit and Investment Company of India (SCICI) as a public limited company on 8 December 1986. SCICI now acts as a channel for providing development finance to private sector shipping companies. Financial assistance to public sector shipping companies is the direct responsibility of the government. The work of recommending ship acquisition approvals, which was previously done by SDFC, is now performed by a new Ship Acquisition Licensing Committee (SALC) for private sector shipping companies.

Despite all the problems, SDFC's contribution to development of shipping cannot be belittled. The soft loans advanced by SDFC since its establishment in 1959 played a major role in the growth of Indian shipping. Out of the total Indian tonnage of 5.76 million GRT as on 31 March 1986, 5.21 million GRT net operative tonnage was acquired with the financial loan and/or guarantee assistance of SDFC. The total loans disbursed by SDFC up to 31 March 1986 amounted to Rs. 1,337.43 crore. The net operative tonnage acquired with SDFC's assistance as on 31 March 1986 was estimated at 52,12,344 GRT. The total SDFC assisted Indian tonnage (operative tonnage) as on 31 March 1986 was reckoned as 90.45 per cent of the then operative Indian tonnage.[1]

The rate of interest on these subsidised loans was 3 per cent per annum, on loans sanctioned on or before 31 March 1971, 4.5 per cent per annum on loans sanctioned on or after 1 April 1971 till and including 9 November 1981. On loans sanctioned on or after 10 November 1981 the rates of interest levied were 6.75 per cent per annum on loans for acquisition of ships built in Indian shipyards and 7.5 per cent per annum on loans for acquisition of new as well as secondhand foreign ships.

The total subsidy on interest given by the government amounted to about Rs. 175 crore, that is, an average of Rs. 7 crore per annum spread over a span of 25 years of SDFC's existence. This is a very small amount, considering that it contributed to the growth of Indian tonnage from 0.7 million GRT to about 6 million GRT. SDFC's contribution to growth of Indian shipping can therefore be termed as a very worthwhile contribution.[2] SDFC, since 1975, had also been acting as an advisory body for considering and recommending for approval proposals for acquisition of ships.

Distortion in SDFC's Loan Policies

It was SDFC's unsound lending policies that were its undoing. Initially SDFC used to grant loans to Indian shipping companies whose purchases of ships were approved by the government to the extent of 90 per cent of the price of the foreign built new ships and 75 per cent of the prices of secondhand ships. At the end of 60s this policy underwent a change. SDFC examined the liquidity position and cash flows of the shipping enterprises applying for loan and if the liquidity position and cash flows were excellent either the loan was not granted or the quantum of the loan was cut down. This was contrary to the criteria followed by the banks and financial institutions that better the liquidity position and the larger the expected future cash flows of the borrower, the greater is their creditworthiness. SDFC preferred to grant loans to those shipping companies which had no cash resources of their own and whose liquidity position was weak. SDFC would lend less or not lend at all to financially viable and sound companies on the ground that they would manage without SDFC finance, and would lend liberally to less viable and financially weak companies on the ground that they were more in need of finance. A need-based approach indeed! In the prolonged shipping depression the government funds became jeopardised more because of this need-based approach.

As a development financing institution it should have been SDFC's objective to lend to efficient companies with sound track records so that development of shipping could be accelerated. This would have also ensured that with a given loan outlay the growth would have been faster and more substantial. The objective of speedy development of Indian shipping companies was therefore ill served by SDFC's loan policy.

One of the important objectives of granting loan assistance at low rates of interest was to place Indian ship owners at par with foreign shipowners in international competition. Due to the fact that most of the maritime countries assist their shipowners in the acquisition of ships by granting loans at low rates of interest, SDFC by denying loan assistance or by giving meagre loan assistance to efficient Indian shipping companies, placed them at a handicap in international competition.

The lending policy also involved discrimination among Indian shipping companies. The public sector Shipping Corporation of India received preferential treatment in getting loans from SDFC. If SDFC's resources were not adequate, the best course would have been to reduce the level of loan assistance uniformly for all shipping companies.

In conclusion, it may be stated that the prolonged shipping depression and the faulty lending policies of SDFC were mainly responsible for the defaults on the part of Indian shipping companies in making payment of interest and repayment instalments to SDFC.

Capital Structure, Freight and Charter Hire Earnings, Profits and Dividends in the Second Half of the Fourth Decade

The paid-up share capital of the company, which was Rs. 25,55,30,408, remained the same up to 30 June 1985. In the year 1984-85, convertible debenture bonds of Rs. 12,77,50,000 were issued. In the year 1985-86, 50 per cent of the convertible bonds amounting to Rs. 6,38,75,000 were converted into equity shares. The paid-up share capital on 30 June 1986 therefore amounted to Rs. 31,94,05,408. There were debenture bonds (50 per cent unconverted portion) of Rs. 6,38,75,000. In the year 1986-87, out of the debenture bonds of Rs. 6,38,75,000, at the option exercised by the debenture bond holders, debenture bonds of Rs. 5,62,02,800 were converted into equity shares. In the same year, International Finance Corporation, Washington subscribed for 2 million equity shares of Rs. 10 each (equity shares of Rs. 2 crore) at a premium of Rs. 3 per share. The paidup equity capital thus amounted to Rs. 39,55,77,850 (apart from share premium account of Rs. 60 lakh). In the same year the company made the rights issue of equity shares to the shareholders. The shares were oversubscribed and 2,48,14,966 equity shares of Rs. 10 each were issued, out of which Rs. 5 per share was paid up and this amounted to Rs. 12,40,74,830 of paid up equity capital. The paidup capital on 30 June 1987 therefore worked out as under:

	Paidup Capital Rs.
3,95,57,785 equity shares of Rs. 10 each	39,55,77,850
2,48,14,966 equity shares of Rs. 10 each, Rs. 5 each per share paid up	12,40,74,830
	51,96,52,680

After deducting allotment money of Rs. 23,79,683 in arrears and adding Rs. 30,358 of forfeited shares, the paidup equity capital on 30 June 1987 was Rs. 51,73,03,355.

In the year 1987-88 debenture bonds of Rs. 69,26,200 were converted into equity shares. International Finance Corporation, Washington, during the year subscribed partly by cash and partly by conversion of loan for 3 million equity shares of Rs. 10 each at a premium of Rs. 6.87 per share. The premium was credited to share premium account. The paidup share capital as on 30 June 1988 after deducting allotment money in arrears and adding forfeited shares amounted to about Rs. 55.61 crore. With the addition of share premium of Rs. 2,06,10,000 collected from International Finance Corporation, Washington, to the previous balance of Rs. 60,00,000, the share premium account went up to Rs. 2,66,10,000.

The freight and charter hire earnings in the year 1983-84 were Rs. 64.87 crore as compared with Rs. 55.90 crore in the previous year. The loss sustained by the company during the year amounted to Rs. 4.28 crore as compared with the loss of Rs. 5.42 crore in the previous year. In view of the loss, no dividend was paid for the year 1983-84. It may be stated that the earnings covered all the interest and almost two thirds of the depreciation charges.

The freight and charter hire earnings for the year 1984-85 were Rs. 63.69 crore. The company returned to the profit making list and made a net profit of Rs. 1.90 crore. A dividend of 7 per cent was paid for the year 1984-85.

The freight and charter hire earnings during the year 1985-86 amounted to Rs. 77.58 crore. The net profit for the year amounted to Rs. 7.08 crore. A dividend of 12 per cent was paid to the shareholders.

The freight and charter hire earnings during the year 1986-87 were Rs. 96.17 crore. The net profit amounted to Rs. 8.07 crore. A dividend of 12.5 per cent was paid to the shareholders.

The freight and charter hire earnings during the year 1987-88 were Rs. 110.17 crore. The net profit was Rs. 19.50 crore. A dividend of 15 per cent was paid to the shareholders.

Profitability Comparison

The returns on capital employed in respect of Great Eastern and four other major Indian shipping companies are given in the following table.

The return has been calculated on capital employed, which is the sum total of paid up capital, reserves and surplus and loans. Profit or total return has been calculated before providing for interest on loans and taxation.

It will be observed from the profitability comparison that Great Eastern Shipping Company had the best profitability among the five major shipping companies in India in the second half of the fourth decade.

Percentage Return on Capital Employed

Name of Company	1983-84	1984-85	1985-86	1986-87	1987-88	Average
Public Sector:						
Shipping Corporation	-1.6	4.9	8.7	6.5	9.6	5.6
Private Sector:						
Great Eastern	2.4	6.3	8.6	9.5	13.7	8.1
Scindia Steam	-10.8	-	-12.5	-11.3	-16.1	-12.7
India Steamship	-8.4	-2.0	1.0	-2.4	1.8	-2.2
Essar	-	-	4.5	9.9	8.1	7.5

Source: Indian National Shipowners' Association

Performance of Major Indian Shipping Companies During Acute Depression

The table given below sets out the data regarding net profit or loss, paidup capital and reserves of major shipping companies in India during the acute depression years viz.1982-83, 1983-84, 1984-85, 1985-86 and 1986-87:

Rs. in lakhs

Name of Company	Year	Net Profit or Loss(-)	Paidup capital	Reserves and Surplus
Public Sector :				
1) Shipping Corporation	1982-83	-2443.76	2794.94	8907.46
	1983-84	-5163.99	6999.94	3742.27
	1984-85	-226.87	6999.94	3968.87
	1985-86	749.66	6999.94	4717.04
	1986-87	776.00	7019.00	3263.00
Private Sector :				
2) Great Eastern	1982-83	-541.90	2555.34	3250.09
	1983-84	-428.00	2555.30	2655.11
	1984-85	189.71	2555.30	2429.10
	1985-86	708.21	3194.05	2766.84
	1986-87	806.85	5173.03	2900.97
3) Scindia Steam	1982-83	-1720.59	1894.59	1159.69
	1983-84	-2504.04	1894.59	Negative
	1984-85	-944.41	1894.59	Negative
	1985-86	-2944.84	1894.59	Negative
	1986-87	-2928.00	1894.59	Negative
4) India Steamships	1982-83	-1609.94	520.00	370.00
	1983-84	-1646.92	520.00	Negative
	1984-85	-1104.41	520.00	Negative
	1985-86	-721.59	520.00	Negative
	1986-87	-1308.45	520.00	Negative
5) Essar Shipping*	1983	NOT AVAILABLE		
	1984	470.59	2017.24	2651.64
	1985	696.38	2439.67	3040.02
	1986	748.82	2514.71	3183.03
	1987	780.00	3536.00	3798.00

*It may be noted that in the case of Essar Shipping, the calendar year was the financial year as the year ended on 31 December of each year.

Out of the five major companies, two companies namely, Scindia Steam and India Steamship sustained losses in each of the depression years, and losses sustained completely eroded their equity (paidup capital and reserves). Shipping Corporation and Great Eastern sustained losses in the first two years, that is, 1982-83 and 1983-84, and were making profits in each of the remaining three years. Essar

Shipping was operating profitably in each of the four years for which the figures were available.

No Defaults During Depression

Whilst the major Indian shipping companies including the Shipping Corporation of India defaulted in payment of interest and repayment instalments in respect of their loan obligations to the SDFC, Great Eastern met its loan servicing obligations to SDFC regularly and punctually during the acute shipping depression. Even the request of Great Eastern to SDFC for reschedulement of interest and repayment of loan instalments was not entertained by SDFC and the company was told that unless a borrower company committed a default, its application for reschedulement of instalments could not be considered by SDFC. The company with its standing and reputation in international shipping and banking circles could not jeopardise its name by committing a default. Instead the company approached the foreign lenders for reschedulement of loans and interest obligations, and they readily agreed to it. The reschedulement however involved considerable cost because of the prolonged foreign exchange exposure in which the rupee declined in value vis-a-vis foreign currencies in which the loans had been taken and the higher interest charges due to the rise in the applicable interest rates when reschedulement was negotiated.

Company Emerges Stronger

In an interview published in *Business World* of 16 February-1 March 1987, Vasant Sheth, the then Chairman stated: "The deep crisis in the shipping industry worldwide—comparable to the Great Depression of the 30s, has taken many companies into bankruptcy and a majority of the Indian companies are very vulnerable. Despite this, during the last 6 years we have repaid Rs. 83 crore on the dot to SDFC and bankers, and paid a dividend aggregating to Rs.10 crore in 4 out of 6 years."

A number of shipping companies in India and abroad went bankrupt or closed their business during the depression. Most of the companies which survived became financially weaker; some of them even became sick units. The net worth of most companies became negative at the end of the shipping depression in 1986-87. There was no question of any debt-equity ratio. Even for those companies which had a positive net worth, debt equity ratios were very high. Most of these Indian shipping companies had piled up arrears of debt and interest instalments which would require to be cleared later and had no cash or liquidity to purchase ships at the low prices which prevailed as a consequence of shipping depression.

Great Eastern, however, enjoyed an improvement in the net worth, debt-equity ratio and cost of fleet as compared with the figures prevailing in 1978-79, which was the first year of the fourth decade. Great Eastern's net worth was Rs. 35.33 crore in 1978-79. It improved to Rs. 59.61 crore in 1985-86, Rs. 80.74 crore in 1986-87 and Rs. 94.78 crore in 1987-88. This was because the losses sustained by it during the acute depression years were comparatively smaller and formed a small part of its reserves. The company also strengthened its equity base by issue of convertible debentures, a large part of which was converted into equity, issue of right shares to the existing shareholders and issue of equity shares to International Finance Corporation, Washington.

The company was therefore in a position to purchase ships at the low prices prevailing in 1986-87 and 1987-88. The cost of its fleet went up from Rs. 186.33 crore in 1977-78 to Rs. 318.80 crore in 1985-86, Rs. 337.79 crore in 1986-87 and Rs. 361.25 crore in 1987-88. The cost of the fleet would include the cost of ships acquired. However, the cost of the ships sold would be deducted for arriving at the cost of the fleet at the end of the year. The purchase of ships at low prices in 1986-87 and 1987-88 resulted in the appreciation of their value with the progressive improvement in the freight markets. Chairman Vasant Sheth in his statement to the shareholders at the Annual General Meeting held on 22 December 1988 stated as follows:

"In the last 2 years your company has purchased 8 vessels comprising of 7 Bulk Carriers and one Chemical Tanker. These ships have been purchased at a total cost of approximately Rs. 40 crore. This Rs. 40 crore investment has been financed by approximately Rs. 25 crore equity and Rs. 15 crore borrowings. Thus the debt equity ratio on these recent acquisitions has been less than 1:1. Moreover, it is heartening to note that the market value of these recent acquisitions is in the region of Rs. 85 crore, that is, an appreciation of Rs. 45 crore. Therefore, you will observe that the equity in these acquisitions has more than doubled in 24 months in terms of the market value."

During this decade the cost of the fleet, that is, the cost at which the ships were acquired, went up from Rs. 186 crore in 1977-78 to Rs. 361 crore in 1987-88, that is, almost doubled itself; the loan liability of the company rose only marginally from Rs. 116 crore in 1977-78 to Rs. 130 crore in 1987-88.

The company's debt-equity ratio was 3.31:1 in 1977-78. The ratio improved to 2.55:1 in 1984-85 and in view of considerable acquisition of ships, which were partly financed by loans, the ratio went up to 2.70:1 in 1985-86 and again improved to 1.79:1 in 1986-87 and 1.37:1 in 1987-88.

During this decade Great Eastern emerged as the largest shipping company in the private sector in India. Its financial position taking into account such parameters as the profitability, net worth, and debt-equity ratio was by far the best among the Indian shipping companies in the private or public sector.

Clear Vision

Great Eastern's management developed keen awareness during the depression that radical changes were required in the shipping industry and the industry needed thorough restucturing. Addressing the Annual General Meeting of the company held on 24 January 1984, Chairman Vasant Sheth called the subject of his speech "New Wave Shipping." In his speech he said: "Periodically every industry undergoes change to fit into the changed environment, to cater to new needs, to take advantage of the latest technology and to provide better services/value to its customers. Sometimes the changes required and called for are radical. Changes have taken place in the past in industries such as steel, motor cars, electronics, communications, aviation, etc. Now I feel that time has come for a radical change in the shipping industry." He added, "We in Great Eastern firmly believe that a totally new wave shipping is called for in the years ahead." Referring to the changes needed he observed that "only the companies with a high capital base, low gearing and lots of liquidity can survive. Buying and selling of ships is an inherent part of the shipping business." The profits made on sale of ships in the case of Great Eastern amounted to one-third of its equity. He also stressed the importance of diversification into non-shipping industries so that the company could have a steady income and have liquidity to take advantage of shipping opportunities during the depression. He also referred to the need for simplification of government controls, regulations and procedures which had affected the industry adversely.

In his Chairman's statement to the shareholders of the company at the Annual General Meeting held on 19 December 1985, Vasant Sheth stated that the policy of excessive borrowing had been both expensive and unwise. In the decade 1965-1975, when shipping was earning well and interest rates were low, for every rupee paid to the shareholders by the company, one rupee was paid in interest to the creditors and bankers. In the decade 1975-1985, when the company was going through a depression and interest rates were high, the company was paying for every rupee paid to the shareholders 4 rupees in interest to the creditors or bankers. He also referred to the fleet expansion which could be achieved by the company at low prices which were prevailing and which carried a very low downside risk. Equity capital could be raised and used for this expansion. He said that the company should be allowed to diversify into non-shipping activities so that it would not be solely dependent in future on the fortunes of the volatile shipping industry alone. He stated: "He is perhaps a brave Chairman who claims that there are still profitable opportunities in shipping, but that is my belief. I am convinced that your industry presents unique possibilities for making substantial profits provided we set about doing so the right way." He added: "We are at the bottom of the valley from which the roads lead only upwards." He therefore invited the shareholders to contribute in the raising of equity for financing a new programme of expansion. One may therefore conclude that even during the dark days of depression the company's management displayed a clear and remarkable vision.

Measures Taken During Depression

The following measures were taken by the company during the depression, which resulted in the improvement in the financial viability and growth of the company despite the effect of depression:

* Restructuring of the company's finances in order to strengthen its equity base, improve its liquidity and keep a

low debt-equity ratio.

* A judicious gradual disposal of the company's older, uneconomical ships which resulted in putting a stop to the losses which were being sustained by the operation of the ships. This also brought about reduction in the loan liability as loans outstanding on these ships were paid off after their sale. There was an improvement in the financial liquidity also as the sale proceeds of the ships after repayment of loans produced surpluses. These surpluses reduced or offset the losses in the years in which the company was incurring losses. They added to the profits in the years in which the company was making profits.
* Acquisition of ships at low prices which were prevailing in the depression. The emphasis in the earlier part of the decade was on modernising of the company's ships by acquiring new or near new sophisticated ships with the latest technology and maximum fuel efficiency. The new generation of ships which were being built consumed about one-third to one-half less fuel than their equivalent sized ships built earlier. In the latter part of the decade the emphasis was on acquisition of secondhand ships at very low prices which were prevailing as a result of the depression. As the then Chairman Vasant Sheth frequently mentioned, "Interest efficient ships were no less important than fuel efficient ships." In view of their low prices the interest and depreciation burden was comparatively small in respect of these second-hand ships. The cost of operating these ships was therefore low. These ships could make profits at low freight and charter hire rates which were prevailing at that time. With the improvement in the freight rates thereafter these ships began to make far higher profits.
* The setting up and registration of a wholly owned susidiary company in the U.K. enabled the company to carry out timely acquisition of ships at bargain prices without being hindered by the regulations and procedures of the Government of India.
* Diversification to other branches of the industry with a steady income. The company acquired offshore supply vessels. Investment was made in an associated company as part of a joint venture for owning and operating oil rigs. The

company also went into the real estate business.

* Stringent cost control and best utilisation of the company's fleet. This was facilitated by the setting up of a Board of Management in which the Chairman, Managing Director, Heads of the Operating Departments, Secretarial, Finance and Accounts Departments met for four hours or more in a meeting every week and discussed and monitored the day-to-day strategy and formulated short term as well as long term plans.

Fixed Deposit Scheme

With the fall in freight rates from mid-1981 and the onset of the shipping depression, the company's liquidity position worsened. In order to improve the liquidity position the Board of Directors at their meeting held on 28 January 1982 decided, in principle, to accept fixed deposits from the public and shareholders. Under the provisions of the Companies Act the maximum amount of fixed deposits that the company could accept at that time was Rs. 15 crore. The fixed deposits placed with the company on an average did not exceed Rs. 5 crore at a time. Although the fixed deposits carried a rate of interest of about 14 per cent per annum, the cost was higher to the company because there were costs to be met not only in respect of advertisements and brokerages but also the costs involved in disallowance of part of interest paid on fixed deposits in the claim for expenditure admissible under the Income Tax laws. The effective cost therefore went up to as much as 17 per cent per annum.

After the issue of convertible bonds by the company of the value of Rs. 12,77,50,000 carrying interest at 13.5 per cent per annum and International Finance Corporation's subscription for shares of the nominal value of Rs. 2 crore at a premium of Rs. 60 lakhs, coupled with improvement in the company's earnings during the year 1986-87, an evaluation of the requirement of funds on fixed deposit and its cost was made. Consequently, it was decided to stop accepting and renewing the fixed deposits from the public and shareholders in the year 1986-87.

Suvibha Investment Co Pvt Ltd

At the end of the year 1983-84 the company acquired shares in Suvibha Investment Co Pvt Ltd, whereby the latter became a subsidiary of the company. The company then transferred its investments in the shares of various companies to the tune of Rs. 13,54,800 to Suvibha Investment Co Pvt Ltd against issue of shares, and also further subscribed Rs. 35,94,400 in cash to the share captial of Suvibha. The total paid up capital of this company inclusive of preference shares of Rs. 2,000 therefore came to Rs. 49,52,200.

There were two objectives in having an investment company as a subsidiary of the company. SDFC, in its loan agreement with the company, had placed restrictions on the investments of the company's funds and the company could not invest its surplus funds in investments yielding good returns without obtaining SDFC's approval. SDFC on their part did not approve the proposals made by the company for investments of its funds. A company of Great Eastern's size having large borrowings and having a schedule of repayments in respect of interest and loan instalments payable to lenders has to keep its funds invested in such a way that they mature for payment when the instalments became due and the instalments could be paid to the lenders out of these funds. However the company's attempts from time to time to obtain SDFC's approval to remunerative investment of the company's funds failed.

At one time the Board of Directors of the company invested funds in the 11 per cent convertible bonds of Tata Engineering and Locomotive Company Ltd (TELCO). This was done with the unanimous approval of the directors present at the Board Meeting held on 18 August 1980 including the SDFC director on the company's Board. SDFC however later issued instructions to the company to disinvest from the TELCO convertible bonds and asked the SDFC director who also happened to be Executive Director of SDFC to resign from the Board of Great Eastern.

Having a subsidiary company which could borrow freely from the holding company and then channel the funds in desirable investments was the only way out of the unreasonable restrictions imposed by SDFC. Secondly, the investment company could also, with an improvement in the company's liquidity position, diversify in the finance and investment business and obtain good returns on the surplus funds which would accrue after return of the normal times in the shipping business. A prolonged controversy developed between SDFC and the company in regard to the company having Suvibha Investment Co. Ltd. as its subsidiary. The controversy came to an end with the winding up of SDFC in 1987.

Important Changes in the Board

Pratapsinh Mathuradas Vissanji, who was a director of the company since its incorporation on 31 August 1948, was pressing for his proposal to retire from the Board. He requested the Board to agree to his retirement at its meeting held on 29 November 1979. The Board of Directors did their best to persuade Pratapsinh to continue on the Board but did not succeed. At the Board Meeting held on 21 January 1980, the then Chairman Vasant Sheth read out to the Board a letter dated 20.11.1979 from Pratapsinh reiterating his desire not to seek re-election at the ensuing General Meeting and the Board had to accede to his proposal. The Board of Directors in their Report to the Shareholders for the year 1978-79 referred to his contribution in the following words:

"We recall the great contribution made by Mr. Vissanji in hundreds of deliberations over three decades of his association with the company and in which he played a significant role in the growth and expansion of this company. His unflinching support and guidance even went to the extent of joining management in business trips abroad to assist in mature solutions of complicated problems. He has been a tower of strength to your Board and the least that we could do is to record our sincere appreciation and deep gratitude and convey the Board's and your good wishes to him for his good health and happiness."

B.H. Bhiwandiwalla, one of the founder-directors of the company, died on 27 March 1981 at the age of 63. A.H. Bhiwandiwalla & Company (Bombay) Private Limited, of which he was a member and director, had promoted the Great Eastern Shipping Company and were its Managing Agents till the cessation of the managing agency system in India in 1970. He played a significant role in the deliberations of the Board. His mature advice was greatly valued by the company's management and he made his contribution to the progress of the company.

Sudhir Mulji, who was a senior officer of the company from October 1961 to 27 June 1974, was appointed as whole-time director of the company from 27 June 1974. He was appointed as Joint Managing Director of the company for a period of five years from 14 August 1974. Mulji was appointed as Managing Director of the company with effect from 14 August 1979. Mulji, who was posted to the company's London office as its President, resigned as Managing Director of the company on 1 April 1980.

Darbari S. Seth, who was Deputy Chairman and Managing Director of Tata Chemicals Ltd, and was associated with the Tata group of companies, was appointed as a director of the company at the General Meeting of the shareholders of the company held on 22 December 1981.

Beginnings of Diversification

In line with the general trend among international shipping companies to move out of traditional shipping into more specialised forms including offshore oil industry requirements, the company acquired two Anchor Handling Tug Supply vessels which were being built in Japan. These vessels were delivered in early 1983. Great Eastern was the first Indian shipping company to acquire the supply vessels for offshore requirements. Further, two Anchor Handling Tug Supply vessels were being built to order at the NKK shipbuilding yard in Japan and were delivered to the company in early 1984. These four supply ships were named after the late K.D. Malaviya, regarded as the father of the oil industry in India. K.D. Malaviya was Vasant Sheth's father-in-law. These four ships were named *Malaviya 1*, *Malaviya 2*, *Malaviya 3* and *Malaviya 4*. These ships were pressed into service with ONGC.

A.H. Bhiwandiwalla & Co. (Bombay) Pvt. Ltd. with which the company had close links, was offering the company participation in a proposed joint venture for owning and operating rigs. The proposal was under negotiation with foreign collaborators and awaiting government clearance for a long time. The Directors Report to the shareholders for the year 1982-83 made a reference to this proposal. It was during the year 1986-87 that the company made an equity investment of Rs. 62.90 lakh which was 24.9 per cent of the equity capital of Great Atwood Ltd., a joint venture company between the Bhiwandiwalla Group and Atwood Oceanics Inc. Great Atwood company had purchased two offshore oil rigs, *Shenandoch* and *Gettysburg*, which were renamed *Kedarnath* and

Badrinath. The rigs were employed for ONGC's work.

The Board of Directors at their meeting on 24 March 1983 approved acquisition by the company of a commercial plot of 4,000 sq. metres in the commercial complex of the City and Industrial Development Corporation of Maharashtra Ltd (CIDCO) at CBD, Belapur, New Bombay for the purpose of construction of an office building for the company. The above acquisition could be considered as the beginning of the company's diversification into the real estate business. The building constructed on the plot of land in New Bombay, named 'Great Eastern Chambers', is considered to be the best building in the locality. The office premises in the building were sold in record time at the top rates prevailing in the locality at the time of sale.

After receiving the approval of the Ministry of Finance, Government of India for the company entering into construction activity in the year 1987-88, the company formed a cell named 'The Great Eastern Developers' for conducting the real estate and construction business.

Strengthening of Equity and Liquidity

The most important reason as to why Great Eastern was virtually the only Indian shipping company to come out financially stronger at the end of the shipping depression was the measures taken by the company during the depression to stregthen its equity base and to improve its liquidity that is, availablity of cash, bank balances and short-term investments which could be readily utilised.

There were two important factors which enabled the company to successfully implement these measures. First, the excellent past track record of the company in respect of profitable operation, payment of handsome dividends and frequent issues of bonus shares had created confidence among the shareholders that the company would fare well. Second, due to the efficient operation of the company's ships during the 1981-86 depression, the company sustained losses only in two years, 1982-83 and 1983-84, and the total loss during these two years was the moderate amount of Rs. 9.60 crore.

Other shipping companies in the private sector would have found it comparatively difficult to raise further equity or loans during the depression. It also required courage on the part of the

Sheths to launch such a scheme of convertible debentures as the company was losing almost Rupees 1 crore every month in 1982-83 and it is only the profit of about Rs. 7 crore on the sale of ships which reduced the losses. In view of the shareholding of the Sheth family, they would have to also perforce invest in convertible debentures which were offered as a rights issue to the shareholders.

The Board decided on 23 November 1983 to issue, subject to sanction of the Controller of Capital Issues and the approval of the shareholders 13.5 per cent secured 12,77,500 convertible debentures of Rs. 100/- each and offer them to the shareholders in the proportion of 1 bond of Rs. 100 for every 20 equity shares of Rs. 10/- each held by the shareholder. After a year from allotment, 50 per cent of the amount paidup on each bond was to be applied towards issue of 5 fully paidup equity shares of Rs. 10 each. After about 3 years from allotment the balance 50 per cent of the amount of each Bond was to be converted at the option of the bondholders into 5 fully paid equity shares of Rs. 5 each. The bonds held by the bond holders who did not exercise such option were to continue as bonds until maturity and were to be redeemed at par on completion of 7 years from the date of allotment.

The convertible bonds issue was oversubscribed between 2 July 1984 and 13 August 1984. The company was able to raise Rs. 12.775 crore from the shareholders and half of the amount was to be converted into equity shares on completion of 1 year. This issue considerably improved the liquidity position of the company and also enabled the company to successfully undertake and implement the further measures such as issue of right shares to the shareholders and negotiation of a financial package consisting of subscription for equity shares and grant of a subordinate loan of US$ 8 million by International Finance Corporation.

In early 1985, the company approached the International Finance Corporation (IFC), Washington, in connection with the company's expansion and modernisation programme, asking IFC to subscribe to the equity of the company and grant a subordinate loan. After a project appraisal by IFC and long negotiations on the terms of financing, an investment agreement was signed between the company and IFC. The financing package with IFC was worked out in two parts, namely IFC's subscribing to the company's equity shares of Rs. 10/- each at a price of Rs. 13/- per share and IFC granting a subordinate loan of US $ 8 million. It is noteworthy that

Great Eastern was the first shipping company in the world in which IFC took equity participation.

The equity subscription of IFC was utilised to acquire a bulk carrier which was named *Jag Vishnu.* The subordinate loan of US $ 8 million was drawn in three instalments by the company. The first tranche of US$ 2,025,000 was drawn on 22.2.1988; the second tranche of US $ 2,737,500 was drawn on 31.5.1988; and the third tranche of US $ 3,237,500 on 27.10.1988. This loan was also used to acquire two ships from abroad on 2.6. 1988 and 22.7.1988 respectively. The ships were named *Jag Vivek* and *Jag Vijay.* The subordinate loan carried an interest rate of 9.25 per cent per annum payable in quarterly instalments.

One of the noteworthy features of this subordinate loan was that it could be used as an open line of credit and the company could use it as and when required. For the borrower this is much better than ship-related borrowing wherein a ship is identified and the shipowner approaches a financing institution to lend against that ship. Specific ship-related borrowing is a time consuming process, whereas under the line of credit there is considerable freedom of action and ability to take quick decisions.

Under the subordinate loan agreement the company further granted an option to IFC to convert part of the subordinate loan into equity shares of the company at a premium as per the formula agreed in advance. The option to convert the subordinate loan into equity was restricted to 6.25 million equity shares of the company. IFC exercised the option in two stages by converting part of its loan firstly into 3 million equity shares of Rs. 10/- each at a price of Rs. 16.87 (Rs. 6.87—premium) per share on 7.6.1988 being the date of allotment and 3.25 million shares at a price of Rs. 26.44 (premium of Rs. 16.44) per share on 6.12.1990 being the date of allotment. IFC in all held 8.25 million equity shares after the conversion. On this shareholding they further got bonus shares in the year 1991-92, which increased their holding by 20 per cent to 9.90 million shares. This was about 11.6 per cent of the company's total paid up equity capital.

During the year 1986-87 the company made a rights issue of equity shares to its shareholders in the proportion of 1 share for 2 shares held. The rights issue of Rs. 20.12 crore was oversubscribed and the company retained an additional 25 per cent from the oversubscription. The rights shares of Rs. 10 each were Rs. 5 per share paid up and the balance amount of Rs. 5 per share was to be called up later. The equity paid up capital therefore went up by about Rs. 12.41 crore.

The Great Eastern Shipping Company (London) Ltd.

The company's branch office in London, as we have seen in earlier chapters, was doing very useful work. Headed by Sudhir Mulji, the London office of the company fixed the employment of the company's OBO carriers on the best terms possible during the depression and monitored their operations. The presence of a knowledgeable and experienced shipping executive in London, which was the nerve centre of shipping markets, not only assisted in the employment of the company's ships during those difficult times but also kept the company abreast of world developments in shipping and was of great assistance in sale and purchase of ships.

In the early 1980s, the ongoing shipping depression together with the time-consuming government procedures and bureaucratic delays affected Indian shipping very adversely. It was therefore felt that the registration and setting up of a wholly owned subsidiary of the company in U.K., which would be comparatively free to operate, would be in the interest of the company. The Board of Directors therefore decided on 24 March 1983 to convert the London office into a wholly owned U.K. registered subsidiary of the company.

The company approached the government and the Reserve Bank of India for permission to convert the company's London office into a wholly owned U.K. registered subsidiary. The assets of the London office were to be taken over by the London company and a small cash subscription to the capital of the company was required to be remitted to London. Whilst the government approval permitted among other things purchase, sale and operation of ships, it laid down a condition that the Indian company would not give financial support or guarantees in respect of the London registered subsidiary.

The company was registerd in U.K. on 15 January 1985. The paidup capital of the company was British pounds 1,60,000, out of which 1,260 equity shares of pounds 10 each that is, of the face value of pounds 12,600 were issued against purchase of assets of London office and 14,740 equity shares of pounds 10 each, that is, of the face value of pounds 147,400 were subscribed for cash, that is, out of remittance by Great Eastern Bombay, to the London company. The company commenced its operations on 1 July 1985. The London subsidiary was most useful in acquiring ships at most competitive prices in 1985-86, 1986-87 and 1987-88, since it was not subject to inordinate delays in getting government clearances. It raised loans abroad on its own and purchased ships and had them registered in Gibraltar. The ships were registered in Gibraltar, which did not impose any restriction regarding nationality of officers and crew, so that Indian officers and crew could run the ships. Some of these ships were transferred to Great Eastern Bombay after getting the Government of India's approval in due course. Great Eastern London not only acquired a fleet of ships but earned handsome profits including profit on sale of ships.

Sudhir Mulji, Chairman of Great Eastern London, was invited by the former Prime Minister Rajiv Gandhi to be Chairman of State Trading Corporation of India (STC). He therefore resigned from Great Eastern London on 31 December 1986 and joined State Trading Corporation of India as Chairman. However, after spending some time in STC he found that in the bureaucratic set-up there was not much scope for initiative and enterprise. He therefore left STC and rejoined Great Eastern London as Chairman. With Sudhir Mulji at the helm of affairs of Great Eastern London, the London subsidiary is growing from strength to strength and playing an important role in the growth of Great Eastern Shipping Company.

Purchase of M.V. Sonid at Auction in Greece to Assist Government in Getting Delivery of Cargo Shipped on the Vessel

Transchart, the government chartering organisation, had arranged shipment of 18,000 tons urea from Rostock to India by m.v. *Sonid.* The cargo belonged to Government of India and it was worth approximately Rs. 4 crore. The ship called at a Greek port called Pylos enroute India, and was arrested with cargo on board as a result of legal action taken by Bank of America as the shipowner had failed to repay the loans borrowed from Bank of America. It was announced that the vessel would be sold by auction on 16 June 1985. The government requested Great Eastern through Transchart to assist the government in getting safe delivery of cargo by bidding at the auction and purchasing the vessel in auction sale.

It was an international auction sale and required great initiative and commercial skill to successfully bid for the vessel at the auction. The government chose Great Eastern because it had confidence in the business skill and competence of the company. The government permitted the company to bid up to US $ 1.25 million and also approved payment of brokerages, legal and other expenses within the overall ceiling of US $ 1.25 million and also gave an option to the company to scrap the ship after completion of the voyage to India. K.M. Sheth, Deputy Chairman, accompanied by K.J. Vesuna, Operations Manager, and S. Govindrajan, Engineer Superintendent, attended the auction and purchased the vessel at a very favourable price of US $ 4,80,000. The vessel successfully carried out the voyage and delivered the government cargo. The government's confidence in the ability of the company to deliver the goods was more than justified. The vessel was renamed *Jag Krishi.* The ship was in a good condition and operated profitably until it was sold in 1988-89 for scrapping for about Rs. 2.6 crore.

Management

During this decade Vasant Sheth was the Chairman, K.M. Sheth Deputy Chairman and Managing Director, and Sudhir Mulji Joint Managing Director up to 14 August 1979 and Managing Director from 14 August 1979 to 31 March 1980. Sudhir Mulji continued as president of the company's London office until the incorporation of Great Eastern London Ltd in 1985, of which he was appointed Chairman.

New Generation

It is in this decade that the new generation of Sheths who joined the company began to shoulder increasing responsibilities of management of the companies.

Vijay Sheth, son of Dr. Kantilal Jagjiwan Sheth and grandson of Jagjiwan Ujamshi Mulji, with a B. Com (Honours) degree, had worked for some time in the 1970s in the company. He later went to Manila and joined the Asian Institute of Management (Harvard affiliated) and obtained a Master of Business Management (MBM) degree. Thereafter he rejoined the company as Senior Deputy Manager. He held the position of Vice President (Commercial).

He was appointed Executive Director for five years from 1 July 1989. He now looks after the offshore supply vessels.

Bharat Sheth, son of K.M. Sheth, Deputy Chairman and Managing Director, and grandson of Maneklal Ujamshi, studied economics and obtained his B.Sc. (Hon) (Economics) degree from Scotland. He joined the company on 1 October 1981. He was appointed as Senior Deputy Manager with effect from 1 February 1984. Thereafter he held the position of Vice President (Commercial). He was appointed as Executive Director with effect from 1 July 1989. Bharat Sheth looks after the shipping activities of the company and is in charge of the Bulk Carriers division.

They have been looking after their departments competently and have made a worthy contribution to the progress of the company in the fourth decade.

Management and Executives

Vasant Sheth, Chairman and K.M. Sheth, Deputy Chairman and Managing Director continued to look after overall management of the company. Sudhir Mulji, who resigned as Managing Director on 1 April 1980 to take over the responsibilities of President, London office and later, on incorporation of The Great Eastern Shipping Co (London) Ltd, became Chairman of that company, also shared in the overall management responsibilities and managed the London subsidiary which also acquired and operated a fleet of ships.

Vasant Sheth's and K.M. Sheth's contribution in steering the company skillfully and successfully in the acute shipping depression and making it the best managed company in India and one of the best managed companies in the world won universal acclaim.

As stated earlier, the younger generation of Sheths—Vijay Sheth and Bharat Sheth—assumed increasing responsibilities of management in this decade. In the early years of the fourth decade D.H.C. Storey and N.L. Narasimhan died. Storey, who had retired as Technical Director and was continuing as Technical Advisor with the company headed the Personnel and Maintenance Department of the company for a number of years. He very competently looked after the repairs and maintenance of the company's fleet and technical work and had played a worthy role in the growth of the company. He died on 15 January 1984. N.L. Narasimhan was a very conscientious, hard working and competent Engineer

Superintendent of the company and rendered meritorious services in looking after the repairs and maintenance of the company's fleet. He died on 13 August 1979. N.G. Kirpalani, who was posted in London office and was looking after the maintenance and repairs of OBO carriers and also advising on maintenance and repairs of other ships whenever reference was made to him in London, resigned from the company's services with effect from 1 July 1980.

N.P. Gidwani joined the company as Group Advisor on 6 April 1981 and assisted the Chairman and the Deputy Chairman and Managing Director in the financial management of the company. He played a worthy role in the company's issue of convertible bonds and rights issues and in successfully negotiating a financial package consisting of subscription to equity shares and subordinate loan with the International Finance Corporation.

S.N. Sanklecha as Company Secretary implemented the convertible bonds issue and equity shares right issue to the shareholders in the lean times faced by the shipping companies in the shipping depression. His expertise in handling of the company's marine hull and P & I insurances contributed to the company's fleet being insured on very favourable and competitive rates and terms. He worked with dedication in all the four decades, having joined prior to the incorporation of the company, and was Company Secretary for 35 years. He was designated as Senior Vice President (Corporate) on 1 April 1987.

P.R. Naware was appointed as Company Secretary on 1 June 1987.

B.N. Adappa, who was heading the dry cargo division of the Operations Department rendered dedicated services to the company in all the four decades. He handled employment and operations of bulk carriers most efficiently to the great advantage of the company. He also looked ofter the supply of bunkers to the ships and brought about savings in the cost of fuel, which is an important component in the operating costs of ships. He was designated as Executive Vice President on 1 April 1987.

K.J. Vesuna, who headed the wet cargo division of the Operations Department, looked after the employment and operations of OBO carriers in the oil trade and tankers and also acquisition/building of ships for his division competently. He was designated as Executive Vice President on 1 April 1987.

N.E. Pardiwala, who headed the company's Personnel

Department after Utamsingh left the company's services, looked after the recruitment, promotions, terms of employment, negotiation of union agreements, staff welfare schemes etc. of employees, both ashore and afloat. He tackled the above aspects with vigour and rigour and organised and streamlined the personnel matters to the satisfaction of the management. After Great Eastern's diversification into the real estate business, for some time he attended to the work of the real estate division also. He was designated Vice President (Personnel) on 1 April 1987.

A.R. Balasubramaniam, who was Chief Accountant of the company for about 25 years, retired on 4 April 1985. He meticulously looked after the accounts of the company which grew in dimensions as well as complexity with the substantial growth of the company. He also handled the company's taxation matters. After his retirement, D.G. Khatri, who had ably and competently assisted Balasubramaniam, became the Chief Accountant. Khatri's expertise in accounts and taxation as well as foreign exchange transactions, which are a very important part of a shipping company's business, proved very valuable for the company. He was appointed Vice President (Accounts) on 1 April 1987.

P.C. Jain, Engineer Superintendent, in charge of the dry cargo division, and M. Aranha, Engineer Superintendent, in charge of the wet cargo and offshore division, who had been competently looking after the work of repairs and maintenance of the dry and wet cargo fleets respectively, were designated Vice Presidents (Technical) of their respective departments. S. Ghosh, Engineer Superintendent, who meticulously attended to the ships in the wet cargo division, was designated Assistant Vice President (Technical) in this decade and as Vice President (Technical) subsequent to the close of the decade.

G. P. Khot joined the Delhi office of the company as Manager on 1 September 1982. By qualification he was a chemical engineer with a B. Tech and M. Tech in Chemical Engineering from L.I.T. Nagpur and I.I.T. Bombay respectively. With a diploma in Industrial Management from Bombay and business experience as an officer in State Trading Corporation and in his own business, he has built up excellent rapport and relations with the government Departments and Ministries with which the company has dealings or has to obtain clearances etc.

Progress During the Fourth Decade

The progress made by the company in a number of areas has been dealt with earlier under the heading 'Company Emerges Stronger.'

At the end of the year 1977-78 the paid-up equity share capital of the company was Rs. 15.33 crore. It was three and a half times higher at Rs. 55.61 crore at the end of the year 1987-88. The reserves rose from Rs. 19.85 crore at the end of 1977-78 to Rs. 39.17 crore at the end of the year 1987-88. The net worth went up during the same period from Rs. 35.18 crore to Rs. 94.78 crore.

The freight and charter hire earnings rose from Rs. 37.90 crore in 1978-79 to Rs. 110.17 crore in 1987-88. The company sustained a loss of Rs. 1.27 crore in the year 1978-79. In the year 1987-88, which ended the fourth decade, the company made a profit of Rs. 19.50 crore, which was the highest in the 40 years of its existence.

The company owned 18 ships of 3,91,690 GRT on 29 November 1978. The number of ships owned by the company increased to 28 and the GRT to 5,60,254 GRT as on 30 June 1988. This does not take into account the ships owned by the company's London subsidiary.

Great Eastern Fleet's Percentage of Indian Tonnage

Date & Year for Great Eastern Tonnage	Indian Tonnage GRT	Great Eastern Tonnage GRT	Great Eastern Tonnage as Percentage of Indian Tonnage
09.11.1978	53,54,388	3,91,690	7
29.11.1979	55,79,793	3,91,690	7
27.11.1980	56,29,478	3,71,181	7
30.06.1981	56,79,436	3,61,761	7
30.06.1982	58,79,288	4,26,658	7
30.06.1983	60,30,178	4,11,432	7
30.06.1984	60,96,038	4,04,182	7
30.06.1985	63,64,004	4,41,731	7
30.06.1986	59,76,165	4,60,059	8
30.06.1987	58,02,877	5,34,684	9
30.06,1988	56,75,180	5,60,254	10

Notes:
1. Indian Tonnage as on 1st January of each year
2. Fractions in the percentage figures have been rounded off to the nearest next integer if the fractions are 0.5% or more.

The preceeding table details the progress in the tonnage (GRT) owned by the company in the context of the increase in Indian tonnage, and percentage share of Great Eastern tonnage in the Indian tonnage

It will be observed from the above table that whilst the tonnage of the Indian fleet was only marginally higher on 30 June 1988 at 56.75 lakh GRT as compared with 53.54 lakh GRT on 9 November 1978, the Great Eastern tonnage at 5.60 lakh GRT was more than 40 per cent higher in mid-1988 as compared with the tonnage on 9 Novemer 1978. Great Eastern tonnage also increased from 7 per cent of the Indian fleet to 10 per cent of the Indian fleet during this decade.

Net Worth Position and Debt Equity Ratio
1988-89

(Rupees in crores)

Name of company	Position as per Balance Sheet as on	Total Capital Employed	Net worth	Debts	Debt-Equity Ratio
Public Sector :					
Shipping Corporation	30/6/88	1355.80	135.47	1277.11	9.43:1
Private Sector :					
Great Eastern	31/3/89	280.44	120.80	159.08	1.23:1
Scindia	31/3/89	217.08	(-)117.27	155.26	-
India Steamship	31/3/89	126.13	(-)57.43	128.04	-
Ratnakar	31/3/89	114.06	(-)50.71	112.04	-
Essar Shipping	30/6/89	305.83	102.56	178.84	1.74:1
South India Shipping	30/9/89	132.82	32.54	100.28	3.08:1

Notes : 1 Total Capital employed includes paid-up capital reserves and surplus, and loans.

2. Net worth includes paidup share capital and reserves which are negative figures in the case of some companies after adjusting losses.

It will be observed from the preceeding that Great Eastern at Rs. 120.80 crore had the highest net worth among the private sector shipping companies. Total capital employed by the public sector Shipping Corporation of India was Rs. 1,355.80 crore as compared with a much smaller total capital employed by Great Eastern in the amount of Rs. 280.44 crore. The net worth of Shipping Corporation as compared with that of Great Eastern was however only marginally higher at Rs. 135.47 crore. Great Eastern had also the best debt-equity ratio amongst all the major Indian shipping companies. Its debt equity ratio of 1.23:1 was far superior to the debt-equity ratio of 9.43:1 of Shipping Corporation.

As stated in the Directors Report for 1987-88, the strategy adopted by the company over the last few years of (a) improving liquidity and achieving reduced gearing through substantial increase in the equity base, and (b) acquisition of good and cheap secondhand tonnage which was available at low prices, had finally paid off.

The company's operating earnings for the first time crossed Rs. 100 crore mark. The company also recorded the highest net profit before tax of Rs. 19.50 crore in its 40-year existence. The then Chairman Vasant Sheth in his statement to the shareholders at the Annual General Meeting held on 22 December 1988 stated: "Subsequent to 1983-84 in the face of many shipping bankruptcies in the world including some of the Indian shipping companies, Great Eastern had managed to earn modest profits and in fact started servicing the shareholders' funds with a small dividend in 1984-85. This was followed by a stronger performance every year since then." The Chairman expressed the belief that the company was not only in a better position to face the challenges for the years ahead, but would reap real benefits from growing prosperity for shipping.

REFERENCES

1. 27th Annual Report and Accounts 1985-86 of SDFC pp.15 and 16.

2. 'Shipping Crisis, Shipping Policy and SDFC' - issued by the office of SDFC Executive Director (Bombay), dated 10 September 1986.

Jagjiwan Ujamshi Mulji

Maneklal Ujamshi

Founders of The Great Eastern Shipping Company.

A.H. Bhiwandiwalla, Founder and Chairman of
The Great Eastern Shipping Company 1948 - 1973.

Group photograph of Great Eastern staff members and a few connected persons in 1956.

Vasant Sheth, President of INSA addressing A.G.M. in 1957. Others in photograph (from left to right) are Lal Bahadur Shastri, Shipping and Transport Minister, Sumati Morarji, Dr. Nagendra Singh and Sir Ramaswamy Mudaliar.

Vasant Sheth, Chairman and K.M. Sheth, Deputy Chairman and Managing Director.

Great Eastern Board of Director's Meeting in early 1981.
Sitting (from L to R) : K.M. Sheth, S.P. Mehta, Vasant J. Sheth, Rusi N. Sethna, S. Jagannathan.
Standing (from L to R) : N.P. Gidwani (Group Advisor), Sudhir Mulji, (President, London Office), S.N. Sanklecha, (Secretary), C. Srinivasan (S.D.F.C. Director).

Vasant Sheth and Asha Sheth with the Indian Ambassador to Japan at the launching of a ship in Japan.

Signing of Ship Building Agreement with Japanese Ship Builders in The Great Easterns' Office. Sitting (L to R) Vasant J. Sheth, A.H. Bhiwandiwalla, and Ship Builders' representative. Standing (L to R): S.N. Sanklecha, T.M. Sanghvi, Sudhir Mulji, and Ship Builders representative.

Group Photograph (1990) of Chairman, Deputy Chairman and Managing Director and Executives of the Company.

Vasant Sheth delivering a Speech.

Vasant Sheth, Capt, Ahuja, founder of Sea Cadet Corps,
K.M. Sheth, Asha Sheth.

Inauguration of Great Atwood Ltd. Seen in the Photograph are
(from left to right) H.T. Parekh, Shankar Dayal Sharma,
R. Venkataraman and Vasant Sheth.

Sale of Great Eastern Ship to Tata Chemicals (1977). Vasant J. Sheth, J.R.D. Tata, and S.N. Sanklecha. (Standing)

Sudhir Mulji, Present Deputy Chairman

Group photograph of Great Eastern staff members in 1952 at a farewell party to Amratlal V. Mehta, Manager, Freight and Operations Department.

K.M. Sheth Present Chairman & Managing Director

6

Change in Scenario for Shipping in Distress

The prolonged shipping depression which hit Indian shipping from 1976 to 1986 (with a two-year break from mid-1979 to mid 1981) brought about gloom and despondency in Indian shipping circles. Great Eastern was one of the very few Indian shipping companies which did not commit a single default in respect of its loan servicing obligations. A number of Indian shipping companies either went bankrupt or turned seriously sick; some other shipping companies although potentially viable made losses and faced serious liquidity crises. They defaulted in the payment of their instalments towards repayment of loans and interest to their largest creditor - Shipping Development Fund Committee (SDFC). SDFC had also stood as a guarantor for numerous loans and credits given by the banks and foreign shipyards. In some cases of default of their borrowers, SDFC was required as guarantor to make payments to these creditors.

The government was faced with the prospect of losing a large part of the funds it had lent for the development of shipping. There was disillusionment in government circles about the role of Indian shipping in the development of the Indian economy. The Shipping and Transport Ministry lost its credibility and clout with other ministries and especially with the Finance Ministry, because large government funds lent to shipping companies were in danger of being lost.

Quite apart from the world shipping recession which had adversely affected the Indian shipping industry, as we have seen in the earlier chapters, it was SDFC's indiscriminate and wrong lending policies which endangered the safety of government funds. SDFC adopted what they called a need-based approach, by which they gave loans to companies which had no funds or liquidity cushions of their own. They denied loans to well managed shipping companies on the excuse that they had some funds and they could manage their ship acquisitions without SDFC's loans.

It is not the author's intention to belittle the role of SDFC in the growth of Indian shipping in earlier years. However, that cannot absolve SDFC from the blame for the great harm it caused in the last 12 years of its existence. When shipping companies were not in a position to honour the borrowers' loan servicing obligations and asked for reschedulement of their loan repayments, SDFC refused to agree to loan reschedulement. It even went to the extent of telling borrower shipping companies that reschedulement could only be considered after the borrowers committed the default in payment. They ignored the fact that many borrower companies in their loan agreements with banks had the usual covenant that default by the borrower in loan servicing obligations with any of its creditors would make him at once liable for the full repayment of the loan to the bank.

SDFC Interference and Government Regulatory Procedures Adversely Affect Shipping Operations

Almost all the Indian shipping companies had the SDFC director or directors on their Board of Directors. They interfered in the working and management of the companies and would not permit them to invest their funds to maximise their earnings. Managing Directors and executives of shipping companies wasted considerable time in answering queries or collecting irrelevant information or trying to persuade the SDFC directors on their Boards not to veto the decisions taken by them in the running of the companies.

SDFC also acted as the Acquisition Committee on the basis of whose recommendations the government approved or disapproved the purchase of ships by shipping companies. The SDFC Executive Director's office in Bombay, which examined and processed shipping companies' applications for purchase of ships, held up the applications for many months by asking for irrelevant information and data, and often for frivolous reasons did not send their recommendations to the Acquisition Committee. Even when recommendations for some of the acquisition proposals were made after much delay, the Acquisition Committee itself further delayed their decisions on these applications. The provisions of Monopolies and Restrictive Trade Practices Act, which made it incumbent on the major shipping companies in the private sector to seek approvals to building or purchase of ships, added another delaying dimension since clearances under the M.R.T.P. Act required six months in the normal course. (The applicability of the M.R.T.P. Act to expansion in shipping was waived in the early 1980s.)

Also, the government did not permit the shipping companies to sell the vessels on commercial considerations and insisted that the ships must be sold only after they had completed their so called normal life. SDFC as creditors also prevented the sale of ships on the grounds that the sale proceeds would fall short of the outstanding loans on the ships. SDFC failed to realise that sale of loss-making ships would put an end to the recurring losses of the borrower companies owning them and their sale proceeds would reduce their debt exposure and debt servicing requirements.

The government restrictions on time-chartering out of Indian ships had prevented Indian shipping companies from time-chartering out their costly large-sized tankers, OBO carriers, bulk carriers etc. when charter rates were good. As a result, the shipping companies were exposed to the full force of the shipping depression and sustained heavy losses. The licensing policy of the government regarding operation of ships in specified trades or routes, restrictions on time-chartering out of Indian ships and chartering in of foreign ships, restrictions on dry-docking and repairs of ships, which prevented shipping companies from carrying this out abroad at the repair yards at far less cost in terms of repair charges and time factor, greatly undermined the efficiency of Indian shipping and increased its operating costs. The *pari passu* obligation of building ships in India at far higher prices and with delayed deliveries against shipping orders placed abroad or ships purchased abroad by Indian shipping companies was suspended for some time during the shipping depression. However, the costly and outdated ships of poor quality which had already been built at Indian shipyards by Indian shipping companies under compulsion or pressure from the government, sustained heavy losses and made the position of their owners precarious during the depression.

Internationally Competitive Shipping

Shipping faces international competition. Therefore the costs of operation of Indian shipping must enable it to compete internationally and attain its growth. If full freedom of operation is not given to Indian shipping it will not be able to operate efficiently.

As shipping is a capital intensive industry, the capital cost, that is, depreciation and interest charges, form a good proportion of the total operating costs. The shipowner must be able to build his ship at a shipbuilding yard anywhere in the world, which gives him the lowest price and best credit terms. If restrictions are placed on the building of ships so that a shipowner has to build some of his ships in India where the shipbuilding costs are high, the quality of ships poor, delivery times inordinately long and only limited types of ships can be constructed, the shipowner will be burdened with far higher capital costs. Similarly, the shipowner must have the freedom to carry out dry-docking and repairs of his ship at a repair yard anywhere in the world which charges the lowest prices for repairs and completes the repairs in good time.

Further, shipping is a cyclical industry with alternating booms and depressions. Prices of ships are influenced by these cycles and fluctuate greatly. If ships are acquired or built when their prices are low, the capital costs, that is, interest and depreciation, also remain low and the operations of ships become viable. Secondly, acquisition of ships when ship prices are low and sale of ships when ship prices are high enable the shipping companies earn substantial profits, which supplement the profits on operation of ships and enable the shipping companies to grow and prosper in spite of the cyclical nature of the industry. Indian shipowners, because of the government restrictions on acquisition and sale of ships, could not take purchase and sale decisions based on commercial considerations and could not avail of this legitimate income on a regular basis.

The licensing restrictions in India under which a shipowner can operate his ships in specified trades or on specified routes also places the shipowner in a strait jacket. He cannot operate his ships freely according to the requirements of the trade or changes in trade and maximise his earnings. Time chartering out of Indian ships to foreigners and taking a foreign ship on time charter freely according to the operating requirements of the shipowner are a *sine-qua-non* of efficient shipping operation. If it is not permitted, efficiency suffers and costs of operation rise.

The government restrictions and regulations which were enforced in respect of shipping therefore placed Indian shipping at a handicap in spite of its low cost structure based on low manning costs as compared with higher manning costs in developed maritime countries. Indian shipping could have grown at a much faster pace if the government had realised the international character of the shipping industry and not placed undue restrictions and controls.

Countries which give freedom of operation to their national-flag shipping, like Greece, Japan and Norway, have achieved substantial shipping growth and prosperity. In order to provide full freedom of operation and lower manning costs, many developed countries have encouraged their shipowners to register their ships under flags of convenience countries such as Liberia and Panama.

It was the Great Eastern Shipping Company which consistently, right from its establishment, pleaded for and advocated more freedom of operation. This did have some educative effect and resulted in a less restrictive regime of government controls, regulations and procedures.

Drastic Change in Shipping Scenario

The prolonged shipping depression in which many shipping companies in India and abroad went bankrupt and very large number of shipping companies everywhere turned sick, came to an end in 1987. Increase in international trade which provides a demand for shipping, decrease in the shipbuilding output and scrapping of a large number of ships which curtailed the supply, largely corrected the imbalance in the demand and supply factors of shipping. The freight markets improved and shipping companies again began to make profits. In India the abolition of SDFC in April 1987 and establishment of The Shipping Credit & Investment Co. of India Ltd. (SCICI) as a financing institution for shipping also brought about a great change in the shipping environment. SCICI has not only been dynamic in its lending operations but has also made a contribution in arranging speedy government clearances of purchase and sale of ships, and by not interfering, as a creditor, in the day-to-day management of the shipping companies. SCICI's role in the growth of Indian shipping has been dealt with later in this chapter.

With the installation of the P.V. Narasimha Rao government in 1991 at the centre when the country was facing acute foreign exchange crisis and was about to default in its debt servicing obligations, there was all round realisation that the country had stagnated economically because of government controls, regulations and procedures. The discarding of communism by Russia and East European countries of the Communist Bloc demonstrated that a socialist economy with its controls, regulations and procedures was a hindrance to the economic growth of a country. Many countries smaller than India in Southeast Asia and elsewhere such as Singapore, Thailand, Malaysia, Taiwan, and South Korea made far greater economic progress and increased their standards of living substantially in comparison with India. They had given more scope to market forces. Our country too has been moving towards a liberalised economy where market forces can play a dominant part. To some extent this has also brought about liberalisation in the shipping policies.

The Shipping Credit & Investment Co. of India Limited (SCICI)

The setting up of SCICI as a development financial institution for shipping on December 8, 1986 coincided with the end of the prolonged shipping depression. The government reviewed the operations of SDFC sometime during the year 1986 and decided to wind up the operations of SDFC with effect from April 3, 1987 in of the SDFC (Abolition) Act 1986. Simultaneously, the government decided that the financial assistance to shipping and deep sea fishing industries should be handled by a new financial institution. The Industrial Credit & Investment Company of India (ICICI) was asked to promote a new company to take over the function.

ICICI, the main promoter of SCICI, subscribed to 20 per cent of the issued capital of the company of Rs. 50 crore. Industrial Development Bank of India, Industrial Finance Corporation of India, Unit Trust of India, Life Insurance Corporation of India, General Insurance Corporation and its subsidiaries, State Bank of India and the four commercial banks joined ICICI in the promotion of SCICI and subscribed to the balance share capital. During the year 1990-91 SCICI issued additional equity capital of Rs.25 crore to the public through a prospectus, increasing the total paid-up capital to Rs. 75 crore.

On a cumulative basis up to 31 March 1992, loan sanctions for shipping activities including ship acquisitions amounted to Rs. 1191.08 crore and actual disbursements to Rs. 664.89 crore. SCICI assistance to the shipping sector covered 112 vessels aggregating 15.46 lakh DWT. SCICI assistance for acquisition of ships covered 34 per cent of the gross tonnage of shipping held in the private sector.

When SCICI came into being, the stake of the government in the shipping industry was very large, with loan and guarantee assistance to private shipping companies as at 31 March 1987 aggregating to Rs.816 crore with overdue principal and interest aggregating to Rs.319 crore. SCICI was given the task on behalf of the government of rehabilitation of sick but potentially viable companies. SCICI constructed appropriate rehabilitation packages.

As a result of the timely extension of rehabilitation assistance and largely due to the buoyant market conditions, there has been a significant flow of funds to the government from the erstwhile SDFC assisted companies. The aggregate recoveries in respect of loans and interest from viable and non-viable shipping companies owing dues to the government, through continuous monitoring and follow-up by SCICI since the abolition of SDFC up to 31 March 1992 amounted to Rs.386.56 crore.

The following comparison of SCICI with SDFC will bring out the role played by SCICI in assisting the progress and growth of shipping since SCICI's inception.

(1) SCICI is committed to provide its decisions on proposals for loan and other assistance very quickly and normally within a period of 6 weeks. The minimum time taken for sanctioning loans was 10 days and 84.56 per cent of the sanctions were within 4 weeks.

SDFC took inordinately long time; in granting loan sanctions and even ship acquisition sanctions which were also done by SDFC. Great opportunities for ship acquisitions at favourable prices were thus lost. The image of Indian purchasers of ships in the international sale and purchase markets was so tarnished that sellers of ships quoted higher prices to Indian purchasers as they were not sure whether the transactions would receive the Indian Government's approvals and would at all go through.

If SDFC had continued and SCICI had not come into the picture, the substantial acquisition of ships by Indian shipping companies in 1987, 1988, 1989 would not have taken place. SCICI also played a role in substantially reducing the time factor for grant of approvals by the Acquisition Committee to the purchase of ships.

(2) SCICI has been monitoring borrowers' operations without interfering with the management of the borrowers' operations and without adversely affecting the efficiency of their operations.

Monitoring of operations was most perverse in the case of SDFC and most adversely affected the efficiency and operations of borrowing shipping companies. SDFC blocked all innovations and avenues of more fruitful employment of spare funds by borrowing companies who also could not avail of freedom of operations.

(3) SCICI has played an important role in arranging foreign exchange borrowings for acquisition of ships. An important feature of SCICI's foreign currency borrowings has been the very fine terms obtained by it, both in terms of rate of interest and maturities, and these remain benchmarks for Indian external commercial borrowings.

SDFC had no role to play in foreign exchange financing except giving guarantees to foreign shipyards and banks for the credits and loans granted to Indian shipping companies. On SAFFAUNS loans too SDFC had no foreign exchange involvement.

(4) SCICI has followed both commercial and development considerations in grant of loans to shipping companies for acquisition of ships. It has brought about acquisition of sizable shipping tonnage with far less resources as compared with SDFC.

SDFC in the 70's and 80's had ignored both commercial considerations as well as development considerations in granting loans for ship acquisitions. Had the same amount of money, which was lent by SDFC, been disbursed prudently it could have brought about far larger acquisition of tonnage and would have also reduced the extent of defaults in repayment by shipping companies during the depression period.

(5) SCICI devised rehabilitation packages which helped the sick shipping companies to turn healthy. These companies have started repaying loans to government.

SDFC took no remedial action to assist sick but potentially viable shipping companies to restore their health. They were therefore also unable to recover any part of the loans from the defaulting companies.

(6) SCICI by its rapport and co-ordination with the government has been instrumental in bringing about wholesome liberalisation

in some government policies which were thwarting the progress of Indian shipping. SCICI has made significant contributions in the following positive changes in government policy which have already taken place or recommended.

(i) The ship acquisition licensing procedure has been drastically streamlined and acquisition approvals are now available to shipping companies within 6 weeks from the date of application. The application form has been rationalised with the assistance of SCICI.

(ii) The licensing policy itself has been significantly liberalised on the recommendation of SCICI.

(iii) Government has recognised that in order to expand national tonnage and increase the exposure of Indian companies to international competition, shipping companies may be allowed selectively to acquire ships for cross trading. This was actively canvassed by SCICI.

(iv) The procedures for granting permission for the sale of ships - for scrapping or for trading - are being streamlined and may be drastically cut short in terms of a recent exercise in which SCICI has been actively involved.

(v) Government has since decided to allow shipping companies to seek the approval of SCICI alone (without a reference to the ECB Division of the Ministry of Finance) for the pattern of financing ship acquisitions for which SCICI would be providing foreign currency loans.

SDFC not only did not play any such positive role but made the government regulations and procedures more cumbersome and time-consuming.

(7) SCICI has formed a Financial Advisory Services Team (FAST) to provide merchant banking and other financial services including consultancy to the industry. These include: assisting companies to raise capital in the market through public issues, placements or otherwise, evaluating projects, promoting of joint ventures between Indian companies entrepreneurs and overseas investors with a view to collecting overseas capital, technology and marketing tie-ups, giving advice on acquisitions and mergers, advising companies in selecting appropriate financing packages especially in foreign exchange, providing leasing and other financial services.

SDFC did not provide any of these services.

(8) SCICI has attempted upgradation of management levels and shipping know-how by arranging seminars etc. which was never done by SDFC.

SCICI'S Loan Assistance to Great Eastern

SCICI has disbursed to the Great Eastern, upto 31.8.92 total loans of Rs. 141.94 crore, out of which foreign currency loans amounted to Rs. 116.59 crore and rupee loans amounted to Rs. 25.35 crore.

7

Great Eastern's Advocacy of Freedom of Operation for Shipping

As we have seen in earlier chapters, it is SCICI's dynamic approach after its establishment at the end of 1986 and later the radical liberalisation of the entire regulated Indian economy from government controls and regulations by the Congress Government at the Centre in 1991, which changed the complexion of Indian shipping.

However, right from 1948, it has been Great Eastern that has played the key role of educating the government as well as shipowners about the importance of removal of restrictions and simplification of regulatory procedures.

Great Eastern right from its early days advocated that shipping was an international industry and freedom of operation should be given to the industry to enable it to compete with shipping of other maritime countries which enjoy freedom of operation. It should, however, be noted that there were two constraints which led to modify Great Eastern's approach to the problem. The entire Indian economy being dominated by government rules, regulations, controls and procedures, there was no way in which the shipping sector could ask for full freedom of operation unfettered by any rules, regulations or procedures. The call for freedom of operation therefore had to be restricted to those vital areas which had a substantial bearing on costs of operations of shipping. Secondly, in those early days Indian shipping operating in overseas trades was divided into two sectors, liner shipping and tramp shipping. Indian liner shipping companies were not in favour of freedom of operation because they were members of conferences and wanted to prevent other Indian shipping companies from entering the liner trades in which they were participating. This could only be done by licensing of ships for the routes or trades by the government. Great Eastern which had its stake in the tramp trades therefore had to restrict its call for freedom of operation tramp shipping.

The plea for freedom of operation in important areas of shipping operation was made in representations to the government and Chairman's speeches. Here the references cited are only those contained in the Chairman's speeches at the General Meetings of the shareholders of the company. A. H. Bhiwandiwalla was the Chairman from 1948 to 1973 and he delivered/issued Chairman's speeches/Chairman's statements during this period. From 1974 onwards Vasant Sheth was the Chairman and the Chairman's speeches/Chairman's statements were delivered/issued by him.

Chairman's speech at the Annual General Meeting (AGM) of shareholders on 30 December 1952:

Compulsion to buy ships from Hindustan Shipyard

"In order to have a planned building programme and continuity of employment for the Yard the Government has decided to finance the Indian shipping companies with loans for the purchase of Visakhapatnam-built ships. This policy is correct so far as it goes. The Government is, however going further and bringing indirect pressure on shipping companies to place orders for coastal ships exclusively with the Visakhapatnam Yard. The Government is also considering, it is understood, of banning purchase of ships from abroad for coastal trade. I shall not be surprised if the Government is persuaded to pass legislation making it compulsory on Indian shipping companies to acquire ships for coastal trading from the Visakhapatnam Yard only. There are two basic considerations which make this policy not only undesirable but positively harmful for the growth of Indian shipping. Firstly there is ample scope, nay, urgent need for expanding the tonnage in the country in shortest possible time. Secondly with limited financial resources it is necessary to augment tonnage not only by new ships built at Visakhapatnam Yard involving heavy capital expenditure but also by purchasing from abroad suitable second-hand ships costing relatively less. If expansion of coastal shipping is made dependent entirely on vessels built at the Visakhapatnam Yard the capacity of which is very limited, the pace of growth of shipping will receive a serious setback."

Chairman's speech at the AGM on 24 December 1953:

Hindustan Shipyard and the Shipyard pricing

"As I pointed out to you last year, shipping companies are being subjected to indirect pressure in order that they may place orders with the Hindustan Shipyard. This pressure has increased this year. It is fully appreciated that the yard must be kept busy and placed on a stable footing. By agreeing to pay the difference between the cost of building at the Yard and U.K. prices the Government has accepted the principle that Indian shipowners should not be required to pay more for their ships than others. It is now essential that the Government should adopt the concept of a world parity price instead of U.K. parity price in fixing the prices of ships built at the Visakhapatnam Yard. Not only the prices in the U.K. but also the competitive prices prevailing in other shipbuilding countries such as Holland, Germany, Denmark, Sweden, Japan, etc. should be taken into account in determining the selling price of ships."

Chairman's speech at the AGM on 25 November 1954:

Freedom to charter ships

"It has been urged from time to time that the chartered tonnage should be eliminated from the coast as early as possible, that we should be self-sufficient at least in coastal shipping. The idea is to build up our own tonnage and also to save the foreign exchange that would otherwise be payable to foreign companies as charter hire. I wholeheartedly endorse these objectives. I also appreciate the need that over-tonnaging on the coast should be avoided and that the owned tonnage licensed for coastal operation should continue to be fixed for each company with this overall object in view. But to insist mechanically that under no circumstances should there be any chartered tonnage employed on the coast would be an unbusiness like approach. It is one thing for a company to use chartered vessels *because it does not possess enough tonnage of its own;* but surely it is an entirely different matter for the company to bring in some chartered vessels *only as temporary substitutes for its owned tonnage* when the latter can for a time be better employed on the overseas trade. What matters is that we should own enough tonnage and also do our best to expand it. Subject to this, however, each company must be allowed to operate with a 'flexible fleet', with freedom to charter as and when the need arises and to employ the whole fleet, including charters, on the coast and on the overseas as the exigencies of business may require. Lack of such freedom can only detract from the efficiency in fleet operation without offering any compensating advantage."

Chairman's speech at the AGM on 16 December 1955:

Ban on letting out of Indian ships

"A *de facto* ban has recently been imposed on letting out Indian-owned cargo vessels on a time-charter basis to non-Indian parties. The purpose of Government loans, it has been held, is to encourage tonnage expansion so that our own cargo may be increasingly carried in our own vessels, whereas hiring them out to other countries would defeat this purpose. This, I regret to say, takes an unduly narrow view of the shipping industry and runs counter to important business considerations. Two-way time-chartering is an integral part of shipping, especially of the tramp trade; at times this is particularly useful in covering business risks; besides, long-term chartering out of ships at favourable rates can directly stimulate tonnage expansion since it widens the opportunities for the gainful employment of vessels and also enables a shipowner to plough back booked profits on a planned basis rather than depend on anticipated profits from trading, which may or may not come true; for all these reasons it has been extensively resorted to by other maritime countries. There is no reason why the same freedom should not be allowed to Indian shipowners subject to whatever reasonable condition may be found necessary to prevent any dislocation of regular trades."

Why Private Sector?

"The Industrial Policy Resolution of 1948 decided to keep shipping in the private sector. This was undoubtedly a wise decision. In shipping efficiency is synonymous with despatch and quickness of decisions. Besides, it calls for an unusually high degree of flexibility and initiative, shrewd business judgement, ability to watch day-today developments as well as to evaluate long-term trends. Consequently, it lends itself far more readily to private enterprise which enjoys inherent advantages in fulfilling these indispensable conditions of success.

Chairman's speech at the AGM on 6 December 1956:

Freedom of operation for tramp shipping

"Your company has taken active interest in tramping right from its commencement. The adventurous enterprising spirit with which shipowners have been imbued from the dawn of history attains its high-water mark in tramping. Your company had to face competition of an international character from well established foreign shipowners; this is an implicit challenge in tramping business. Owing to the ignorance and apathy on the part of Indian shipowners, as well as the Government in this country, about the importance of tramping business and its requirements, we had to face not only lack of co-operation, but actual hostility and obstruction, in the form of numerous restrictions that were placed on our `Freedom of the high seas'. The position has improved with the Government's recognition of the role of tramping in the country's economic life. I am, however, sorry to say that the majority of Indian shipowners interested in the liner trade have not yet, to say the least, appreciated its significance. Liners and tramps are like two wings, each equally indispensable to the life and growth of India's shipping industry.

"In view of this prevalent bias against tramp shipping, the Government has been influenced and swayed by the liner interests and prejudices, and conditions for the creation and growth of the tramp fleet in this country have not been established. It is hoped that the Government will consider the matter dispassionately and allow the same freedom of operation to tramp owners in this country as is enjoyed by successful tramp-owners in other maritime countries.

"There is a lot of confusion and far from clear thinking about the economics of shipping in this country. In normal peace times and in the absence of emergencies the maximum operational efficiency and the optimum utilisation of tonnage should guide and govern the employment of ships. There is nothing sacrosanct about the carriage of India's exports or imports in Indian ships.

What matters is the rapid growth and development of Indian tonnage plying on the high seas. This can only be brought about if the Government does not interfere with the employment of vessels and permits tramp operators to follow considerations of operational efficiency and gainful employment which will assist the rapid expansion of the merchant fleet. If some of the Indian ships do not carry part of India's imports or exports, the country will no doubt have to pay the freight charges in foreign currencies. But the Indian ships, which are more gainfully employed in other trades, will earn more foreign exchange than will be paid to foreign ships for carrying part of India's imports and exports. It is the net difference in foreign exchange that matters. The astonishingly rapid progress made by Norwegian and Greek shipowners in recent years would not have been possible if the Governments of those countries had imposed the restrictions which are fettering the Indian tramp operators at present.

"The Government restrictions on letting out Indian ships on time-charter to foreigners have acted as a restrictive influence on expansion of Indian tonnage and foreign exchange earning without doing an iota of good to the country. If an Indian shipping company wants to expand rapidly it must make sure of gainful employment of at least some of her ships for a period of time. Time-chartering out of ships provides this sort of employment for an assured period and makes the shipowner immune from the risks of fluctuations in the freight market. With such a hedge he can afford to take the risks of the freight market by building and/or purchasing more ships at the prevailing high level of prices in the place of those chartered out. Moreover tramp operators have to judge the freight market and at times to cushion off the risks of a fall in the market by letting out some of their vessels on a time basis. The only difference between letting out a ship on a time basis and fixing her for a voyage is the difference between the wholesale selling of freight and the retailing of freight. Whilst the Government has no objection to the retailing of freight, it has prohibited wholesale selling of freight to the great detriment of the shipping industry. May I earnestly appeal to those in authority to examine this question dispassionately and exempt at least tramp operators from the restriction on letting out their vessels on a time basis?"

Chairman's speech at the AGM on 28 November 1957:

Wisdom behind freedom of operation

"The Company would have achieved still better results if it had enjoyed unrestricted freedom of operation. Right from the beginning, we had been urging on the Government to recognise the importance and special problems of tramp shipping. In spite of the all-round ignorance of and consequent prejudice against the requirements of tramp shipping, we not only pioneered but also persevered in this branch of shipping. As the liner interests and prejudices influenced and dominated the Government decisions, our path was strewn with many difficulties and obstacles. I am, however, glad to say that, subject to our Government keeping up their commitment made in 1956 and permitting purchase of two cheap second-hand vessels for our coast, we would establish a small nucleus of three large tramp ships. With the operation of such a tramp fleet the Government is also realising its peculiar problems and lends a sympathetic ear to the requirements of tramp shipping.

Complete freedom of operation is enjoyed by tramp shipowners all the world over, and has been responsible for the rapid and spectacular growth of shipping in countries such as Norway and Greece. Two years ago, from this very forum I had made the following observations:

"Two-way time-chartering is an integral part of shipping, especially of the tramp trade; at times this is particularly useful in covering business risks; besides, long-term chartering out of ships at favourable rates can directly stimulate tonnage expansion since it widens the opportunities for gainful employment of vessels and also enables a shipowner to plough back booked profits on a planned basis rather than depend on anticipated profits from trading which may or may not come true.'

"If these words had been heeded and ban on time-chartering out of Indian ships had been lifted, our `Jag-Laxmi' could have been time-chartered out for one or two years at the very favourable rates prevailing in the first half of 1957. This vessel alone then would have earned the net foreign exchange annually of the order of Pounds Sterling 375,000. Your company would have earned back the whole cost of the ship namely, Rs.1.20 crores in about 2-1/2 years. The company's net earnings and the country's net foreign exchange in 2-1/2 years on this vessel would have been sufficient to purchase another ship costing as much as `Jag-Laxmi'. The foreign exchange famine has jeopardised the success of our Five-Year Plan itself and it saddens my heart that owing to the dogmatic approach on the part of the Government, such splendid opportunities for earning foreign exchange were missed.

"My observations are not intended to lament the past, but to draw the pointed attention of the authorities to the correct approach to this problem in future. The fallacy of the Government attitude can be further evidenced by the fact that whilst we can time-charter foreign ships for overseas trading, we cannot time-charter out Indian ships to foreigners. This means that whilst we can buy freight wholesale, we are not allowed to sell it wholesale. When the freight markets are likely to fall, the tramp operator must sell wholesale part of his shipping space at the prevailing favourable rates. If he is not permitted to do so, he is bound to sustain losses in retailing freight voyage by voyage at the progressively declining rates. Lately this subject has been discussed personally with high Government officials and I am glad to say that the Government is realising that their rigid attitude in the past prevented the country from earning foreign exchange. May I express the hope that in future whenever opportunities present themselves again, the Government will permit the tramp operators to time-charter out some of their ships for a period trading at the favourable rates and help book the profits for the company and foreign exchange for the country?"

Chairman's speech at the AGM on 12 December 1958:

Importance and special procedural requirements of tramp shipping

"I am going to deal at some length with the requirement for the development of tramp shipping and also with the question of discrimination between the public sector and the private sector in shipping, not only because of their bearing on the development of Indian shipping but also because of their relevance to the contribution your company can make to the development of shipping.

"Although the importance of developing tramp shipping in India has been recognised by the Government, the policies followed by them do not show that there is adequate appreciation of the vital role that tramp shipping can play in the economic development of the country. Development of tramp shipping is the quickest way of increasing our participation in the overseas trade. If we wait till the main Conferences admit us as Members with substantial tonnage, we shall have to wait indefinitely. Growth of tramp tonnage is also the quickest way of building up of our overseas tonnage which is an essential perquisite for admission to the various Conferences. Tramping offers much better opportunity for fuller employment of the available tonnage because of the unrestricted freedom which tramps enjoy for carrying bulk cargoes from one port to another all over the world. The Study Group of the Consultative Committee of Shipowners appointed to examine the shipping target for the Second Plan estimated that, excluding the substantial oil trade, over a crore of tons are being carried as bulk commodities in the international trade of India and observed that 'there is a wide field for Indian tramp tonnage to participate in this trade.' Finally, development of tramp shipping would ensure a recurring big saving or earning of precious foreign exchange involved in payment of freight bills year after year.

"As the liner companies constitute the majority interest in Indian shipping and we perhaps are the only tramp shipping company, the Government thinking and policy is influenced and conditioned by the liner companies. There is lack of an adequate appreciation on the part of the Government of the peculiar problems posed by tramp shipping and its actual operational requirements. In fact, we submitted a memorandum in April 1955 to the Director General of Shipping on the subject of Special Requirements of a Tramp Shipping Company and the need for procedural and other changes. However, up to now the matter has not received due attention from the Government.

"It is difficult to believe that even now in peace-time the Government exercises a rigid licensing control over the employment of ships under the Control of Shipping Act in much the same way as is exercised in times of war. For every voyage or fixture we must have the licence of the Government. I am unable to find a single valid reason for the exercise of this war-time control in peace-time. The officials merely continue to exercise control and powers to which they have become accustomed. Our liner friends who have set and scheduled services can easily comply with such a procedure. It is, however, next to impossible for tramp operators to function efficiently within the framework of the present licensing procedure.

"Efficient tramping postulates that there must be unrestricted freedom of operation. Tramp operators all the world over carry on their business on the basis of either (1) voyage fixtures, that is on a short-term voyage basis or (2) long-term fixtures with a commitment to carry several shiploads of cargo. Long-term fixtures may comprise contracts for the carriage of a particular quantity of cargo in a number of shiploads or charters on time basis. The tramp shipping companies in other countries also enjoy the full operational flexibility under which they not only employ their own vessels on voyage charters and time-charters to others but also sometimes take vessels of others on voyage or time-charter basis to fulfil their own commitments efficiently.

"Further, tramping requires that the best opportunity for employment is seized without delay. Frequently, sudden enquiries are received over the telephone or by cablegram from our agents on the Baltic Exchange in London or from a shipper requiring a ship at a particular port on a particular day either on voyage charter or time-charter basis. Generally these offers are open for acceptance within 12 or 24 hours. On the Baltic Exchange there is international competition and if decision is not communicated promptly, the business would be lost to tramp operators of other countries who are well placed to give quick decisions since they are not governed by licensing procedures. We are therefore frequently placed between the horns of a most uncomfortable dilemma: to abide by the prescribed official procedure and lose our legitimate business or to by-pass the procedure in the interest of securing the business. At present the situation for tramp operators is critical. For want of employment opportunities many tramp operators are laying up their tonnage. If an employment opportunity is lost for want of receipt of Government approval in time, tramp operator would be probably faced with the question of idling or laying up of the vessel involving him in heavy financial losses and the country in foreign exchange losses. We had therefore to take the liberty of informing the Government and closing the business before receiving their approval which takes some time, in the confident hope that the Government would indulgently consider such technical breaches, if any, arising out of the exigencies of tramp operation. The more so as the Government has unequivocally declared itself in favour of developing tramp shipping, which, however, cannot be fostered if the rules, as they now stand, are to be literally followed in every single case.

"As tramping involves international competition we cannot compete with foreign tramp operators unless we possess the same unrestricted freedom for adjusting the movements of our vessels, as is enjoyed by our foreign competitors. If tramp shipping is to be developed in this country it is most essential that Government should modify, if not abolish, their licensing procedure and rules so as to suit the peculiar requirements of tramp shipping. In fact, some time ago the Government were considering the issue of global licenses to ships. I suggest that Government introduce the system of global licences for tramp operators' ships and give the tramp operators full freedom to give on voyage or time-charter their own vessels to others and take on voyage or time- charter others' vessels according to their requirements. As there is foreign exchange scarcity at present the question of release of foreign exchange to Indian operators chartering foreign vessels will have to be considered. I would suggest that the Indian tramp operators should be allowed to charter foreign vessels and the necessary foreign exchange be released to them if they have reasonable expectations that the business for which this chartering is done will not result in a net foreign exchange loss to the country. Subject to this condition applicable only in respect of chartering of foreign vessels by tramp operators, the Government must allow full freedom of operation to tramp operators. I submit that the existing Government rules and procedure which are not compatible with development of tramp shipping and which act as a restraining influence on the growth of tramp shipping be modified and adjusted so as to suit the special requirements of tramp shipping."

Statement of the Chairman for the year ended 30 June 1960 :

Freedom of operation for tramp operators

"Year after year I spoke at your Annual General Meetings about the great part that can be played by tramp shipping in our country's economy. I also discussed threadbare the special requirements of tramp shipping. Last year I gave expression to my feeling that there was better understanding and appreciation in Government quarters of the special problems of tramp shipping. I also pointed out the necessity of enunciation and announcement of Government's policy in order that tramp shipping operators were certain about the Government policy and proper climate was created for the expansion of tramp shipping. No such policy announcement has been forthcoming. We are still subject to rules, regulations and procedure which no maritime country would impose on tramp shipping. We have to obtain licences for every voyage we carry out; we are not allowed to time-charter vessels when we consider the market favourable and we are not permitted to give our vessels out on time-charter without the Director General of Shipping's permission. Tramp shipping cannot be built up unless there is freedom of operation for tramp operators. Every tramp owner is required to take a view of the market and to arrange the fixtures of his vessels on short-term or long-term basis in accordance with his view. He is also obliged to deplete or supplement the fleet under his operation by giving out ships on charter or by hiring others' ships on charter. In this way alone tramp ships could be fully employed without running risks and further ships could be acquired for tramp operation.

"In spite of the basic procedural handicaps we have built up our tramp fleet and we are proud of its survival under such difficult environment and circumstances. `The survival of the fittest' is the challenge with which shipowners plying ships in international tramp trades are confronted; we like this challenge and we accept it. However, when Government policies bind and fetter our hands and feet, odds are heavily against us in this unequal international competition where only the fittest can survive and succeed. The tramps also provide the cheapest vehicle of transport and the freight bill of the Government and other big shippers and consignees in the country must go down substantially if tramps are given a free hand to play their useful role.

"Although senior-most officials of the Government say that tramps should be the future ships in our country, freedom of operation has not been conceded to tramp operators. In the year 1956-57 we entered into a long-term contract of carriage and were given permission to fulfil our contract by taking foreign vessels on charter whenever necessary for operational reasons. Even this limited freedom of operation ensured gainful employment for our tramp ships and marginal earning of about Pound Sterling 500,000 in foreign exchange for our country. Placing of trust in us and grant of freedom of operation to enable us to give our ships on charter and hire foreign ships on charter whenever necessary for short-term or long-term periods for operational reasons will go a long way in building up a growing and prosperous national tramp fleet and earning valuable foreign exchange for the country."

High cost of ship's stores and repairs in India

"In our country the cost of ship's stores and repairs is very much higher than that prevailing in foreign countries such as U.K., Germany, Hong Kong, Japan, etc. For example steel renewals in India cost Rs.5,000 to Rs.6,000 per ton as compared with Rs.2,500 to 3,000 per ton in Japan. The high cost of maintenance and repairs of ships therefore is another factor which places an Indian shipowner at a disadvantage as compared with his competitor in foreign country.

"It is estimated that the level of repair cost in India is 25 per cent higher than that in other maritime countries such as the U.K. or Japan. In the last 12 years we have spent about Rs. 230 lakhs on repairs. Assuming that at least 50 per cent of the repairs were carried out in India, the excess 25 per cent charges paid by your company on repairs would amount to Rs. 28.75 lakhs and to that extent your company is at a disadvantage as compared with its foreign competitors."

Chairman's speech at the AGM on 21 December 1961:

Discrimination in Favour of Shipping Corporation of India in the Japan-India Trade

"In any economy, mixed or otherwise, the units which should be encouraged most are those which are most efficient. The only way to gauge the competitive efficiency of 2 units is to permit free and fair competition between them and to apply the same criteria to both units. In India, the public and private sector can easily develop together because the demand of the nation is very great. There is no need for one sector to eclipse the other; there is no need for one to be given more favourable treatment than the other. If, therefore, any policy of the Government divides the public and the private sector, if there is a schism in the nation dividing the two sectors, we shall undoubtedly waste our energies in the most fruitless occupation of unrealistic ideological differences, and leave the task of rebuilding the nation behind. I would far prefer the State to run an industry than to see its development hindered by arguments between the public and private sector. I am convinced that the most important job before us today is to increase our production and efficiency. We can then consider how to share the benefits. To put it simply, let us first bake the cake before deciding who is to eat it.

"All Government cargoes are offered first to the Shipping Corporation of India, and, if there is any overflow, it is offered to the Great Eastern Shipping Company or any other Indian line. Frequently this policy is inconvenient to the consignees of cargo as it has to wait for the Shipping Corporation's vessels before it is shipped. Besides, the Government today is perhaps the largest single importer in this country. If, therefore, they follow a policy of preferring the Shipping Corporation of India to other Indian companies, there will come a stage when the only Company that can expand with any degree of confidence will be the Shipping Corporation of India. Although we welcome the expansion in the public sector, we believe there is room for expansion for the private sector as well provided the Government encourages them both equally.

"As for giving us lower freight-rates than the Corporation, there really seems no valid reason for doing so. We are providing the Government and the shippers with exactly the same service as the Corporation. We give them as many sailings and as regularly as any Conference line does. It is, therefore, very unfair of the Government to treat us as outsiders and, consequently give us lower freight-rates when we have applied for membership to the Conference. Besides, if Great Eastern refuse to carry the cargo at this reduced freight-rate, the Government will be forced to pay the same freight-rate as they are paying to the Shipping Corporation to a foreign shipping company. They will not only, therefore, have to pay the same rate but also they will lose that much foreign exchange which they could save through us.

"Besides, it would be a most unfortunate policy for any Government to follow to discriminate in favour of independent public sector units in a mixed economy. If public sector steel mills use public sector banks and Government Ministries use public sector shipping companies regardless of all commercial considerations then there seems to be no point in setting up independent public sector corporations; they may as well become a supply depot to the Government."

Chairman's speech at the AGM on 29 December 1962:

Great Eastern ousted from Japan-India Trade

"In the overseas trade, during the year under review, our ships mainly participated in the India-Japan and Japan-India trade. Your Company has established itself in these trades after six years of hard work and effort. It was, therefore, shocking to find that we were badly let down in the Japan-India trade. Our interests were not taken into account nor were we consulted before an arrangement in regard to the Japan-India trade was stated to have been arrived at under the auspices of the Government.

"The Estimates Committee of the Parliament in their Report declared that the Government-owned Eastern Shipping Corporation Ltd., which is now the Shipping Corporation of India Ltd., would support our membership of the Conference catering to the trade between Japan and India. In view of this pronouncement we were trying for the last two years to secure membership of the Conference. Pending our admission to the membership of the Conference, our ships were only given overflow of the Government cargo moving from Japan to India after the ships of The Shipping Corporation of India Ltd., were filled up. Since we were likely to secure admission to the Conference, we refrained from encroaching on Conference cargoes which we could have, by quoting lower rates of freight. We confined ourselves to the 'overflow' and carriage of full load cargoes which could be carried economically by tramp ships. Not only our application has been rejected but also the present trend of Government thinking appears to be towards offering the overflow cargoes to foreign Conference Members and not to us which is contrary to what was done in the interim period. The Members of the Conference, with the exception of the Shipping Corporation of India Ltd., which is the only Indian Company, are foreign shipping companies. If this arrangement remains unchanged we shall be wiped out of existence from the Japan-India trade. It is sincerely hoped that notions of prestige will not be allowed to stand in the way of retracting the wrong step and we shall be allowed to play our useful role in the Japan-India trade."

Chairman's speech at the AGM on 20 December 1977:

Issue of global licenses and freedom of operation for tramp fleets

"The acquisition of ships has been encouraged by the Government with the intent of providing Indian trades with adequate shipping space. In the process the Government of India has evolved a policy which in effect denies Indian tramp shipping companies the normal protection of hedging against the fluctuations in the freight market by chartering out vessels for a period to international companies. The policy is particularly rigorous when demand for shipping space is high that is when major oil and steel companies are willing to offer long-term commitments to shipowners. At that time normally Indian requirements also are substantial so that domestic needs lead to the imposition of conditions preventing profitable long-term contracts. The freight rate on Government cargoes is based upon the current spot rate applicable to single voyages without any assurance of long-term period employment. So long as Indian imports are plentiful employment is available but the need for dampening the amplitude of revenue fluctuations is not solved. Even in normal times, therefore tramp shipping companies in India face a great deal of uncertainty in their flow of income. The excellent domestic grain harvests combined with a steady improvement in the production of fertilisers has curtailed imports into India from the high figure of 11 million tones of grain in 1966-67 to a negligible quantity in 1976-77.

"A similar, if less dramatic story, is true of fertilisers, petroleum products, rice and other goods that traditionally move in full shiploads. Indian shipping companies at present also employ their ships for third-flag trades but at rates of freight or hire which are excessively low. The loss of a securely based employment with the excessively low freight market is now taking a devastating toll of the profits and revenues of Indian shipping companies. In the present shipping depression, due to scarcity of Indian cargoes, the Government is liberal in permitting the employment of Indian ships for third-flag trades or period employment. If the Government had followed this policy earlier, Indian tramp shipping would have been in a much better position. The purpose of this address is not recrimination but to derive lessons from the past experience. I earnestly hope that the Government will evolve a long-term policy (not confined to the present depression only) of permitting Indian tramp companies the freedom to employ their ships for third-flag trades or on long-term period charters which will give them not only assured employment but provide them with a hedge against the vagaries of the tramp freight market and to some extent save them from the plight in which they find themselves in the present shipping depression. In the past I have advocated from time to time the issue of global trading licences to Indian tramp ships and unrestricted freedom to employ ships on long-term charters and I trust that the Government with the experience gained in the present depression will suitably modify their policies to permit unrestricted trading including long-term period chartering even in normal times."

Making Indian shipping more competitive by abolition of controls and restrictions

"The acute shipping depression which has shaken the shipping industry to its foundations provides an excellent opportunity to Indian shipping with its lower cost structure to come to the fore. The developed maritime countries possessing large shipping fleets have received a rude jolt and their shipping because of its higher cost structure is facing more adverse weather and stormier seas. The Japanese have set the trend. Japanese controlled tonnage in 1969 consisted of 84 per cent tonnage in owned ships and 16 per cent tonnage in chartered ships; today it is 55 per cent owned and 45 per cent chartered. Japan has also the largest seaborne trade (in terms of tonnage) in the world. I believe the trend on the part of the developed countries of owning less tonnage and chartering in more tonnage will ultimately be accelerated by the shipping depression. We in India have to gear ourselves by economising on all cost components that go into the running of a ship and make ourselves most competitive. Excellent opportunities, therefore, lie ahead for countries like India which can increasingly cater to the world sea-borne transportation by owning larger fleets which could be chartered out to shippers, charterers or shipowners in developed countries. This will minimise the cost of transportation for the countries concerned and also benefit our country. This can only be done if the Government gives up its inhibitions and allows freedom of operations such as unrestricted chartering in and chartering out of ships, freedom to enter into long-term freight contracts and also to enter into suitable arrangements with the shippers, charterers and shipowners in developed countries. I earnestly appeal to the Government to have a fresh look at the Government policy and abolish those controls and restrictions which come in the way of legitimate expansion of Indian shipping.

"The Government should provide automatic release of foreign exchange for repairs, spares and stores of ships on an annual budget basis as ships earn or save foreign exchange. The Government has also to some extent liberalised the terms of the *pari passu* clause under which Indian Shipping Companies are obliged to place orders for ships with Indian shipyards whenever they buy new or secondhand ships from abroad. I would suggest that the pricing and other terms for construction of ships at Indian shipyards should be formulated in such a way that orders are placed by Indian Shipping Companies voluntarily on a commercial basis with Indian shipyards. The compulsion under the *pari passu* clause is not in the interest of development of Indian shipping and should be done away with."

Chairman's speech at the AGM on 30 December, 1978:

Licensing of ships

"My predecessor in his Chairman's speeches to you in the fifties dealt at great length on the many harmful effects of the Government's licensing policy in respect of Indian ships. I also spoke on this subject to you last year. It is not necessary, therefore to cover the same ground again. However, I would just summarise the very adverse effects of the restrictive licensing policy followed by the Government:

a) Whilst the licensing policy restrains the Indian Shipping Companies from carrying cargoes, it cannot prevent foreign shipping companies from lifting this cargo with the result that cargo is increasingly diverted to foreign ships.

b) In respect of carriage of dry and wet bulk cargoes, foreign flag ships enjoy freedom of operation and capacity to operate world-wide which make their operations efficient. Indian-flag ships which do not have this freedom of operation are placed at a great handicap as compared with their foreign competitors and are not able to compete on equal terms in this highly competitive international business. Unless a shipping operator employing his ships for the carriage of bulk cargoes (dry bulk cargoes as well as oil) has the freedom to let out his ships on time-charter and charter-in ships belonging to others if required for carriage of his contracted cargoes, he cannot maximise his operating efficiency. Licensing is a hindrance in this regard.

c) The international freight markets for bulk cargoes are highly competitive and fluctuate widely. The shipping operator operating a fleet of tramps, bulk carriers and tankers must therefore be allowed to hedge in good times against the fall in the freight market by giving part of his fleet on long-term time-charters and/or entering into forward contracts of affreightment. Licensing comes in the way of these legitimate hedging operations.

d) The routes or trades which are indicated to the Government in the application for securing approval of the purchase of a ship may not remain profitable after lapse of time as trading conditions change continuously. In such circumstances, insistence that the shipping operator must ply his ship only on the route or trade which he had originally indicated is very unreasonable. It not only prevents the shipping operator from changing over from unremunerative trades or routes in the context of the changed circumstances, but also results in uneconomic and under-utilisation of ships which are national assets.

e) As far as general cargo or liner trades are concerned, licensing has imposed a monopoly of a few Indian companies on certain important Conference routes and also on those trade routes covered by our country's bilateral trade agreements with Russia and other East European countries. These trades are barred to other Indian shipping companies.

f) Licensing for shipping companies having more than one ship out of which one or more ships are compelled t) engage in coastal trading by licence has meant that the shipping operator has no option or choice but to continue in the trade in which he is making losses. He is even without the option of selling the ship and giving up the losing trade because the Government will not permit him to sell the ship unless he agrees to put one of the remaining ships as a substitute in the losing trade.

"May I therefore again earnestly appeal to the Government to abolish restrictive licensing with immediate effect and issue global licences to Indian ships. I trust that the Government will also permit tramp shipping operators unrestricted trading including long-term period chartering."

Chairman's speech at the AGM on 22 December 1981:

Shipping companies around the world becoming more and more international

"Shipping companies around the world are becoming so to say more and more `international' every day. Often you find a shipping company is registered in one country, its ships are registered in another country (flags of convenience) where laws are particularly favourable for shipping, the ships are however operated out of London, New York, Hongkong or Tokyo, the crews come from yet another country, the ships are financed from international borrowings and they sail the seven seas. Today approximately 31 per cent of world tonnage (in terms of dead weight) is registered under flags of convenience.

"An international shipowner can take decisions on whether to charter his vessel for a short period or for a long period stretching over several years; he can borrow internationally, spend internationally, buy and sell tonnages he wishes and take advantage of every opportunity with total freedom and absolute speed at his sole discretion".

India - A controlled economy and therefore unavailability of freedom of operation

"India is a controlled economy and hence we do not have the

same freedom of action that is available to international shipowners. Let me discuss some of these aspects:

"As shipping is a capital intensive industry it is not surprising that over 90 percent of the private sector shipping tonnage in the country is with monopoly houses as defined by the Indian MRTP Act. But really are we a monopoly? Approximately 55 percent of the Indian Merchant fleet is owned by public sector companies. The balance 45 percent owned by the private sector is spread out between 60 odd companies. Great Eastern owns approximately 6 percent of the Indian Merchant fleet and India in turn owns approximately 1 percent of the world fleet!! As I said earlier we operate in international markets against international competition.

"There have been recent press reports that Government is thinking of liberalising MRTP and also of removing shipping from the purview of MRTP altogether. If this is done, it would certainly go a long way to help speed up decisions for expansion and we would be able to seize opportunities for buying ships at the right time.

"Our expansion of Rs. 200 crore was conceived in February/March 1981. Thereafter it was developed through detailed discussions among the Senior Managers. In May 1981 the plan was crystallised and we submitted it to the Ministry of Shipping and Transport.

"The Ministry recommended our plan to MRTP around mid-October 1981. We have not yet had our MRTP hearing. We hope that the hearing will take place fairly soon. On this basis the earliest we will get our MRTP clearance is in February/March next year.

"As you can see it will take a full one year before we can even think of implementation. Sometimes I marvel at our track record under this unique regulatory framework. I must confess that good luck or Dame Fortune must be playing its role.

"In addition to MRTP clearance we need specific approvals for sale or purchase of ships from the Government of India. The Director General of Shipping makes his recommendations and this is then considered by an Inter-ministerial Committee.

"It is well known in international shipping circles that Indian shipowners pay a premium on price to international sellers for delays in getting Government of India approval.

"In the international arena selling ships in times of booming freight rates and secondhand tonnage prices is a common practice to generate funds for further acquisition and expansion. This is not a venture in speculation but through judiciou: purchase and sale of ships one can strengthen the net worth of the Company and in turn enable the Company to substantially increase its risk bearing capacity and borrow further and increase its investment in ships."

Other Controls

"Indian shipowners also require Government permission for:

a) Repair to ships overseas - Though obviously Indian Yards have to be encouraged and supported but there should also be a very positive attempt to make Indian Yards truly cost effective.

b) Ordering of spares - There has been a considerable amount of liberalisation recently but a lot more can be done.

c) Chartering of ships to foreigners particularly on long term charters - Due to the fluctuations in the freight rates large international shipowners have part of their tonnage on long term charters. This is not always highly profitable but is a steady income and therefore acts as a buffer to the fluctuation in the fortunes of the Company. Furthermore a long term charter is an assignable asset and can be pledged with Banks for financing acquisitions."

Chairman's statement to the shareholders for the year 1981-82:

Advantages and disadvantages of Indian shipping

"As I see it, the main advantages are:

1) Financial assistance from the Government on soft terms;
2) Very good cargo support from the Government; and
3) A highly skilled and technically qualified population of Officers and Seamen at competitive costs in relation to international shipping.

"These advantages are very significant. The developed nations by and large do not have all these advantages. This is why the developed nations are losing a major portion of their tonnage to Flags of Convenience who can achieve certain amount of cost benefits. The real advantage of Flags of Convenience is the total freedom and mobility which they enjoy and which is so essential to this International Cyclic Industry. The attraction to put ships under Flags of Convenience has been so great that almost one-third of the world's tonnage is under these Flags. In an attempt to arrest this exodus some of the developed nations have given full operational freedom and a subsidy based on manning costs.

"To my mind the main disadvantage to Indian shipping is the lack of this mobility and freedom. This disadvantage may more than offset all the advantages that we have. India is a controlled economy and, therefore, mobility and freedom that we would be able to achieve would be nothing like what the Flags of Convenience enjoy; but nevertheless, a certain amount of freedom is essential and should be allowed for this industry, if not to prosper, at least to survive."

Speed of Government Decisions

"The heart of ship owning business is `correct timing', of sale and purchase of ships. Ships bought in times of depression and sold in booms can provide not only the much needed reserves but actual cash to make down payments which quite often attract subsidised funds of foreign Governments which are attached to new buildings. The key to success is speed with which both sales and purchases can be put through. In fact, speed in taking decisions generally, in this industry, is a key to success. This is were India lags far behind.

"Today when Indian shipping is in deep difficulties and when large scale Government funds lent to companies are in danger, it is time to reflect as to where the Indian Flag has failed."

"Let me take you through a couple of procedures and then recommend remedies:

1) When we wish to buy a ship, we have to apply to the DG Shipping, with 29 extra copies of the application, who makes his recommendations to the Ministry of Shipping & Transport; the Executive Directors — SDFC also makes his recommendations to the Ministry; the application alongwith the recommendations are considered by an Acquisition Committee of the SDFC who then make their recommendations; the matter is then referred to the Finance Ministry. In addition, of course, MRTP approval is required. Eventually the Ministry of Shipping & Transport directs the DG Shipping in Bombay to issue the necessary permission.

2) When one wants to arrange any sort of foreign exchange finance, once again we have to make an application to DG Shipping

who makes his recommendations to the Ministry of Shipping & Transport, who in turn refer the matter to the Finance Ministry; who then, after consulting the Reserve Bank of India return the papers back through the same channel through which they were received.

"What I am advocating is that there should be a single point approval. The Government should lay down its policy on acquisition, on financing, etc., and the DG shipping or an equivalent authority should administer that policy. All applications which fit into the policy laid down by the Government should be cleared at the DG level. Only exceptional and extraordinary applications should be referred to the Ministries at Delhi. Furthermore, Shipping must be removed from the purview of MRTP altogether.

"There are several other areas too where simplification, speed, etc., can be had.

"I must hasten to add that at times we are able to get decisions very quickly from the Government of India, even if it involves inter-ministerial liaison or consultation, but more often than not, it is very time consuming. Furthermore, most shipping decisions are time bound. For example, when one wants to buy a ship the seller invariably wants the prospective buyer to give his decision within a stipulated number of days. Very rarely an Indian owner declares Government of India approval within the stipulated date. Invariably, extensions are sought and even the extended date cannot always be met because one just does not know how long, which Ministry and which department will take to clear the proposal.

"I must also add that I have not known many proposals submitted to the Government to have been rejected. They have, more often than not, been approved may be with marginal modification and hence all the more reason why a one point approval is workable and will benefit the industry enormously."

Chairman's speech at the AGM on 24 January 1984:

Trading in ships

"The mini boom of 79/81 was the right period for getting rid of old ships at good prices. Some in fact did sell but many felt the boom would last longer and missed, so to say, the bus. Recently about nine world famous names in shipping have entered into the short term business of trading in ships. Broadly they have called for fresh capital to buy ships in distress with the purpose of selling them at a small to reasonable profits."

Buying and selling of ships

"Buying and selling ships is an inherent part of a shipping company's business. Ship's prices, particularly secondhand ship's prices fluctuate with freight rates. Ships have to be sold in times of boom to cash in the profits, thereby again strengthening the capital base which in turn strengthens the foundation of this industry. Very few Indian companies have been selling off their ships. The average age of the Indian fleet (reckoned in number of units) is over 11 years as compared to the average age of say the Norwegian fleet which is 6 years. About 38 percent of the fleet is over 15 years and about half of that is over 20 years old. Therefore, not only have Indian Shipping Companies not cashed in their profits, but have partly an obsolete fleet on their hands.

"Great Eastern is probably the only exeption. We have bought 58 ships and sold 38 ships in our 35 years of existence. We have made an overall profit from sale of ships of about Rs. 16.28 crore that is, 28 percent of our net worth. Today the average age of Great Eastern's fleet is 8.5 years."

India - a Controlled Economy

"India has a controlled economy and for all permissions one has to go to Delhi. As the complexity of our economy grows, the manner in which the controls are being administered becomes more and more impractical. I feel that policy should be laid down by Government in Delhi and the administering of that policy should be decentralised at Bombay (where over 95 per cent of the industry is based) with the Director General of Shipping. In fact, the Merchant Shipping Act envisages and provides for the DGS administering and overseeing implementation of the policy of the Government.

"Other industries operate only in India and therefore also have a protection of the market, hence several of them can survive and prosper. Shipping in an international industry competing against foreign shipowners from the four corners of the world. One cannot go running to Delhi for approvals all the time. When we buy a ship it takes us as much as 8/9 months at times to clear proposals. Selling a ship can take 2/3 months. In the meantime markets change and opportunities are lost. It is well known that Indians buy at a premium and sell at a discount essentially because of delays in getting Government approvals. What puzzles me is that the permission is always given but why does it take to long? Carrying on from this argument if the permission is always given, then there is all the more reason to support my suggestion to delegate the administering of controls to a single authority in Bombay rather than files travelling from Ministry to Ministry in Delhi."

Building of ships in India under the* Pari Passu *Clause

"Every time an Indian shipowner buys a ship from abroad he must place an order for an equivalent tonnage with an Indian shipyard. Unfortunately, Indian shipyard prices are most uncompetitive. Even after discounting the price with the benefit of the soft loan given the prices are still very much higher than the international market. Fixed price Contracts are not given by the Indian yards and the price is eventually decided by the Government at the time of delivery which is several years after the placement of the order. Furthermore, the quality of the product is nowhere near that of the leading international ship builders and there are inordinate delays in delivery.

"Great Eastern has suffered a great deal on this aspect. On four ships built at Indian yards, we have had to pay almost Rs. 9 crores extra. Those who have placed orders today with Indian yards are suffering even further. To give an example a panamax bulk carrier can easily be bought from a Japanese or Korean Yard at about Rs. 16 crore. In India one has to pay almost double this amount. Several shipping companies who have been forced to place their orders at these exorbitant prices can only make losses which again will affect their long term viability."

Quick approval for purchase and sale and approval to diversify

"Quick approvals are absolutely essential. Wherever Government funds are not involved, at least in those cases, the approving authority should be where over 95 percent of the industry is based, that is, in Bombay with the Director General of Shipping. Even when Government funds are involved, the SDFC should clear the proposals quickly. If the Government accepts my suggestions on finances and norms I see absolutely no reason why approvals cannot be had promptly.

"Similarly on sales too, approvals must be given fast. We as managers in the shipping industry are best to judge the timing of sale and the Government has to have faith in this judgement."

Approval to diversify

"Currently SDFC funds and guarantees are only given to shipping companies and not to companies that have other industrial activity. To my mind the decade ahead requires strong financial health. The new entrants into the shipping industry, that is, the composite companies, have the financial infrastructure to do well. I therefore feel that shipping companies should now be allowed to diversify into non-shipping activities. This is bound to help the industry. They should be allowed to retain the existing funds support that they enjoy from SDFC and SDFC should continue to support them even after they have diversified."

Chairman's statement to the shareholders for the year 1983-84 :

Times have changed

"The strength of Great Eastern has been its willingness to accept change; never an easy thing to do. Government, some industries and Unions have often refused to face the fact that old industries die and new ones are born. We must realise that the shipping industry that we knew is dead and a new shipping industry is in the process of being born.

"Gone are the days of steady growth in bulk seaborne trade. Sizeable profits from the sale of older ships, as a result of steady inflation in new building prices, are also a thing of the past. There is a dramatic and continuing fall in new building prices which are in most cases subsidised by Government, of countries where ships are being built. Volatile currency markets and widely fluctuating freight rates have put an end to low capital bases and high gearing. The New Industry calls for sophisticated, specialised and fuel-efficient ships, `tied in' cargoes, a strong capital base, high liquidity and low gearing and far greater and sharper skills on the part of Managers than ever before.

"I feel that Indian shipping has a very important role to play in the new industry. It must be clearly appreciated that around 45 per cent of the world fleet is with Flags of Convenience and with low cost countries including India and it is this fleet which in future will have a competitive edge over those of the traditional maritime nations. The fleets of these advanced nations are receiving heavy subsidies from their Governments which will sooner rather than later disappear placing them at a further disadvantage. This is what gives me confidence in the future of Indian shipping. It may even be possible for India to attract foreign investment for shipping subject to the Government following an 'Open Policy'.

"It will take some time before we can avail of this natural advantage. Internationally the crisis facing the industry must abate. Though the economies of the developed world are looking up, laid-up tonnage is still high at 10 percent of world fleet. It is my opinion that for a variety of reasons such as costs, technological advancements etc., a significant part of this laid-up tonnage may not be recommissioned. This is another silver lining which must give us hope. In the interim we should all revamp our shipping activities and be prepared to look at the future with renewed hope."

Diversifications

"Diversification will be with a view to providing stability to the profit cycle and certain amount of growth. We have identified two areas for diversification so far, namely :

"1. **The Area of Energy** : This has been dealt with in the Directors Report and all I would like to add here is that this area is a high priority one for the Government and with continuous technological changes, it offers great challenges and vast scope. It could also be the catalyst for a second industrial revolution in India.

"2. **Housing Development** : There is a crying need for good housing in this country. The Government of India has set up a Housing Development Finance Corporation and is also receiving international assistance. It is also a priority area for Government. The skills required in housing development are similar to those for shipping where you construct houses, lease them out and/or sell them as compared to constructing ships, chartering them out and eventually selling them.

"For some of you who wonder why we are looking at an industry like this which has various connotations and implications of a non-professional nature, I must assure you that I believe that things have changed significantly and I do believe that we will be able to run a clean and professional outfit in this area. It is on this basis that I am contemplating this diversification."

Chairman's statement to the shareholders for the year 1985-86:

Complying with Government procedures constitutes the most expensive item in the purchase and chartering of ships

"International shipping is an extremely complex business. It is affected by factors which cannot always be predicted or quantified such as socio-economic and political events over the globe, growth or decline in world sea-borne trade, wars, droughts, famines, oil prices, commodity prices, interest and currency exchange rates and several other such factors. Shipowners, therefore, have to assess each factor and act quickly in order to achieve low costs. This is essential not only to bolster our exports, but to compete internationally.

"To highlight the point - over 50 per cent of the standing costs of Great Eastern are related to the purchase price of ships. In the case of new ships, probably as much as over 70 per cent of the standing costs relate to the purchase price. The strains on the cash flows are significantly greater. Therefore, Indian shipowners must be in a position to buy ships cheap. From time to time there are magnificent opportunities available in the international market. In fact, presently, there are tremendous opportunities of buying not only cheap tonnage, but buying near new tonnage (with all the technological advantages) at almost throw away prices. To give an example, several Indian shipowners went for handy sized bulk carrier in 1980-82 at prices ranging between $ 18 million and $ 22 million per piece. The same ships today are available internationally at prices ranging from $ 2.5 million and $ 5 million per piece. I estimate the difference in the standing costs to be in the region of $ 4000 per day. Incidentally, the saving itself is probably higher than the daily rates that these ships can possibly earn in today's market. These opportunities may not be available for long, and, therefore, we have to act with speed.

"Government authorities, therefore, must recognise that delays on account of complying with the Government's present procedures constitute the single most expensive item in the purchase or chartering of ships. I cannot believe that a country gains very much from the multiple sanctions of different authorities. It is difficult perhaps for the authorities to make an exception for the shipping industry, but they must recognise that in the international markets even very large investments in shipping are made within hours. In comparison, the Indian system of Government approvals is too slow and consequently all good opportunities are lost to Indian shipowners. I, therefore, urge the Government to revamp their procedures to allow shipowners more freedom for not only purchase and sale of ships but in all other areas of operations, to achieve lower costs and higher efficiencies. Government must appreciate that if we are to be unpampered it is but fair that we also be unhampered or else it will not be possible to achieve the required goals."

Monopoly and distortion in the oil sector

"Cargo protection of course is invaluable to Indian shipping. However, it is competition that will bring down costs and improve efficiencies. I, therefore, feel that Indian shipowners should not seek subsidies but they are entitled to ask for open and fair competition where Indian lines are treated as equal. Unfortunately, this is not so in the oil sector which has distortions in favour of the Shipping Corporation of India. This has proved very detrimental. The corporation has used its monopoly powers to exploit the market by deliberately over-building to squeeze the private sector out of the oil trade: besides the absence of competition combined with a cost plus system has succeeded in providing Indian oil companies with possibly the most expensive oil sea transportation in the world. They have been able to do this because the Government has denied competition even among Indian shipping lines.

"We do not seek Government financial assistance. We graciously accept cargo support but recognise that this cannot be at the cost of our trade and above all we are willing to compete and provide a better service. In turn, all I ask of Government is to revise its policy and procedures in two major areas — firstly to allow us the freedom

— to buy and sell and to operate efficiently, and secondly, to treat all Indian shipping lines equally and encourage a healthy competition between them."

8

Areas in Which Great Eastern Scored

It is relevant to seek a answer to the question - What were the circumstances and factors which contributed to Great Eastern's success?

Entry in High Growth Tramp Shipping

Great Eastern's entry into and increasing participation in tramp shipping, that is, bulk cargo shipping, provided excellent scope for growth. At the dawn of independence, tramp shipping was a virgin area of shipping in India. Indian shipping companies were seeking entry into the coastal trades or overseas liner trades which had very limited possibilities for growth. Liner shipping in India's overseas trades was controlled by the Conferences which were overwhelmingly dominated by foreign lines. Only two companies, Scindias and India Steamships, were admitted as members of the conference and were given a small share of trades. In post-war years, bulk cargo trades, both dry cargo and oil cargo expanded greatly. India's overseas trade also consisted largely of bulk cargoes in terms of volume. It is the volume of cargo (as distinct from value of cargo) which provides employment for shipping. Therefore there was great scope for acquiring ships for carriage of bulk cargoes in India's overseas trade. Great Eastern who were pioneers and the first substantial participants in the carriage of bulk cargoes could expand well in this growth sector of shipping.

Trading Skills and Tramp Shipping

It is interesting to record why Great Eastern went for tramp shipping. The promoters of Great Eastern A.H. Bhiwandiwalla and Company were large importers of sugar and traders in commodities.

For importing sugar, which is a bulk cargo, from Java (Indonesia) to India they had to charter tramp ships and they had acquired a know-how of operating tramp ships. Great Eastern therefore could easily operate the tramp ships. Further, with the expected blocking of entry into liner shipping and with the modest financial resources at its disposal which could only buy secondhand tramp ships, Great Eastern had a quick realisation that it could play an effective role in operating tramp ships.

The tramp shipping market was based on competition and involved bargaining, unlike liner shipping which had fixed freight tariff schedules and allocated liner route sailings. The business acumen and trading skills of Great Eastern's promoters and directors who were traders, were very useful in employing and operating tramp ships. It is the same business acumen and trading instincts which enabled Great Eastern to score over other Indian shipping companies which started operating tramp ships.

In the initial years, that is, in the 1950s, whenever there was a dearth of cargoes, the trading background enabled Great Eastern to purchase and sell cargoes either through the medium of A.H. Bhiwandiwalla and Company or Jagat Trading Company, which was a subsidiary of Great Eastern, so that they could provide employment to Great Eastern's ships.

Moving with the Times

Great Eastern could fare well in good times and emerge unscathed, perhaps with better financial strength, after the prolonged depression because it always moved with the times and took timely action to meet the requirements of the changed environment of the shipping industry from time to time.

Although Great Eastern was predominantly in the coastal trade in the initial period, it substantially reduced its participation in the coastal trade after the 1960s. This was because operations in the coastal trade were no longer profitable and led to losses. Other Indian Shipping Companies were not so quick in the realisation that coastal trade was not likely to be profitable because of the stagnation in the coastal trade and government control of coastal freight rates.

When the company reduced its stake in the coastal trade, it saw an opportunity to start the liner service from the west coast of the

U.S.A. and Canada to India. The company's ships which were carrying iron ore cargo from India to Japan proceeded in ballast to the west coast of the U.S.A. and Canada and loaded general cargo for India. This liner service, started at the end of 1962, earned well for the company for a few years. After the cargo availability dwindled (due to stoppage of aid cargoes) on account of the increasing unfriendly attitude of the U.S.A. Government and the increase in competition for the smaller volume of cargo with the entry of Scindia Company in this trade, Great Eastern withdrew its ships from this trade.

The prolonged depression which commenced in 1975-76 vividly brought out the cyclical nature of the shipping industry. Great Eastern therefore acquired supply vessels for serving the offshore oil industry in 1982 and through a joint venture company also purchased rigs for the same industry a little later. It also entered the real estate business. The objective was to have more stable income from this diversification when traditional shipping was going through lean years.

In the quarter century from 1948 to 1973, world sea-borne trade, which provided demand for shipping, increased annually at the average rate of 8 per cent. The supply of ships however did not keep pace with demand. In view of this great rise in the world sea-borne trade, shipping passed through a period of good earnings and large expansion. Those who borrowed money and acquired ships benefitted. The Greek shipowners such as Niarchos and Onassis and Norwegian shipowners borrowed heavily and built very large shipping fleets. Great Eastern also joined the merry league of borrowers, acquired ships and expanded its fleet. During this period of two decades Great Eastern's net worth grew from a mere Rs.20 lakh in 1948 to Rs.3.07 crore at the end of the year 1957-58, Rs.8.94 crore at the end of the year 1967-68 and Rs.19.04 crore at the end of the year 1972-73. At the end of each decade the net worth of the company grew substantially.

The OPEC crisis at the end of 1973, with the quadrupling of oil prices, had a dramatic effect on shipping. World sea-borne trade stopped growing. Gigantic orders placed prior to 1973 for new ships got executed and thereby an abundant supply of shipping tonnage came on the market.

This resulted in the prolonged depression. It started in the tanker sector in 1974-75 and dry-cargo ships sector in 1975-76.

Shipping companies with heavy borrowings faced most difficult times. The interest and loan repayment instalments could not be paid and most companies with high debt-equity ratios came into serious trouble. It is at this time that Great Eastern realised that strengthening of the company's equity base was necessary to avoid cash flow problems and defaults in servicing of loans to creditors. Even during the depression the Great Eastern managed to strengthen its equity base and augmented its cash flows. This enabled the company not only to meet its commitments to the creditors but also to have money for acquiring ships at the low prices they were available at then.

This enabled Great Eastern to make good profits especially after lifting of the shipping depression on the operation of these low-priced ships with low interest and depreciation charges. None of the other Indian shipping companies could strengthen their equity base during the depression.

Purchase and Sale of Ships

There was another area of purchase and sale of ships where Great Eastern had an edge over other Indian shipping companies. In a cyclical industry like shipping where the average rate of return over the good years and the bad years is not high, the profits made on sale and purchase of ships greatly supplement the operating earnings. This is considered as part of the shipping business by international shipowners.

In India, due to the rigid Government control on purchase and sale of ships and the generally held view in Government and shipping circles that trading in ships was a speculative business and not part of the legitimate shipping business, Indian shipping companies refrained from consciously engaging in this business. Great Eastern on the other hand within the four corners and fetters of Government regulations and controls always regarded sale and purchase activity as a valuable adjunct of shipping business. Great Eastern therefore could make good profits on sale and purchase of ships. Now the Government as well as Indian shipping companies have realised that sale and purchase of ships and profits made on them are legitimate part of the shipping business.

Great Eastern Chairman Vasant Sheth at the 35th Annual General Meeting of the shareholders held on January 24, 1984 stated that

Great Eastern had bought 58 ships and sold 38 ships in the 35 years of its existence. It made an overall profit on sale of ships of about Rs. 16.28 crore, that is, 28 percent of the company's net worth of Rs. 58.05 crore at that time. At the end of the financial year 1991-92 the profit on sale of ships right from the inception of the Company amounted to about Rs. 47 crore which is about 18 percent of the present net worth of about Rs. 247 crore.

Tax Planning and Management

The income tax impact is one of the most important financial matters in a shipping enterprise. Ships registered under the flags of convenience and in countries such as Greece pay no taxes on their income. In many maritime countries investment allowances, free or accelerated depreciation provisions, tax free reserves, tax holidays etc. obviate or substantially reduce the tax liability of shipping companies on their income. Since shipping is an international business exposed to international competition provisions for tax relief and tax planning play an important part in the affairs of shipping companies.

Great Eastern has paid meticulous attention to tax planning and tax management. The Company in its 44 years of existence therefore paid taxes in a few years only. Tax planning due to tax reliefs available to shipping has improved the after-tax earnings of Great Eastern and made its operations more viable. It has also brought about its growth and expansion at a faster pace.

Even with tax reliefs available under Indian tax laws which were less favourable than those in many maritime countries it was possible to embark upon planned acquisition of ships and sale of ships and not pay taxes most of the years.

As corporate income was taxed in India at more than 50 per cent, with no tax liability the after-tax income more than doubled itself. The cash flow which consisted of after-tax income plus depreciation rose substantially. The net present value and the internal rate of return on the discounted cash flow basis on the existing shipping projects improved greatly. It also became worthwhile to undertake new projects and expand because of their improved economic viability.

Great Eastern also took advantage of certain tax reliefs to shareholders of shipping companies like Section 80 K-relief (now abolished) which could make dividend or part of dividend tax-exempt in the hands of the shareholders. This could be done if there was Section 80J income out of which Section 80 K income could be distributed to shareholders. Great Eastern in a number of years paid fully tax-free or partly tax-free dividends to shareholders. The investment in Great Eastern shares therefore became attractive to investors.

Foreign Exchange Transaction and Foreign Exchange Liability Management

Shipping is an international business par excellence. A shipping company may order its new ships or buy secondhand ships in different countries. The prices payable may be in currencies of the countries in which the shipbuilding yards are situated or the sellers of secondhand ships are located. The loans arranged for financing the aforesaid capital outlays may be in some other currencies. The shipping company's cashflows arising from freights or charter hires in respect of its ships from which it will meet the capital cost payments or loan instalment payments may be in still other currencies.

There was great uncertainty prevailing in recent years on account of fluctuations in the values and parities of different currencies. Therefore the shipping companies were exposed to great financial risks. This was an important field in which proper planning and coordination of the currencies to be specified in shipbuilding contracts, the currencies in which loans were to be drawn and provisions for payment in currencies in charter parties, freight contracts and freight fixtures could eliminate or minimise foreign exchange risks. It was necessary in this connection for the management of the shipping company to pay constant attention to international monetary and currency developments and to have necessary expertise on obtaining of foreign exchange covers, entering into hedging transactions and arranging if necessary optimal currency holdings.

At present there is awareness of the importance of foreign exchange liability management and SCICI provides expert guidance to its customer shipping companies in this matter. It also undertakes swap transactions for interest as well as currencies with the objective of realigning the liability profile of its customer groups on a dynamic basis taking into consideration the changes and prognostication for various currency and interest rates in the world market. This is however post-1987 development.

In the pre-SCICI years, however, there were a few companies having the expertise in foreign exchange transactions and foreign exchange liability management. Great Eastern had acquired the expertise in this area. It not only covered the foreign exchange risks but also resorted to devices such as taking new loans on better terms and with the loan proceeds repaying the foreign exchange loans taken earlier, arranging for substitution of floating rates of interest by fixed rates of interest, changing currencies of loans under multi-currency options in respect of Euro-currency loans, and even cancelling foreign exchange covers if it was gainful for the company to do so. Foreign exchange risk management by Great Eastern gave it an edge over other Indian shipping companies.

London Office and U.K. Registered Subsidiary

The opening of a London office in the prolonged depression provided the company with a window on the international developments in shipping. It enabled the company to fix the employment of its OBO carriers which were heavy loss making units in the depression, at better rates because of the company's presence in the London market. The company also was well-informed on the ship sale and purchase market, shipping finance availability, charter markets etc. because of the valuable information provided by the London office.

Later a subsidiary of the company was incorporated in London on January 15, 1985. The time-consuming government regulations and procedures became worse during the depression years because the recovery of government funds lent through the SDFC to the shipping industry was endangered. The Shipping and Transport Ministry lost its clout with the Finance Ministry and other Ministries of the Government. The acquisition proposals etc. referred by the Shipping and Transport Ministry to other Ministries would not be cleared for a long time.

Unfettered by the cumbersome government restrictions and procedures the London company was able to raise loans and buy ships promptly at the low prices prevailing at that time when the shipping industry was about to come out of the depression. Great

Eastern, the Indian company also, when it did not get or did not expect to get the government approval in time for the ships purchased, arranged the purchases through the London company and bought the ships from the London company when the government approvals were at long last available. The registration of the subsidiary company in London not only enabled it to have a fleet of ships which could be acquired and operated with full freedom of operation but also enabled Great Eastern to acquire some ships through the London company. Otherwise due to the inordinate delays in getting government approvals these ship purchase transactions would have failed to materialise.

Management

Great Eastern's management, consisting of Vasant Sheth, K.M.Sheth and Sudhir Mulji owed their position partly to the family connection but predominantly to the experience and expertise they had acquired in building up the company and operating its growing fleet. They had the trading tradition of the family and leadership quality. They also selected managers without sectarian considerations of religion, caste, province etc. Storey, Sanklecha, Adappa, Balsubramanian, Vesuna, Pardiwala were with the company for many years. Gidwani who joined later and remained with the company for about a decade was competent and well-versed in financial matters and handled his portfolio efficiently. The experience and expertise of these managers who worked with a sense of dedication made a worthy contribution to the profitability and growth of the company.

Strict Business Culture

The strict and no-nonsense business culture of the company was helpful in improving the financial results of the company and contributed to its growth. However, the lack of flexibility which this culture involved also had its disadvantages. The following anecdote will illustrate the point:

M.G. Pimputkar, ICS, a very competent, upright and strict officer, was the Shipping and Transport Secretary in the early 1970's, and also held the post of Lieutenant Governor of Delhi. His uprightness can be seen from the fact that the imported limousine with a liveried chauffeur which he used as a Lieutenant

Governor, was not used by him as Transport Secretary. He would go to the Transport Bhavan in a self-driven small car. It was during his tenure that the government officers in his ministry who did not take action or reply to the letters in three days had to give an explanation for the delay to Pimputkar. The entire Transport Ministry was functioning in a disciplined and efficient way.

He was very well disposed towards Great Eastern due to its dynamism. He also asked Sanklecha to prepare a few notes for him on shipping subjects. At that time the Finance Ministry and Planning Commission did not release rupee loans or foreign exchange for acquiring ships which were to operate in international cross trades. Therefore he asked Sanklecha to prepare a paper on the desirability of Indian ships participating in international cross trades and gave all the data needed by Sanklecha. The paper was published by Sanklecha in *Indian Shipping* under the title 'Indian Shipping in International Cross Trades.' Sanklecha had free access to Pimputkar and was not required to take an appointment to meet him.

The company, subject to availability of loan from SDFC wished to place an order for 2 OBO carriers of 122,350 DWT each at an estimated cost of Rs. 57.35 crore and 1 product carrier of 32,360 DWT at an estimated cost of Rs. 13.16 crore. Pimputkar as Transport Secretary indicated that the loan assistance from SDFC would be forthcoming. The Company placed the order and SDFC decided to grant loans of Rs. 2246.90 lakh for financing 30 per cent cost of OBO carriers and 40 per cent cost of the product carrier. Meanwhile the government faced a financial crunch and therefore the disbursement of loans was postponed. The Company was assured that the loans would be forthcoming as soon as the financial resource position of the government improved.

At this time there was a shortage of ships for carriage of coastal coal cargo due to the uneconomic freight rates. The government therefore pressurised Indian shipping companies to berth their ships for carriage of coal even at a loss. As Great Eastern did not offer any ship for carriage of coastal coal, Pimputkar tried his utmost that Great Eastern offered at least 1 or 2 ships. However Great Eastern did not offer a single ship for this carriage as it was a loss-making proposition. This completely upset Pimputkar. When Sanklecha met him for some work Pimputkar told him that he should stop writing his articles on national interests involved in development of shipping. He said that Great Eastern approached government for loans at concessional rates of interest and other facilities. However, he felt, the Company, which was a prosperous one, was not prepared to make even a small sacrifice in the national interest. Even small companies had agreed to berth ships although their shoulders were not as broad as those of Great Eastern to bear the burden of losses.

Pimputkar was transferred from the Transport Ministry. Subsequently SDFC went back on its loan commitment to the Company. A few years later Pimputkar remarked to a friend that although he was not in the Transport Ministry he would have forcefully conveyed to SDFC that the commitment made when he was Chairman of SDFC should be honoured. However he was disillusioned by Great Eastern's refusal to berth 1 or 2 ships for carriage of coastal coal and he would not go out of his way and try to persuade SDFC to honour its loan commitment. If SDFC made a reference to him he would communicate his views to them and recommend that SDFC should disburse the committed loans to Great Eastern. Perhaps a little more flexibility would have earned far greater returns to the company.

9

Public Sector in Shipping

The Eastern Shipping Corporation Ltd. which was formed in March 1950 as a joint sector corporation with 74 per cent equity participation by government and 26 per cent equity participation by Scindia Company, to be managed by Scindia Company, became a completely government owned undertaking in 1956. The other government-owned corporation - The Western Shipping Corporation Ltd., was established in 1956. The public sector - private sector controversy goes back to that time. These government-owned corporations were merged into The Shipping Corporation of India Ltd. which was established on 2 October 1961.

Industrial Policy Resolution of 1956

The Industrial Policy Resolution of 1956 of the government classified shipping in the category of industries under Schedule B, namely industries which will be progressively state-owned, and in which, therefore, the state will generally take the initiative in establishing new units, but in which private enterprise will also have the opportunity to develop in the field either on its own or with state participation. This Resolution forms the basis on which the public sector has become the dominant sector in shipping.

Before the passing of this Industrial Policy Resolution of 1956, in the post-Independence period up to the early 1950's, it was considered by the government that state participation would inspire confidence in Indian companies and encourage them to expand their activities in shipping. With this end in view and with a view to ensuring development of Indian shipping with the active co-operation of private enterprise, the government decided to set up two or three shipping corporations, including the joint sector Eastern

Shipping Corporation.

However, the above policy of the government was more or less reversed by the Industrial Policy Resolution of 1956 and it was stated: "The responsibility for the development of Indian shipping now rests squarely on the public sector."[1]

Even after the passing of the Industrial Policy Resolution of 1956, however the government's policy on the issue was not clear.

Lal Bahadur Shastri, who was then Minister of Transport, stated in Bombay in 1956: "I may also state it very clearly in this context that it is not our intention that shipping in the public sector should run in competition on routes on which existing private shipping companies have established themselves." In July 1958 S.K. Patil, Minister of Transport, stated: "Today we want leadership and we look to it in the private sector where most of the work of the shipping industry in the last 40 years has been done." Pointing out the part that the two sectors should play in developing shipping he observed: "The public sector in shipping is just in the position of your younger brother, and I assure you that you will always remain the elder brother or the elder sister, whatever you call it."

The Estimates Committee 1958-59 of the Parliament (Second Lok Sabha) in their 38th Report on Ministry of Transport and Communications, published in April 1959 dealing with Eastern Shipping Corporation Ltd. and Western Shipping Corporation Ltd. stated that the government policy was stated to be as follows:

"Shipping in the public sector should not run in competition with private shipping companies on routes on which the private shipping companies have established themselves. The corporations should operate only in those trades in which the private shipping companies are unwilling or unable to operate successfully, owing to uncertain prospects, or inadequency of resources or any other reasons."

The committee however felt that the government policy was expressed in negative terms and lacked a positive approach. It recommended a redefining of the policy in the changed context. The role of the government in the field of shipping according to the committee was no longer to play the supplementary role but the main role itself.

It was in pursuance of this new approach that Dr. P. Subbarayan as Minister of Transport in June 1960 observed that "the sooner the private shipowner recognises this fact, the better it will be for the continued co-operation of the two sectors."

Role Assigned to Public Sectors in Successive Five Year Plans

The Committee on Public Undertakings (3rd Lok Sabha) in the 3rd Report on Shipping Corporation of India published in April 1965 expressed the expectation that there would be progressive increase in the shipping tonnage in the public sector from Plan to Plan. The committee felt that in keeping with the government policy, an upward revision of the expansion programme of the Corporation during the Fourth Plan period would be necessary. This would require that an adequate percentage of the future additions to the country's shipping tonnage is reserved for the corporation so that its share in the country's tonnage shows a perceptible rise at the end of the Fourth Plan period. In regard to the development of shipping in the public sector during the Fifth Plan period, the committee was informed by the government as follows:

"The thinking of the Planning Commission on the subject is that ultimately 50 percent of the national fleet must be owned by the public sector. Though the Government's policy in this regard is to be finalised there is considerable strength in the contention of the Planning Commission. In any case, it is the definite policy of the Government to expand the public sector on a much larger scale than hitherto done." The Committee were also given to understand that a Planning Group set up by the Planning Commission had recommended that efforts should be made to secure for the public sector 50 percent of the country's total tonnage holding by 1975-76.

It may be stated that the allocation of increase in share in the acquisition of ships to the Shipping Corporation continued in the sixth and seventh Plans. The following extract from the *Final Report of the Working Group on Shipping for the Seventh Five Year Plan* 1985-1990 issued in December 1984 would bring out this point :

Ratio Between Public Sector and Private Sector

"5.11 The public sector has continued to play a predominant role in the Indian shipping industry. At present the public sector comprises 3 shipping companies viz. The Shipping Corporation of

India, The Mogul Lines and the Poompuhar Shipping Corporation (owned by the State of Tamil Nadu). The Mogul Lines is expected to merge with the Shipping Corporation of India by the commencement of 7th Plan period, and the tonnage owned by the Poompuhar Shipping Corporation is negligible at present. The public sector would, thus, effectively comprise only the Shipping Corporation of India. The Shipping Corporation is the largest shipping company in India, and is, in fact, one of the largest shipping companies in the world, and the total tonnage owned by the Shipping Corporation at present is more than the total tonnage owned by the entire Indian private sector shipping fleet put together. In view of its broad base, and the varied nature of operations, the Shipping Corporation appears to be the company with the best potential for growth in the 7th Plan period.

"5.12 Historically, the Government has accorded higher weightage to the public sector in the sectorial allocation for acquisition of tonnage and according to the policy laid down during the 6th Plan, the ratio of tonnage between the public sector and the private sector is to be maintained at 55:45 of the total operational tonnage of 6.36 million GRT as projected to exist at the end of the 6th Plan, nearly 3.58 million GRT, or 56.29% of the total tonnage would be in the public sector, and 2.78 million GRT, or 43.71% of the tonnage would be in the private sector. At the end of the 6th Plan, inclusive of the estimated tonnage on order, the public sector will have about 65.5% of the total tonnage. In view of the greater potential for growth in the public sector as compared to the private sector, as mentioned in para 5.11 above, it is proposed that the ratio between the public sector and the private sector may be kept at 65:35 in the 7th Plan. As a result, from out of the anticipated 10 million GRT operational tonnage at the end of the 7th Plan, the public sector would own 6.50 million GRT, and the balance would be owned by the private sector."

"The Report of the Working Group on Shipping For the Eighth Plan stated that the public sector has played a crucial role in the development of national shipping tonnage and the performance of the public sector company was good. The Shipping Corporation of India (SCI) was a strong and viable company. Thus a significant portion of the national tonnage in future should also be acquired by the public sector.

"It also quoted with implied approval from the Report of the

Steering Committee for Perspective Planning for Transport Development (August 1988) that the public sector would acquire between 60% to 70% of the national tonnage in the time frame of the Eighth and Ninth Five-Year Plans and the private sector would require to raise large sums of money over the time period for acquiring 30% to 40% share in the national tonnage. The Report also goes on to mention the public sector share in the various types of ships which would be acquired as follows:

"The Government is presently following the policy of allowing the public sector to acquire the entire crude oil tanker tonnage required to cater to national needs. For petroleum products, the policy is that the public sector is allowed to acquire one third of the total product tanker tonnage. In addition the public sector has the option of acquiring another one third of the product tanker tonnage and the remaining one third is allocated to the private sector shipping companies. For liner trade, at present, the public sector caters to a very large percentage of the national liner movement. All companies at present are permitted to acquire bulk carrier tonnage.

"The Government will continue to follow the existing policy for tonnage acquisition in relation to crude oil, petroleum products and dry bulk cargoes. The Government would follow the policy of allowing public sector to acquire at least 75% of the total liner tonnage requirement. For specialised ships and offshore vessels and structures, the Government will follow a policy whereby the public sector will have the option to acquire another one third with the balance one third being allocated to private sector companies."

Why was Shipping Covered Under Schedule B of the Industrial Policy Resolution of 1956?

Perhaps the reasoning contained in the following extract from the 38th Report of Estimates Committee of Parliament 1958-59 (Second Lok Sabha) can be given as the possible justification by the government for inclusion of shipping industry under Schedule B of the Industrial Policy Resolution of 1956 :

"Under the Shipping Policy of 1947 development of shipping was left to private companies and the responsibility of Government was limited to rendering assistance to them to achieve the targets. But the growth of tonnage was slow. The opportunity of building up the tonnage in the immediate post-war period was not availed of. Shipping is considered to be a highly competitive and changing industry: the fortunes of those engaged in this industry varied particularly during the pre-independence period for various reasons. Private companies were chary of putting money to the extent it was required. As such it became necessary that the resources of the private entrepreneurs or the savings forthcoming from private quarters should be supplemented by Government."

The growth of Indian tonnage in the post-Independence period up to the early 1950s was slow because the government policies of the time were faulty. There was limited scope for shipping companies to participate in coastal trade and in the overseas liner trades. The cargo availability in the coastal trade which was reserved for Indian shipping companies was not high and therefore a very large tonnage was not required to cater to the coastal trade. As for the overseas liner trades, the Conferences of liner shipping companies dominated by foreign lines controlled India's liner trades. They gave a small share to a couple of companies, namely Scindias and India Steamships and there was no opportunity available for Indian entrepreneurs to acquire ships for liner trades. The bulk cargo trades, both dry and wet, which provided great scope for development of shipping were ignored by the government and the government policies also were hostile to the development of the bulk cargo trades. The Great Eastern Shipping Company purchased a tanker in 1956. The government however laid down a condition that Great Eastern would have to hand over the tanker to a public sector corporation, if decided by them. The company was not allowed to acquire further tankers.

The world over, shipping in the post war years was financed predominantly by borrowed capital. In most maritime countries the funds, either directly provided or indirectly arranged by the government, were lent to shipping companies in the private sector for acquisition of ships. Although in the 1950s the government was disbursing loans for acquisition of ships on an ad hoc basis, it was not on an adequate scale. It was only after the Shipping Development Fund Committee was established in 1959 that loans for acquisition of ships were regularly disbursed to shipping companies for acquisition of ships. For these reasons it may be observed that private sector companies were not at fault for the slow growth of Indian shipping. It appears that on ideological grounds the public sector was given importance under the Industrial Policy Resolution of 1956.

Government Controls and Measures of Assistance Ensured Shipping Corporation's Growth

It may therefore be observed that the government had already assigned a pre-determined dominant role to the public sector corporation. The approvals for purchase of ships, allocation of loan funds for acquisition of ships, the licensing of ships for operation in particular trades, reservation of some vital shipping sectors which were controlled by the government for the public sector ensured that the public sector in shipping could only expand substantially and at a fast pace and left no room or scope for private sector shipping companies to expand in accordance with the efficiency and profitability of their shipping operations and the quality of their entrepreneurship.

The purpose of the above comment is not to cast any aspersions on Shipping Corporation but to put developments in the proper perspective in view of the implied as well as explicit claims made by spokesmen of Shipping Corporation that private sector companies did not have the same level of enterprise and dynamism as SCI. Vice Admiral R.K.S. Ghandhi, the then Vice Chairman and Managing Director of Shipping Corporation, in his article entitled "Role of Public Sector In Development of Indian Shipping" published in *Indian Shipping* (Vol.36, No.4-5/1984) has provided a table on the growth of Shipping Corporation and three major Indian shipping companies in the private sector from 31.3.1962 to 31.3.1983. He has recorded the following conclusion based on this table. "The share of these companies (Scindia Steam Navigation Co., India Steamship Co. and Great Eastern Shipping Co.) in the Indian fleet was 28.8 percent, 15.3 per cent and 9.3 per cent respectively as on 31st March, 1962. By 31st March 1983 their share had fallen to 9 per cent, 3.4 per cent and 7 per cent respectively. Over the same period, the number of ships in the Scindia fleet declined from 52 to 38 and the number of ships in the fleets of India Steamship and Great Eastern Shipping increased only marginally from 19 to 20 and from 15 to 19 respectively." As against this, Shipping Corporation fleet on 31.3.1962 consisted of 19 ships comprising 1.38 lakh GRT which constituted about 14 per cent of total Indian tonnage increased to 143 ships of 30 lakh GRT which constituted 50 per cent of the total Indian tonnage on 31st March 1983.

Vice Admiral Ghandhi has mentioned in his observations the number of ships as well as tonnages and their percentage shares of Indian tonnages in respect of Shipping Corporation, but has omitted the tonnage figures in respect of the private sector shipping companies. From 1962 to 1983 the sizes of ships increased substantially. Therefore although the number of ships declined or increased only marginally, their tonnages increased considerably. The number of ships in the case of the Scindia Company declined from 52 to 38 but their GRT went up almost 2 times from 2.88 lakh GRT to 5.42 lakh GRT. India Steamship's tonnage increased one-thirds from 1.53 lakh GRT to 2.02 lakh GRT and Great Eastern's tonnage grew four times from 0.93 lakh GRT to 4.22 lakh GRT. As regards the decline in their percentage shares of the Indian fleet, it may be stated that total Indian tonnage grew 6 times from 10 lakh GRT to 60.05 lakh GRT. The predominant share of this increase in Indian tonnage was, according to government policy, allocated to the Shipping Corporation in the successive Five-Year Plans of the government and implemented accordingly by government controls and regulations.

"The SCI Story", brought out by Shipping Corporation perhaps in 1987, states that Shipping Corporation's tonnage grew 26 times in 25 years from 1.92 lakh DWT in 1961 to 50 lakh DWT in 1986. As Shipping Corporation sailed towards its silver jubilee, its share in Indian tonnage grew from 14 per cent in 1961 to 56 per cent in 1987, the balance 44 per cent being distributed between 46 Indian shipping companies in the private sector. "The largest shipping company in the private sector owns about 8 per cent of the Indian tonnage." Referring to the growth of Shipping Corporation, The SCI Story says: "Few Companies in the world and none in India matched this dynamic growth". It has been overlooked by "SCI Story" that in India's controlled economy the predominant share of the shipping industry was reserved for Shipping Corporation who were greatly assisted in achieving the planned growth by government controls and measures which were highly discriminatory in favour of the Shipping Corporation. The same comments would apply to the following quotation from the paper of L.M.S. Rajwar, the then Chairman and Managing Director of Shipping Corporation presented at the International Seminar on Shipping and Ports at the Turn of the Century in Bombay on April 21, 1986 and published under the caption "Trends in Indian Shipping" in *Indian Shipping* (Vol. 38, No.5. of 1986): "Even though between 1951 and 1986 the private sector shipping tonnage increased 7 times, its share in the total tonnage declined from 96 per cent to 43 per cent. By contrast the public sector tonnage increased over 214 times."

Discriminatory and Preferential Treatment of Shipping Corporation

Taking up the threads again of how government having decided on ideological grounds to allocate the dominant share of the growth of the shipping industry to the Shipping Corporation, assisted it to achieve this by utilising its regulatory regime and measures of assistance such as grant of loans, cargo support etc.

Indian shipping companies could not acquire ships without getting government approvals. Grant of approvals to purchase of ships of various categories was based on sector-wise (public sector-private sector) allocation of ship acquisitions in the successive Five-Year Plans. The loan assistance for acquisition of ships by Shipping Development Fund Committee (SDFC) was also according to the sector-wise allocation of funds in the successive Five-Year Plans.

The Monopolies and Restrictive Trade Practices Act (MRTP Act) was made applicable only to the private sector companies. In shipping the public sector corporation had the dominant share of expansion and it could expand without any let or hindrance as the provisions of the M.R.T.P. Act did not apply to its expansion. The private sector shipping companies were numerous and the extent of expansion of large private sector companies like Scindias or Great Eastern as per the requirements of the Five-Year Plans had to be moderate. The private sector companies however had to seek the approval of the government even in respect of these moderate expansion proposals under the provisions of the M.R.T.P. Act. Many times the applications for expansion were rejected. Even when they were eventually approved, it involved a time factor of six months. By then the opportunities of acquisition of ships were lost in some of these cases.

SDFC granted loans for expansion as per requirements of the Five-Year Plans to the public sector corporation and to private sector companies. The private sector companies therefore could not hope to get loans for acquisition of ships to the same large extent as Shipping Corporation. After 1970 SDFC adopted what was termed as a need-based approach in respect of grant of loans to shipping companies in the private sector. Efficient and profitable companies like Great Eastern which had some liquidity of their own were denied loans or were given far smaller amounts of loans for acquisition of ships on the excuse that they could manage the expansion without the loans or with small amounts of loans. In the case of Great Eastern which had undertaken a large expansion of about Rs. 100 crore in the early 1970s on the basis of loan commitments from SDFC, SDFC went back on its commitments and denied the loans. This placed the company in a very difficult situation since the shipping depression hit the industry after 1975. This matter has been discussed at length elsewhere in this book. Shipping Corporation did not face this problem of denial of loans on perverse need-based considerations, and could freely get the loans and expand substantially and smoothly.

Cargo Support

Great Eastern had applied for membership of the very important Conference which controlled the India-U.K. Continent liner trade. Neither the government nor the two Indian lines namely Scindia Company, and India Steamship supported Great Eastern's application and Great Eastern was denied membership of the Conference and participation in India's most important liner trade. However, Shipping Corporation's application for membership of this liner conference which was made subsequent to Great Eastern's application was strongly supported by the government and by the two Indian lines at the behest of the government and Shipping Corporation was admitted as a member of the Conference. Allocation of Indian lines' share of this liner trade between the Indian lines was made in favour of Shipping Corporation in a progressively increasing proportion at the cost of Scindia Company and India Steamship.

It has also been discussed elsewhere in this book how Great Eastern, which had a contract of affreightment with Japanese steel mills for carriage of iron ore from India to Japan, had built up its participation in the return Japan-India trade. Great Eastern's ships were given rates of freight on the Government cargoes which were 15 per cent lower than those given to ships of Shipping Corporation and other foreign members of the Conference. Although the Estimates Committee of Parliament in its Report had stated that Great Eastern's application for admission to membership of Japan-India Conference would be supported by the Shipping Corporation, the government and the Shipping Corporation arranged matters in such a way that not only did Great Eastern not get membership of the Conference but was ousted from the Japan-India trade.

In respect of coastal coal shipments from Calcutta in the 1950s and early 1960s, the Coal Commissioner and Director General of Shipping, who allocated coal shipments to Indian ships, discriminated in favour of Shipping Corporation in fixing the discharging ports. A large proportion of the government-owned Corporation's ships were assigned the port of Madras as the discharging port. Madras, in view of its proximity to the loading port of Calcutta as compared with ports like Tuticorin, Cochin, Bombay and Saurashtra, ports and with a comparatively favourable freight rate having regard to the distance involved was preferred by all Indian shipping companies as port of discharge for their ships carrying coal from Calcutta.

Reservation of Certain Vital Shipping Sectors for Shipping Corporation

Although Great Eastern acquired the first tanker in India in 1956 the government laid down a condition at the time of its acquisition that the tanker would be transferred to the government-owned corporation if the government so decided later in the matter. Thereafter the government prohibited the private sector shipping companies from acquiring tankers. The tankers were acquired by the public sector companies. There was a short interlude when Jayanti Shipping Company came on the scene and was permitted to acquire tankers. Ratnakar Shipping Company was also permitted to acquire a tanker at this time. Thereafter, again the tankers for the carriage of India's oil imports were permitted to be acquired by Shipping Corporation only. Shipping companies in the private sector barring Essar Shipping Company were not permitted to acquire tankers for this important growing trade.

There was not only reservation of this trade for Shipping

Corporation, but freights or charter hires were paid to tankers of Shipping Corporation on a cost-plus basis. This freighting arrangement on a cost-plus basis arose, it is stated, because International Development Association (IDA), an affiliate of the World Bank in 1972 sanctioned a loan of U.S. $ 83 million to Shipping Corporation for the purchase of 4 tankers and 2 product tankers and laid down a condition to ensure repayment of the loan that freights or charter hires will be paid on a cost-plus basis. It was not in the ambit of private sector shipping companies to get such a huge loan (very huge in the context of the value of money at that time) and expand their fleets. Whatever the origin and reason for the payment of freights on a cost-plus basis, this arrangement ensured that Shipping Corporation, on a large fleet of tankers, did not get affected by the prolonged shipping depression and made some money. Without this cost-plus basis formula, the Shipping Corporation's results would have been worse during the depression. Incidentally, the payment on cost-plus basis on transportation of crude oil imports, when transportation could have been arranged at far lower prevailing freight rates, resulted in the most expensive oil transportation system for the import of oil in the country.

Even for product tankers, specialised vessels and offshore vessels and structures and liner ships, Shipping Corporation has been given preferential treatment in respect of their acquisition and operation. The Working Group's Report on the Eighth Plan for shipping has allocated one-third share of ships of the above categories (excluding liner ships) for Shipping Corporation and further one-third share to be allocated to Shipping Corporation at its option, leaving only one-third share by way of firm allotment to all the private sector shipping companies taken together. It also says that the government would follow a policy whereby the Shipping Corporation would acquire 75 per cent of the total liner tonnage requirement.

Important Yardstick of Profitability on Capital Employed

In Chapters 3, 4 and 5, the percentage returns on capital employed in respect of major Indian shipping companies in each of the three decades from 1957-1958 to 1987-88 have been given. In Chapter 10, the percentage returns on capital employed in the latest 3 years that is, 1988-89, 1989-90 and 1990-91 have been given.

This is a very important yardstick by which the comparative profitability and efficiency of shipping companies can be judged. The percentage return on capital employed in respect of Shipping Corporation and Great Eastern have been reproduced below:

Profitability as Percentage Return on Capital Employed

	Shipping Corporation	Great Eastern
Percentage of average return from 1961-62 to 1970-71 10-year period.	8.2	9.3
Percentage of average return from 1968-69 to 1972-73 5-year period	6.3	11.6
Percentage of average return from 1973-74 to 1977-78 5-year period	5.5	8.6
Percentage of average return from 1978-79 to 1982-83 5-year period	3.0	9.2
Percentage of average return from 1983-84 to 1987-88 5-year period	5.6	8.1
Percentage of average return from 1988-89 to 1991-92 3-year period	9.6	19.5

It will be observed from the above table that Great Eastern consistently had a considerably better profitability than that of Shipping Corporation right from the time Shipping Corporation was formed to the latest years for which figures are available.

Creditable Achievements of Shipping Corporation

It is the purpose of this chapter to put the comparative performance of the public sector corporation and the Great Eastern Shipping company in proper perspective and not to belittle the remarkable growth and achievements of Shipping Corporation. The government has invested crores of rupees in large government-owned undertakings in various important industries. Many of these government-owned corporations are sustaining losses. Even in a large number of government-owned corporations which are making profits, the profits are low having regard to the large capital invested in those industries. There are a very few government-owned large corporations which are making adequate profits and have achieved the growth envisaged for them in the successive Five Year Plans of the government. Shipping Corporation of India is one of the very few such government-owned profit-making corporations which have fulfilled the targets allocated to them in the Five-Year Plans.

The inter-company comparison between the financial performance of Shipping Corporation and Great Eastern in no way detracts from the great role played by Shipping Corporation in bringing about the very large growth of Indian shipping. Shipping Corporation's financial performance and efficiency by and large over the years has been superior to most of the other shipping companies (other than Great Eastern) in the private sector. Then there have been constraints under which Shipping Corporation had to work. It was required to place orders for the construction of ships with Indian shipbuilding yards at unfavourable prices and unduly long delivery times in order to provide employment to Indian yards. Private sector shipping companies have placed shipbuilding orders with Indian shipyards mostly under the compulsion of the *pari passu* obligations (related to ships purchased abroad) which were also not enforced in the last decade. Therefore the adverse impact of the acquisition and operation of Indian-built ships was much greater in the case of Shipping Corporation than in the case of private sector shipping companies. Shipping Corporation had also to operate, at the behest of the government, essential services or start promotional services which produced meagre profits or even caused losses.

It would therefore do well to remember that Shipping Corporation which enjoyed preferential treatment from the government as compared with its competitors in the private sector had also to operate under handicaps and constraints which did not apply to private sector companies.

The success of Shipping Corporation is all the more remarkable because shipping is an international industry, and shipping companies face international competition. It is a capital intensive industry and involves both operations and regular purchase and sale of ships, large scale financing in various currencies and a close monitoring of cash flow and profitability. It calls for a lot of commercial feel and acumen and is an industry whose fortunes are dependent on international political and economic events. It necessitates speedy decisions both on the operations and on the capital fronts. It is also a cyclic industry. In view of these factors and considerations, it is private enterprise and not government-owned corporations which have been the most successful shipowners and operators in world shipping. Greeks, Norwegians, Japanese and others who occupy the leading positions in the maritime world operate through private sector enterprises and companies and not through state-owned corporations. Therefore for a public sector shipping corporation which has to follow certain time-consuming procedures which result in opportunities lost simply because of complicated methods of taking commercial decisions, the success achieved by Shipping Corporation as one of the largest and successful shipping companies in the world is a great achievement. Shipping Corporation operated well and efficiently in an internationally competitive shipping environment and built up a very large and diversified Indian shipping fleet.

Shipping Corporation, when formed in 1961, had 19 ships with a Deadweight Tonnage of 1.92 lakhs. In 1991 it owned 126 ships with 4.91 million DWT. Its tonnage has increased 26 times in 30 years. The gross investment in the fleet has increased 74 times from Rs. 27 crores in 1961 to about Rs. 2,100 crores in 1991.

Shipping Corporation has a very large diversified fleet consisting of the following types of ships:

(a) Break bulk general cargo ships
(b) Container-oriented cargo ships
(c) Bulk carriers
(d) Ore-Bulk-Oil Carriers
(e) Very Large Crude Carriers
(f) Crude Tankers
(g) Product Tankers
(h) Passenger-cum-Cargo Ships
(i) Timber Carrier
(j) Offshore Supply Vessels (OSVs)

Dr. C. P. Srivastava's Great Contribution

The success and growth of Shipping Corporation is in a very large measure due to Dr. C. P. Srivastava who as Chairman and

Managing Director for 10 years made a substantial contribution to the rapid expansion and successful operation of Shipping Corporation's fleet. With his most worthy contribution in making Shipping Corporation one of the largest shipping companies in the world and his subsequent momentous 16-year tenure as Secretary General of International Maritime Organisation (IMO), he has placed India on the world shipping map. Srivastava's outstanding and distinguished services as Secretary General of IMO for improving the standards of maritime transport including safety at sea, prevention of pollution of seas by ships, maritime education and training have won him international recognition. He has been the recipient of Honorary Knighthood from the Queen of England and several decorations and honours by various countries including U.K., France, Germany, Poland, Norway, Sweden, Italy, Greece, Portugal, Liberia etc. Even after his retirement from IMO he has been designated as Secretary General Emeritus of IMO and Chancellor Emeritus of World Maritime University which was established mainly through his efforts.

The Padma Bhushan Award was conferred on him in 1972. The National Maritime Day Celebrations Committee consisting of representatives of government, shipowners and sea farers has also given him the Varuna Award for his most meritorious and invaluable services to the shipping industry.

Srivastava has been closely associated with maritime training in India and was the Chairman of the Committee on Maritime Education and Training set up by the government. He is presently Chairman of the Indian Register of Shipping.

It must also be recorded that most of Srivastava's successors who have headed and managed the Shipping Corporation did well and played their part in the smooth operation and expansion of the Shipping Corporation. Shipping Corporation has been also served by a number of dedicated and devoted officers who made a worthy contribution to the good working and large growth of the Corporation.

Abolition of Distinction Between Public Sector and Private Sector in Shipping

Many knowledgeable people in shipping have been advocating that there should be no distinction or discrimination between the public sector and the private sector in shipping. Both should be regarded as part of the national sector and should be given equal opportunity and equal treatment. The public sector corporations should tap the capital market for their capital requirements. The investors would then judge the comparative efficiency and performance of the shipping companies including the Shipping Corporation and it would provide the motivation to improve the performance to attract funds from the capital market. What the late Vasant Sheth advocated more than 5 years ago is now accepted as part of the new economic policy of the government.

It is reported in the press that Shipping Corporation has sought government's permission to offer its shares directly to the public and its shares will be listed on the Stock Exchange.

It would be appropriate to close this chapter by quoting the following extracts from Vasant Sheth's note which was appended to the Report of Planning Group on Shipping (Rajawar Committee) of which he was a member. The Report was titled "Indian Shipping in the Time Perspective of 2000 A.D.", and was issued in September 1987:

"I have advocated that there should be no distinction or discrimination between the public sector and the private sector in shipping. Both the sectors should be regarded as a national sector and the Government should give equal treatment for the public sector company as well as the companies in the private sector in respect of acquisition of ships, carriage of cargo, and the applicable Government regulations or procedures.

"As regards financing of ships acquisition the Report states that the public sector company can go on drawing on Central Government's budgetary funds for equity. I would suggest that a limit or ceiling for the State's equity contribution in the public sector company should be laid down and once this limit is reached, the public sector company like companies in the private sector should be required to raise equity funds from the public by tapping the capital markets i.e. Stock Exchanges in India. There are other important budgetary expenditure requirements and also resources required for other competing priority sectors and the Central Government's budgetary funds cannot be at the disposal of a public sector company without a limit. This will ensure that the public sector company would have to improve its efficiency and profitability and establish a track record of management in order to attract equity funds from the investors. Recently a report has appeared in newspapers regarding the recommendations of the Standing Committee of Public Enterprises. (SCOPE) a representative body of all public sector undertakings. It has suggested that 49 per cent of the equity be offered to the employees of the organisation or the public and quoted on the Stock Exchange. The capital markets in India provide enough scope for the public sector companies to raise a large part of their equity capital requirements. The popularity of the shares with the investors and the market quotations of shares will also provide a yardstick for judging the comparative performance of various Indian shipping companies."

REFERENCES

1. Estimates Committee of Parliament 1958-59, Thirty-Eighth Report (Second Lok Sabha) Ministry of Transport and Communications dealing with Eastern Shipping Corporation Ltd. and Western Shipping Corporation Ltd. p.4.

10

Beginnings of Fifth Decade 1988-1992 and Future

The improved economic climate in 1988 brought about an increase of 6 per cent in the world sea-borne trade in that year, compared with 2 per cent in 1987. Measured in ton-miles the growth was even slightly higher. The key commodities in this upturn were record shipments of iron ore (345 million tons as compared to 309 million tons in 1987) and of coal (298 million tons from 283 million tons in 1987) as well as crude oil movement, up by 80 million tons to a 1988 total of 1050 million tons, the highest since 1981. With this increase in demand, freight rates were higher for almost all dry and liquid bulk and liner commodities resulting from a significantly increased tonnage balance in almost all shipping markets encouraged by near stability (small expansion) in the world shipping fleet. It is estimated that the surplus world shipping tonnage declined from 83.4 million DWT to 62.6 million DWT from mid-1988 to mid-1989. The surplus tonnage as a percentage of the world merchant fleet declined from 13.3 per cent in mid-1988 to 9.8 per cent in mid-1989

The improvement in the balance between supply and demand in world shipping may be attributed to a substantial decline in new buildings in 1987-88 showing the lowest figures for the last decade, intensive demolition of old and inefficient ships from 1982-1986, when the amount of tonnage sold for breaking fluctuated at the level between 28.3 million DWT to 41.7 million DWT per annum, and a remarkable increase in world trade in 1988 and 1989. In 1988 the total volume of world seaborne trade had risen to approximately the 1980 level (3.7 billion tons) and exceeded it in 1989 (3.9 billion tons).

The volume of world seaborne trade increased by 5 per cent in 1989 and 3 per cent in 1990. In terms of ton-miles the growth was still higher in both the cases. The world seaborne trade in 1990 was about 4 billion tonnes. The world shipping fleet on January 1, 1988 was 588 million DWT. It increased to about 594 million DWT on January 1, 1989 and 609 million DWT on January 1, 1990. The increase in tonnage was very small. The laid-up tonnage which had already declined from 16.3 million DWT in 1987 to 6.7 million DWT in 1988, further decreased to 4.5 million DWT in 1989 and marginally increased to 4.9 million DWT in 1990. The very small, almost negligible figures of laid-up tonnage in 1989 and 1990 indicate that the shipping markets were doing well.

The following per day time charter rates in U.S. dollars for the 12 months time charter for dry cargo bulk carriers of 35,000 DWT, 60,000 DWT and 1,20,000 DWT are cited for the years 1986 to 1990 to give an indication of how the freight markets firmed up. They are not representative of the entire freight market which also includes tankers of different sizes, break-bulk general cargo ships, container ships and other dry cargo ships excluding the bulk carriers of the three sizes which are being covered here.

	US$ PER DAY				
Bulk Carriers	1986	1987	1988	1989	1990
35000 DWT	3500	4800	8600	8900	7800
60000 DWT	4400	6800	11900	13200	10700
120000 DWT	5500	8100	14900	16900	15200

Source : "Review 1990" by Fearnleys.

National Scenario

There were three important factors which greatly affected the development and operation of Indian shipping.

1. **Foreign Exchange Crisis :** The balance of payment deficits, depletion of foreign exchange reserves of the country, the downgrading of the credit rating of the country internationally, the apprehensions regarding the defaults in servicing the foreign exchange borrowings and meeting foreign exchange payment commitments produced a foreign exchange crisis for the country in 1990 and 1991 which most adversely affected the growth of Indian shipping. The restrictions imposed by the Reserve Bank of India in March 1991 on availability of free foreign exchange for

acquisition of ships brought ship acquisition to a virtual standstill during the year 1991. It also became well-nigh impossible for Indian shipping companies to raise foreign exchange loans abroad for acquisition of ships. Indian shipping tonnage which stood on 1.4.91 at 6.07 million GRT (9.98 million DWT) decreased to 5.91 million GRT (9.64 million DWT) on 31.3.92

2. **Liberalisation :** The liberalisation of the Indian economy announced by the government included proposals for abolition or minimisation of government controls and time-consuming procedures, sweeping reforms in the industrial and trade policies, relaxations in the Foreign Exchange Regulations Act, introduction of partial convertibility of the rupee as a prelude to full convertibility.

The objective was to convert the state controlled economy into a market driven economy based on competition and to intergrate it into the global economy. As a result of the initial wholesome impact of the new policy, availability of assistance from International Monetary Fund and the World Bank, the foreign exchange reserves position improved considerably. The government also agreed to release free foreign exchange for 30 per cent of the cost of acquisition of a ship provided the concerned shipping company could raise this amount in rupees from its own resources and was able to arrange the foreign credit or loan to finance the balance 70 per cent cost of the ship. Therefore there has been a slight improvement in the ship acquisition position. During the three months from 1.4.92 to 30.6.92 six overseas vessels and six coastal ships totalling 217,655 GRT (346,624 DWT) have been acquired by Indian shipping companies.

Impact of Liberalisation on Shipping Policies : In an industry like shipping, which has to face international competition and has to be globally competitive, the impact of progressive liberalisation in respect of shipping is bound to be very beneficial. Freedom of operation makes the shipping industry most competitive. Earlier government controls, regulations and procedures applicable to Indian shipping very adversely affected its efficiency and placed it under a great handicap in international competition. Liberalisation of procedures for acquisition of vessels, sale of ships, relaxation in licensing to Indian shipping companies to operate on liner routes, permission to Indian shipping companies to time/trip charter their ships abroad without obtaining prior approval of the government etc. will enable Indian shipping companies to achieve more efficient and cost effective operation of their ships.

3. **Devaluation of the Rupee :** It is the devaluation of the rupee vis-a-vis the dollar in two successive instalments in July 1991 which enabled the Indian shipping companies including Great Eastern to earn larger profits in rupees in the year 1991-92.

Following the Finance Minister's announcement in his 1992 Budget speech, the Reserve Bank of India brought into force effective from 1.3.92, the Liberalised Exchange Rate Management System (LERMS) as per which the rupee was made convertible for all approved external transactions, and Exchange Control Regulations were liberalised. A dual exchange rate came into being. The foreign exchange receipts from all current account transactions (exports of goods and services and invisible receipts) were subject to surrender of 40 per cent at the rate of exchange determined by RBI from time to time which was around Rs. 26 per U.S. Dollar and 60 per cent at market determined rate of exchange which varied between Rs. 29 to Rs. 31 per U.S. Dollar. Foreign exchange was being made available for all imports of goods and services (including travel abroad) at the market determined rate of exchange except some specified essential goods. Under this dual exchange rate system, receipts and payments on capital account including import of ships continued to be subject to controls, and exchange rates for such permitted transactions were at the market rate of exchange. This substantially increased the capital and debt servicing rupee costs of past and future ship acquisitions abroad. It adverserly affected Indian shipping companies' competitive strength in their international operations. If and when the full convertibility of the rupee replaces the partial convertibility of the rupee, this great disadvantage to Indian shipping companies would disappear.

Capital Structure, Freight and Charter Hire Earnings, Profits and Dividend

The paid-up share capital of the company, which stood at Rs. 55,61,02,451 as on 30 June 1988 went up to Rs. 64,84,58,493 as on 31 March 1989 as the balance amount of Rs. 5 per share on partly paid 2,48,14,966 equity shares was called up during the year (9 month period) ended 31 March 1989. The call money in arrears not paid up by the shareholders upto 31 March 1989 amounted to Rs. 3,21,23,510.

The paid up share capital as on 31 March 1990 went up to Rs. 67,79,06,599 as the outstanding calls in arrears payable by the shareholders were reduced, due to the payments made by the shareholders, from Rs. 3,21,23,510 to Rs. 26,97,235.

During the year ended 31st March 1991 International Finance Corporation exercised their last conversion option by converting part of their outstanding loan into 3.25 million equity shares of Rs. 10 each at a premium of Rs. 16.44 per share. The paid-up share capital therefore stood at the increased figure of Rs. 71,21,22,869. The share premium account which stood at Rs. 2,66,10,000 as on 31 March 1990 went up by Rs. 5,34,30,000 due to the realisation of premium on shares of International Finance Corporation. The share premium account stood at Rs. 8,00,40,000 as on 31 March 1991. The total share holding of International Finance Corporation in the company went up to 8.25 million equity shares of Rs.10 each as on 31 March 1991.

The company allotted on 28 June 1991 bonus shares to the shareholders in the proportion of 1 bonus share for every 5 of the existing shares held by the shareholders by capitalising part of the share premium account and part of the general reserves. The paid up share capital therefore went up from Rs. 712,122,869 to Rs. 855,480,806 as on 31 March 1992.

The company, on the recommendation of the Board, decided at the Extraordinary General Meeting on 22 July 1992 to increase the paid-up capital by about Rs. 90 crore by issuing right shares as a 1 for 1 right at par and by issuing shares worth about Rs. 4.28 crore to the employees and working directors of the company. The nominal value of the share of Rs. 10 had a market value of over Rs. 150 at that time. The company therefore could have issued the rights shares at a high premium instead of at the par value. The action taken by the company to issue the rights shares at par enhanced its image and popularity among the shareholders and investors. K. M. Sheth, the Chairman and Managing Director, who took over as Chairman after the passing away of Vasant Sheth, in his letter dated 17 July 1992 to the shareholders also conveyed the Board's intention of going to the international markets with a Euro issue of up to US$ 100 million which was to be priced, unlike rights issue at par, at the best obtainable value at the time of the issue.

With the issue of rights shares, the paid up share capital of the company would go up to Rs. 175 crore on 31 March 1993. With the proposed Euro issue of US$ 100 million in equity shares and/or securities convertible into equity shares, even on the conservative basis of pricing of the issue at par, the paid up equity capital will eventually go up by about Rs. 300 crore. The paid-up capital is therefore expected to increase to Rs. 475 crore over the next 4 years.

During the period ended 31 March 1989 (9 month period) the freight and charter hire earnings amounted to Rs. 111 crore. During the 9 month period the net profit before tax amounted to Rs. 27.12 crore and the net profit after tax amounted to Rs. 22.74 crore. A dividend of 12 per cent was paid to the shareholders in respect of the 9 month period ending 31 March 1989.

For the year 1989-90 the freight and charter hire earnings rose to Rs. 207 crore. The net profit before tax was Rs. 47.49 crore and the net profit after tax Rs. 39.84 crore. Initially the directors recommended dividend of 12.50 per cent and proposed issue of bonus shares in the proportion of 1 bonus share for every 5 shares held. However, a number of shareholders present at the Annual General Meeting of the company held on 20 September 1990 felt that the dividend should have been higher than that recommended by the Directors. The Directors therefore decided to reconsider their recommendation regarding dividend and adjourned the Annual General Meeting. The Directors after reconsideration recommended a dividend of 20 per cent and it was sanctioned by the shareholders at the adjourned Meeting held on 9 November 1990.

The freight and charter hire earnings during the year 1990-91 amounted to Rs. 275.70 crore. The net profit was Rs. 37.14 crore. No provision for tax was required for the year 1990-91. A dividend of 24 per cent was paid to the shareholders.

The freight and charter hire earnings during the year 1991-92 were Rs. 331.77 crore. The net profit amounted to Rs. 93.74 crore, out of which profit on sale of ships was Rs. 13.33 crore. No provision for tax was required for the year 1991-92. A dividend of 30.05 per cent was recommended by the Directors. The net profit of Rs. 93.74 crore was the highest profit made by the company during its existence. The net profit exceeded the amount of paid-up capital of the company.

Profitability Comparison

The returns on capital employed in respect of Great Eastern and six other major Indian shipping companies are given hereunder:

Percentage Return on Capital Employed

Name of Company	1988-89	1989-90	1990-91	1991-92	Average
Public Sector					
Shipping Corporation	8.9	12.9	7.3	9.4	9.6
Private Sector					
Great Eastern	13.0	19.6	15.6	29.7	19.5
Essar	14.6	16.2	11.5	8.6	12.7
India Steamship	11.9	7.5	-2.0	3.5	5.2
Scindia Steam	4.2	4.0	-3.2	3.0	1.9
Varun	15.7	18.8	15.7	14.1	16.7
Chowgule	8.3	11.8	5.0	13.3	9.6

Notes : 1. Capital employed includes paid-up capital, reserves and surplus, and loans.

2. For the purpose of calculating the return, gross profit before providing for interest on loans, guarantee commission, investment allowance reserve has been taken into account. It will be observed that Great Eastern Shipping Company had the highest average profitability among the seven major Indian shipping companies.

Growth and Profitability

At the end of the four decades of its existence and in the early years of the fifth decade, Great Eastern has emerged not only as the largest private sector shipping company in India but also the most profitable among the public sector as well as the private sector shipping companies in India.

This success has been largely due to the issue of convertible bonds and rights issue of shares by which the company strengthened its equity position and improved its liquidity in the shipping recession. As the late Vasant Sheth, the company's then Chairman stated at the 40th Annual General Meeting of shareholders held on 22 December 1988, some of this money was utilised for purchase of eight ships comprising seven bulk carriers and one chemical tanker "in the last 2 years." "These ships have been purchased at a total cost of approximately Rs. 40 crore. This Rs. 40 crore have been financed by approximately Rs. 25 crore Equity and Rs. 15 crore borrowings." The debt-equity ratio on these acquisitions was less than 1:1. As these vessels were purchased when the tonnage prices were low, they had appreciated in value and their market price was about Rs. 85 crore at that time. The equity in these acquisitions had more than doubled in 24 months.

The Directors' Report for the year 1988-89 to the shareholders stated that the fleet owned by the company over the last 3-4 years had almost doubled both in number and tonnage. The market value of the fleet was placed at Rs. 470 crore, which was almost Rs. 210 crore more than their written down value of about Rs. 260 crore as on 31.3.1989.

The Directors' Report for the year 1989-90 to the shareholders whilst referring to the Directors' dividend policy stated that out of the total capital of Rs. 68.07 crore as on 31 March 1990, Rs. 43.52 crore had been paid by the shareholders and the balance of about Rs. 25.50 crore consisted of bonus shares issued by the company. Out of Rs. 43.52 crore contributed by the shareholders, Rs. 1 crore was paid before 1985 and Rs. 42.52 crore in instalments between 1985 and 1989. The 1989-90 profit of Rs. 47.20 crore before tax was over 100 per cent of the capital contributed by the shareholders. This excellent result was achieved within five years of the financial restructuring of the company which was carried out when shipping shares were friendless.

In his statement to the shareholders at the 42nd Annual General Meeting of the company on 20 September 1990, the late Vasant Sheth, Chairman listed the three advantages in which the strength of the company lay. "Our gross and net block consists of well-timed investment in medium vintage fleet with little or no downside risk on value of ships purchased. The consequence of this is that we can run a fleet at half the cost of a competitor who has acquired a new building ship requiring higher interest and depreciation to be provided in his books.

Finally it is comforting to know that at the current level of earnings, 2 years cash inflow could make our company totally debt free."

The Directors' Report for the year 1990-91 to the shareholders recorded that the asset value of the entire fleet after the devaluation was an all-time high of over Rs. 750 crore. It was more than double the written down value of the fleet of Rs. 311 crore as at 31 March 1991.

The Directors' Report for the year 1990-91 to the shareholders estimated that residual debt by 31.3.1992 will be matched by almost same amount of hard rupee cash generated with the company and therefore the company's strength was better than ever before. In fact the cash flow for the year 1991-92 amounted to Rs. 135 crore (net profit plus depreciation); the residual debt on 31.3.1992 was Rs. 111 crore including the amount of Rs. 21 crore due to a foreign shipbuilder under Deferred Payment Agreement.

Some Financial Ratios

The financial ratios given below bring out the financial strength of the company :

Debt : Equity Ratio 1988-89 to 1991-92

(Rs. in lakhs)

Year	Equity	Reserves	Net Worth (Equity Reserves)	Debt	Debt : Equity Ratio
1988-89	6484.58	5594.96	12079.54	15964.17	1.32:1
1989-90	6779.07	8189.33	14968.40	16654.67	1.11:1
1990-91	7121.23	10867.73	17988.96	16217.19	0.90:1
1991-92	8554.81	16139.87	24694.68	11130.02	0.45:1

Whilst the net worth went up from about Rs. 121 crore in 1988-89 to Rs. 247 crore in 1991-92 an increase of over 100 per cent, the debt declined considerably that is, from Rs. 160 crore to Rs. 111 crore. The debt-equity ratio declined from 1.32:1 to 0.45:1. The company's borrowings are less than half of its equity which is not only evidence of the strength of its financial structure but also indicates great scope for expansion of its fleet even on the basis of its present equity by capital gearing if required.

Gross Profit, Net Profit per share and as percentage of Net worth

	1991-92	1990-91	1989-90	1988-89 (Annualised)
1. Gross Profit per Share* (In Rs.)	15.75	11.37	11.50	10.22
2. Net Profit per Share (In Rs.)	10.88	5.58	5.81	5.09
3. Gross Profit as a % of average net worth	63.17%	47.69%	57.87%	51.51%
4. Net Profit as a % of average net worth	43.62%	23.40%	29.25%	25.66%

* (The face value of a share is Rs.10/-.)

Death of M.R. Ruia and A. H. Bhiwandiwalla

M.R. Ruia, who was director of the company since the inception of the company in 1948, passed away on 10 May 1989. He was an eminent industrialist and had held such important positions as President, Indian Merchants' Chamber, President, East India Cotton Association and President, Federation of Indian Chambers of Commerce and Industry. He held the Directorship in the company for about 41 years and made an excellent contribution in the deliberations of the Board and towards the growing prosperity of the company.

A.H. Bhiwandiwalla, Founder-Director of the company, who was Chairman from 1948 to 1973, died on 29 April 1991. An account of the great and most invaluable contribution made by him to the growth of the company has already been set out in chapter 4.

Changes in the Board of Directors

Ghanshyam S. Sheth, son of Sevantilal M. Sheth and grandson of Maneklal Ujamshi, - Founder Director of the company was appointed on 9 May, 1989 as an additional Director by the shareholders in the Annual General Meeting held on 25 September 1989. Ghanshyam Sheth is a graduate in commerce and has 12 years of experience in reputed organisations. He had been looking after the real estate business of the company.

A. K. Parikh was appointed as an additional Director by the Board on 29 June 1989. He was elected as a Director by the shareholders at the Annual General Meeting held on 25 September 1989. A. K. Parikh, B.Com., B.A. (Cambridge) and Bar at-law had held important executive positions in India and was a Director of a number of reputed companies.

K. P. Byramjee was appointed as in additional Director by the Board on 29 June 1989 in the casual vacancy caused by the death of M. R. Ruia. He was elected as a Director by the shareholders at the Annual General Meeting of the company held on 20 September 1990.

The appointment of Vijay Sheth (son of Dr. Kantilal Jagjiwan Sheth and grandson of Jagjiwan Ujamshi, founder of the company) as Executive Director of the company with effect from 1 July 1989 has already been referred to in chapter 5. He continued to look after offshore supply ships.

The appointment of Bharat Sheth (son of K.M. Sheth who was Deputy Chairman and Managing Director at the time, and grandson of Maneklal Ujamshi, founder-Director of the company) as Executive Director of the company on 1 July 1989 has already been dealt with in chapter 5. He continued to manage the dry cargo ships and OBO carriers in the dry cargo trade.

Death of Vasant Sheth - End of an Epoch

Vasant Sheth had his first bypass operation in Houston in the U.S.A. in October 1980. Thereafter he led quite a normal and active life, and set himself a regular work schedule which was free from strain. In March 1992, after a visit to Madras where he had a very strenuous day full of meetings, he had a heart attack. He was hospitalised at the Breach Candy Hospital in Bombay and was treated for a few weeks at the hospital. After his return home, he was attending office for a few hours every day. It was however felt necessary that he should have a medical check up in the U.S.A., where he went in April 1992. He was advised surgery and had a second bypass operation in Houston on 6 May 1992. He was in the Intensive Care Unit for seven days, but he passed away on 13 May 1992. His body was brought to Bombay.

The great loss suffered by India's shipping industry in the death of Vasant Sheth was spelt out in the obituary carried in well-known international shipping journal, *Fairplay*, published from London in its issue dated 4 June 1992, under the caption 'India's Loss.' It stated:

"Just once in every generation there is a formative character. Indian shipping has just lost that man, Vasant Sheth. He died on May 13, after surgery in the US. He founded the Great Eastern Shipping Company, and he was the first Indian to realise the potential for bulk cargoes there. He bought the first Indian tanker, the first Indian OBO and the first clear vision that India could have a private sector shipping fleet, despite all the restrictions that a single minded socialist government could put in his way. It is ironic that he should die now, when Indian shipping is about to enjoy the very freedom that he devoted his life fighting for."

The growth of Indian shipping took place after the advent of independence in 1947. Indian shipping companies which were in existence in the early post-independence years had the very limited objectives of operating in the narrow grooves of the coastal shipping or seeking participation in India's liner trades which were controlled by liner conferences dominated by foreign shipping lines. The scope for growth in India's liner trades therefore was very restricted. It was Vasant Sheth who pioneered the carriage of bulk cargo trade in India and opened up avenues for expansion in this important area which held very large scope for expansion and profitable operation for Indian shipping companies. It would have also served as a stepping stone to Indian shipping's participation in international cross trades in bulk cargoes, but for the government's regulatory policies and procedures. With the liberalisation of government policies in shipping and a little more aggressiveness on the part of Indian shipping companies, Vasant Sheth's vision of Indian shipping companies owning 20 million GRT, or about 30 million DWT (5 per cent of world shipping tonnage), can be achieved.

K.M. Sheth - New Chairman

The Board of Directors of the company at their meeting held

on 28 May 1992 unanimously appointed Deputy Chairman K.M. Sheth as Chairman of the company. As K.M. Sheth was Managing Director also, he became the Chairman and Managing Director of the company. On abolition of the Managing Agency system in the country, K.M. Sheth was appointed as the company's Managing Director on 3 April 1970 and Deputy Chairman and Managing Director on 3 April 1975. K.M. Sheth had over 40 years experience in shipping. The late Vasant Sheth's and K.M. Sheth's qualities and temperaments were complementary to each other and together they constituted, in the words of a business magazine, "a formidable combination." K.M. Sheth with his organising and administrative ability and his expertise and skill in fixing employment and operations of ships had made a great contribution to the growth and progress of the company over the years. Therefore with K.M. Sheth at the helm of the company's affairs, the company is poised for substantial growth and expansion in its activities.

Sudhir Mulji - Director and New Deputy Chairman

Sudhir Mulji was appointed as additional Director and Deputy Chairman at the meeting of the Board of Directors held on 17 June 1992. Mulji became a non-executive Director of the company. Mulji was Chairman and Managing Director of the company's London subsidiary. Previously he was Joint Managing Director and thereafter Managing Director of Great Eastern before he shifted to London. Mulji's long experience in all aspects of shipping, his expertise in economic and financial matters and his brilliance as a negotiator would be of great assistance to K.M. Sheth in the discharge of his onerous responsibilities. He was elected as a Director by the shareholders at the Annual General Meeting of company held on 6 October 1992.

Mrs. Asha V. Sheth - Director

The Board of Directors appointed Asha V. Sheth, wife of the late Vasant Sheth, as additional Director of the company on 17 June 1992. She was elected as a Director by the shareholders at the Annual General Meeting held on 6 October 1992.

Operating Divisions and Subsidiaries of the Company

The main business of the company being shipping, the dry cargo operations and the wet cargo operations are the most important operating divisions of the company.

The wet cargo department, which operates OBO carriers, product tankers etc. is under the overall and close supervision of the Chairman and Managing Director K.M. Sheth who is also in overall charge of the entire business of the company.

Bharat Sheth, who is Executive Director of the company, heads the dry cargo division of the company. The dry cargo division looks after the acquisition, employment and operations of all dry cargo ships including bulk carriers and OBO carriers in the dry cargo trade.

Another factor which would impart long-term stability to the cyclical fortunes of the shipping business of the company is the diversification in the company's activities by increasing participation in the offshore business and housing development. In the year ended 31 March 1991 the company acquired 5 ships, out of which 1 was a bulk carrier and the other 4 were offshore supply vessels. The company now owns 8 supply vessels and is the largest private sector offshore supply vessel owner in India. Vijay Sheth is the Executive Director in charge of the offshore supply vessels division.

Great Eastern Developers - Real Estate Division

As an overall strategy the division has classified various kinds of projects which it intends to undertake into 3 major categories.

Category A: Properties located in the heart of the Urban Centres which have all the necessary infrastructural facilities. The demand for these properties is very high and therefore such properties are difficult to find, but once undertaken yield very quick results. Great Eastern's projects in South Bombay fall in this category.

Category B: These are properties which are located in areas which are in the development stage where the infrastructural facilities are being provided by the government, but the area itself would take some time to develop. A good example of this is New Bombay, the satellite city for the township of Bombay where the division has made substantial investments.

Category C: These properties are large tracts of land without any basic infrastructural facilities. Development of such properties would entail providing basic infrastructural facilities as are required for the development of a township such as schools, hospitals, clubs etc.

The division intends over a period of time to have a fair mix of properties from these categories which would provide both good short term results and long term benefits.

Apart from its focus in striving to have a diverse mix of properties, the division also places a lot of emphasis on bringing professionalism into the project and the activities it undertakes. Value for money in terms of excellent quality, and timely delivery are the main features of any project that the division undertakes. The division intends over a period of time to establish a strong brand franchise built upon these hallmarks and carve out a niche for itself in the real estate business.

Projects on Hand: The division has about 5 lakhs sq. ft. presently in various stages of implementation. It is developing a super deluxe multi-storied residential complex in the heart of the city in South Bombay at Tardeo; a twin building commercial complex of 1,70,000 sq. ft. at CBD Belapur, New Bombay, and a residential building in Juhu - a premium suburb of Bombay very close to the seashore. It also has in the pipeline a major project in the city in South Bombay of about 1,20,000 sq. ft.

Having consolidated its position with prime properties in well located areas, the division is now turning its attention on acquiring properties which would involve development on a much larger scale from multi building residential complexes to township sized projects.

Ghanshyam Sheth, who is a Director on the Board of Great Eastern, looks after the housing and real estate division of Great Eastern which has been named as "The Great Eastern Developers."

U.K. Subsidiary

The company's U.K. subsidiary, The Great Eastern Shipping Co. London Ltd., proved very useful for timely acquisition of ships when acquisition of ships in India bristled with difficulties and delays due to the government regulations and procedures. The U.K. company under the management of Sudhir Mulji has not only grown on its own but also provides to the Indian company the most valuable insights in international freight and tonnage markets as also world maritime developments.

During the year ended 31 December 1990, the U.K. subsidiary made a net profit of $ 397,604. In the year ended 31 December 1991 the U.K. subsidiary made a net profit of $ 395,473 which exceeded the amount of paid-up capital of the company which stood at $ 301,600. It paid a dividend of $ 197,737. The dividend per share amounted to about $ 12. The paid up amount per share was about $ 19.

Prime Securities Ltd

Another subsidiary of the company, Suvibha Investment Company Ltd. which was renamed as Prime Securities Ltd. ceased to be a subsidiary of the company during the year 1991-92.

Retirement of S. N. Sanklecha and B. N. Adappa

S.N. Sanklecha, Senior Vice President (Corporate), retired on 31 May 1990 after 42 years of service with the company. B.N. Adappa, Executive Vice President, also retired on 31 May 1990 after 40 years of service with the company.

Company Executives

K. J. Vesuna, Executive Vice President, has been looking after the wet cargo division. Product tankers and OBOs in the oil trade are managed by him. With experience and expertise that he has attained over the years he has contributed to profitable operation and growth of the wet cargo division which has been doing very well.

N. E. Pardiwala, Vice President (Personnel), has been meticulously looking after the ships personnel as well as the office personnel of the company.

D. G. Khatri, Vice President (Accounts), has been efficiently managing the accounts and finances of the company. He has also acquired proficiency over the years in regard to management of foreign exchange aspects which form a very important part of the finances of a shipping company.

P. R. Naware, Company Secretary, has been looking after the secretarial work including Company Law work, meetings of the

Board of Directors and shareholders. It is his responsibility to obtain government approvals for purchase and sale of ships, obtaining loans and documentations in respect of the loan work. He is also looking after the share department, hull and machinery, P & I and War Risk insurances. By efficient handling of the aforesaid work he is making a worthy contribution.

M. Aranha, Vice President (Wet Cargo - Technical), P. C. Jain, Vice President (Dry Cargo - Technical) and S. Ghosh, Vice President (Dry Cargo - Technical), with experience and expertise acquired by them over a number of years, have been efficiently managing the maintenance and repairs of the company's ships and also looking after and solving the technical problems which arise in regard to acquisition and operation of ships.

Future

India's new economic policy envisages liberalisation in a number of areas. The new economic policy in respect of shipping envisages abolition of the regime of government controls, licences, restrictions regulations and procedures which have hampered the development of shipping industry in India. If this new policy is implemented it will have a most beneficial impact on the growth of the shipping industry in India. Freedom and flexibility of operation is most essential for shipping to operate successfully in competition with shipping of other maritime countries. Indian shipping is under a great handicap in international competition as it does not enjoy the freedom of operation which shipping in other maritime countries possess.

Great Eastern Shipping Company, over the years, has been urging the government (a) to grant more freedom of operation in a number of areas such as purchase and sale of ships, chartering in of foreign ships and chartering out of Indian ships, (b) to remove restrictions on routes where ships have to be operated thus enabling the shipping companies to maximise their profits by plying their ships on routes and trades of their choice, (c) to remove reservation of cargo such as crude oil for the public sector shipping companies, (d) to remove compulsion on Indian shipping companies to place orders for building of ships in Indian shipyards and to get the ships repaired in India irrespective of cost and time factors etc. It is therefore a matter of gratification that liberalisation of shipping policy will bring about freedom of operation for Indian shipping.

With the proposed liberalisation of shipping policy, the Great Eastern Shipping Company, with a strong equity base and liquidity, a low-cost and diversified fleet of ships, and with its expertise built over the years in the management of the shipping operations and sale and purchase of ships should be able to make tremendous progress in the present decade.

The net worth of the company which was hovering between Rs. 35 crore in 1978-79 to Rs. 95 crore in 1987-88 has increased to Rs. 180 crore in 1990-91. At the end of the year 1991-92 the paid up share capital has gone up to Rs. 85.55 crore and the reserves have increased to Rs. 161.40 crore. The net worth therefore has increased to Rs. 247 crore as on 31 March 1992. With the rights issue of Rs. 90 crore in 1992-93 and the expected addition of Rs. 75 crore to the company's reserves, the net worth is expected to increase to over Rs. 410 crore on 31 March 1993.

The company has a Rs. 800 crore ship acquisition plan to be executed in two phases of about Rs. 400 crore each. The first phase implementation will be financed with the right issue collections of about Rs. 90 crore and Rs. 50 crore out of "ploughed back" funds in the company's general reserves which are over Rs. 160 crore at present. The balance Rs. 260 crore will be financed by foreign exchange credits or loans. The company is already in the process of tying up a U.S. $ 60 million (Rs. 180 crore) loan from the International Finance Corporation, Washington. The second phase will start after the company goes to the international market for Euro issue of up to US $ 100 million (Rs. 300 crore). The company intends to price the issue at the best possible value which can be obtained at that time. The proceeds of the issue will therefore exceed Rs. 300 crore. The company will thus be able to finance easily the second phase of the Rs. 400 crore ship acquisition programme. If the expansions are timed correctly and if the freight markets improve as believed by the company, the company's gross block of Rs. 536 crore will go up two and half times to about Rs. 1,350 crore in the next 4 years. The company's assets which are predominantly in ships are at present worth at market prices about Rs. 800 crore. The assets after implementation of the expansion will exceed Rs. 1,600 crore.

In this connection it is interesting to refer to the estimate made by N.C. Singhal, Vice Chairman and Managing Director of SCICI in an interview with *Economic Times* (9 March 1992) about the finance requirements for Indian shipping in the Eighth Plan and also the finance requirements of a shipping company owning 10 per cent of Indian shipping tonnage in the Eighth Plan. As Great Eastern is owning about 11 per cent of Indian tonnage, Singhal's estimate is almost tailor-made for estimating Great Eastern's financial requirements on a pro-rata basis. Singhal's estimate is quoted below :

"According to the Eighth Plan working group on shipping, the replacement requirement is 2.97 million deadweight tonnes (DWT) while that of additional tonnage is 4.77 million DWT — a total of 7.74 million DWT. The capital cost of acquiring this tonnage on the basis of 1989 prices was $ 5.87 billion. The private sector will be required to raise roughly $ 3 billion for this acquisition programme, of which about $ 900 million of promoter's contribution will have to come in through equity and cash accruals. The remainder has to come in the form of loans from institutions like SCICI, commercial banks, deferred yard credit, foreign banks, international institutions, cross-border leasing, bareboat chartering, etc.

A typical shipping company that owns around 10 per cent of the country's fleet will be required to raise roughly $ 18 million (Rs. 45 crore) by way of equity and internal accruals and $ 42 million (Rs. 105 crore) by way of loan annually. I think the Indian shipping industry does not have an insurmountable problem provided it is mentally prepared to meet this challenge."

As per Singhal's estimate, the company will have to make an annual investment of Rs. 150 crore for the 5 years that is, Rs. 750 crore in all. As against this estimate Great Eastern is planning to invest Rs. 800 crore in the next 4 or 5 years.

The tonnage target recommended by the working group on shipping has been pruned down. The Eighth Plan Document accepted by the National Development Council has fixed the tonnage for the next 5-year period 1992-93 to 1997-98 at 7 million GRT (as against the Indian fleet of 5.91 million GRT as on 1.4.1992) with a reduced replacement target of 1.5 million GRT (against 1.9 million GRT overage tonnage) and additional acquisitions of 1 million GRT. Incidentally the tonnage target for the Eighth Plan at 7 million GRT is less than the targets of 7.5 million GRT fixed for both the Sixth and the Seventh Plans.

Although the target recommended by the Eighth Plan Working Group in DWT and the target accepted in the Eighth Plan Document in GRT are not directly comparable, the extent of reduction in the target can be broadly estimated. The total acquisition of ships in the Eighth Plan is 2.5 million GRT consisting of 1.5 million GRT for replacement of old tonnage and 1 million GRT by way of additional tonnage. This may amount to deadweight tonnage of 3.75 million to 4.5 million DWT as compared with 7.74 million DWT recommended by the Eighth Plan Working Group on shipping. A substantial reduction in the target is accompanied by postponement of the Eighth Plan period from 1990-95 to 1992-97. In view of this substantial reduction in the Plan Target the total financial requirements of finance will also go down. If Great Eastern maintains its investment target of Rs. 800 crore, its percentage share of Indian Shipping may go up from 11 per cent to 15 per cent in 4 to 5 years.

GREAT EASTERN GROUP FLEET
AS ON 31 OCTOBER 1993.

Sr. No.	NAME	YEAR BUILT	DWT (MT)
Bulk Carriers			
1.	m.v.JAG VIKRAM	1980	27461
2.	m.v.JAG SHANTI	1972	27071
3.	m.v.JAG SHAKTI	1972	27071
4.	m.v.JAG LEELA	1976	124100
5.	m.v.JAG VIVEK	1977	27012
6.	m.v.JAG VIJAY	1977	24718
7.	m.v.JAG RANI	1976	34134
8.	m.v.JAG RAHAT	1977	36255
9.	m.v.JAG RATNA	1977	35666
10.	m.v.JAG RAVI	1977	36762
11.	m.v.JAG VIKAS	1977	26780
12.	m.v.JAG RASHMI	1981	40505
13.	m.v.JAG RAHUL	1984	37607
14.	m.v.JAG VASANT	1977	26449
15.	m.v.JAG LATA	1973	104746
16.	m.v.POOJA	1983	41501
17.	m.v.KME BARBARA	1989	43664
18.	m.v.JAG VIDYA	1977	27481

19.	m.v.JAG VISHNU	1977	27481
20.	m.v.JYOTI	1968	29138
21.	m.v.SANGITA	1969	23589
22.	m.v.MALINI	1969	29158
23.	m.v.GOPALI	1977	18608
24.	m.v.LADY MOYNE	1974	65051

Tankers

25.	m.t.JAG PRAKASH	1974	25481
26.	m.t.JAG PRIYA	1975	32878
27.	m.t.JAG PREETI	1981	29138
28.	m.t.JAG PARI	1982	29138
29.	m.t.JAG PALAK	1985	27402
30.	m.t.JAG PRABHAT	1985	27397
31.	m.t.JAG PRAGATI	1985	27400
32.	m.t.JAG PRABHU	1978	7260
33.	m.t.JAG PADMA	1982	47801
34.	m.t.JAG LAXMI	1976	124100
35.	m.t.JAG LAADKI	1992	144993

Off Shore Supply Vessels

36.	m.v.MALAVIYA ONE	1983	1090
37.	m.v.MALAVIYA TWO	1983	1101
38.	m.v.MALAVIYA THREE	1984	1271
39.	m.v.MALAVIYA FOUR	1984	1271
40.	m.v.MALAVIYA FIVE	1982	1180
41.	m.v.MALAVIYA SIX	1981	1167
42.	m.v.MALAVIYA SEVEN	1982	1052
43.	m.v.MALAVIYA EIGHT	1982	1052
44.	m.v.MALAVIYA NINE	1983	1194
	Total Deadweight Capacity		1,475,374

Appendix to 10th Chapter

Since financial figures for the year 1992-93 were available when the book was under print, the statement showing debt equity, cost and written down value of the fleet for the years 1987-88 to 1992-93 has been included here.

Some financial highlights showing revenues, cash profits after Tax, dividend payout for the years 1989 (1988-89) to 1993 (1992-93) and decadewise percentage return on the shareholder's funds have also been included here.

STATEMENT SHOWING DEBT : EQUITY, COST AND W.D.V. OF FLEET

(Rs. in lakhs)

Year	Equity	Reserves	Net Worth	Debt	Debt: Equity	Cost of Fleet	Written Down Value (W.D.V.)
1987-88	5561.02	3917.02	9478.04	12974.47	1.37:1	36134.80	21942.17
1988-89	6484.58	5594.96	12079.54	15964.17	1.32:1	41767.17	25938.99
1989-90	6779.07	8189.33	14968.40	16654.67	1.11:1	46844.72	28465.82
1990-91	7121.23	10867.73	17988.96	16217.19	0.90:1	53417.76	31141.30
1991-92	8554.81	16139.87	24694.68	11130.02	0.45:1	51717.69	27005.86
1992-93	17490.47	23952.06	41442.53	17392.60	0.42:1	66,266.18	38234.40

SOME FINANCIAL HIGHLIGHTS

Revenues*

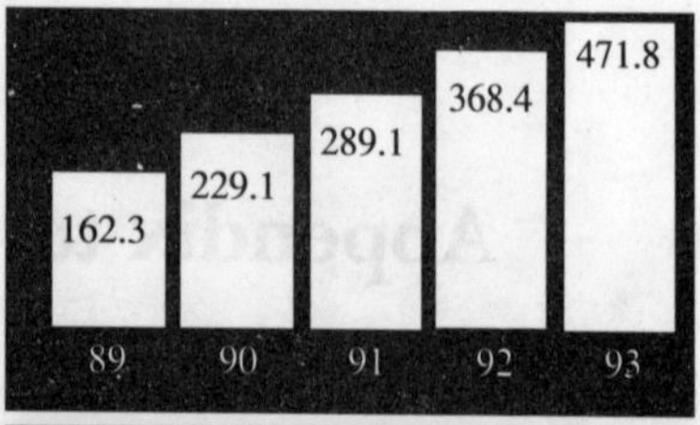

Cash Profits (After Tax)*

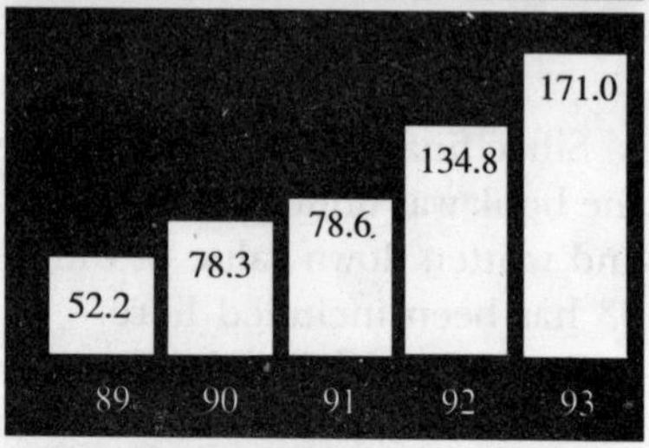

Dividend Payout*

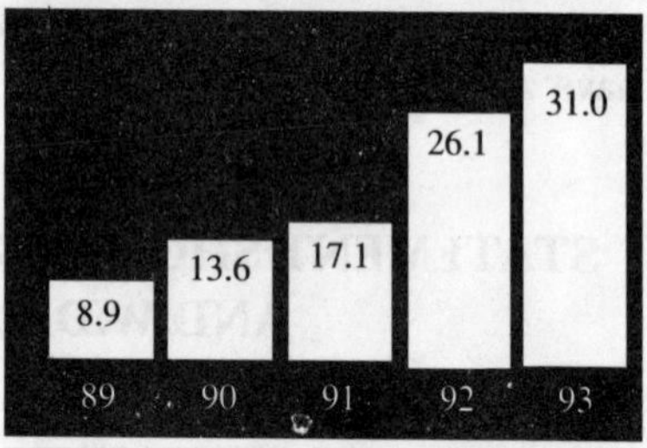

Debt-Equity Ratio

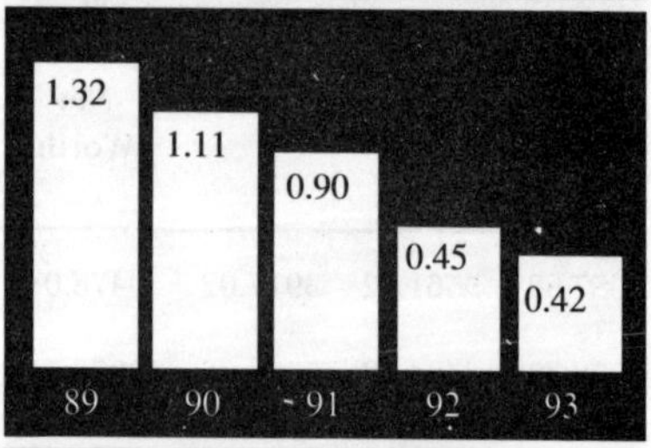

Percentage Return on
Shareholders' Funds**
(Decade Wise)

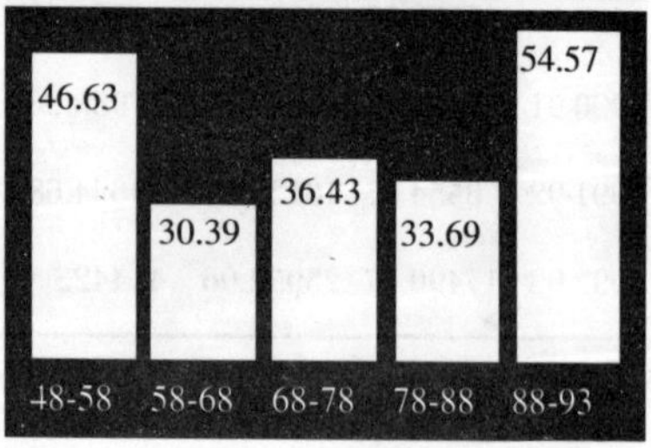

*Rupees in Crores
**Cash Profit / Net Worth

11

Vasant J. Sheth

Vasant J. Sheth

10 December 1927 - 13 May 1992

Vasant J. Sheth was born in Santacruz, a suburb of Bombay, on December 10, 1927. He was the youngest son of Jagjiwan Ujamshi Mulji.

Maritime Education and Training

Vasant Sheth did not pursue higher education in a college or university. He did however cultivate his mind through the exposure he could get on his frequent international travel. He developed an avid and wide-ranging taste for reading and remained a life-long student, always keen to learn more and add to his knowledge. He underwent the Advanced Management Programme (A.M.P.) at the Harvard University when he was well past 50 with interest and put in a great deal of effort in carrying out case studies for the course. He was greatly interested in maritime education and training, which in his view were most essential for the efficient running of Indian shipping in India. He helped Capt. Ahuja in forming the Sea Cadet Council for promoting the love of the sea in all its aspects in school going boys and girls. He was Trustee-Treasurer of Sea Cadet Council for over 30 years. He founded the Great Eastern Cadet Academy for training navigating officers. It was the first cadet academy started by an Indian shipping company for imparting pre-sea training for cadets and mid-sea training for navigating officers. He was also interested in the development of well-trained manpower on board as well as on shore for the shipping industry. He was working closely with Dr. C. P. Srivastava and Dr. N. P. Tolani towards the establishment of an Indian Maritime Foundation for the promotion of maritime training, education and research, but he died before this work could be completed.

Vasant Sheth married Asha Malaviya, the daughter of Keshav

Deva Malaviya, a scion of the family of the illustrious Pandit Madan Mohan Malaviya, and the pioneer and founder of the oil industry in India. It was Keshav Deva Malaviya, chosen by Prime Minister Jawaharlal Nehru as his Minister for Petroleum, who strove for promoting oil exploration and self-sufficiency in oil resources for the country. He fathered India's oil industry from prospecting, production, refining to marketing.

Vasant Sheth's great role in the building of the Great Eastern Shipping Company and the pivotal role he played in the growth of the Indian shipping industry has been dealt with at appropriate places in the various chapters of this book. He acquired the first ship, *Fort Ellice,* renamed *Jag Vijay,* and managed the company right from its establishment until his death. Assisted by K.M. Sheth and Sudhir Mulji, he built up the company, which became not only the largest Indian shipping company in the private sector but also the most profitable shipping company in India. Great Eastern Shipping Company acquired the reputation of being one of the best managed shipping companies internationally.

Contribution to Growth of Indian Shipping

In post-Independence years Indian shipping companies were acquiring ships for the coastal trade and overseas liner trades. The growth possibilities were therefore restricted because coastal cargo was not sufficient to employ a very large fleet and in the liner trades Conferences dominated by foreign shipping lines precluded adequate Indian participation in those trades. It was only the bulk cargoes, which constituted over two-thirds of India's overseas trade in terms of quantities of cargo, which offered scope for employment of a large number of ships. In the post-war years, internationally too it was the bulk cargo trades, dry as well as wet, which offered great scope for growth of bulk cargo shipping (known in earlier years as tramp shipping). Vasant Sheth pioneered bulk cargo shipping in India, and despite the hostile policies of government for the growth of tramp shipping, acquired ships for the bulk cargo trades. Great Eastern fared well because of its participation in the bulk cargo trades. After Great Eastern's success, other Indian shipping companies in course of time acquired ships for bulk cargo trades. This led to the substantial growth of Indian shipping.

Great Eastern, unlike many other Indian shipping companies in those years, achieved very satisfactory financial results. Great Eastern shareholders therefore greatly benefited by receiving handsome dividends and by the issue of bonus shares from time to time by the Company. This gave a stimulus to the flotation of a number of shipping companies in India. Because of Great Eastern's results and servicing of shareholders, shipping shares also became popular and shareholders invested money in the new shipping companies.

Shipping is a service industry in which there is international competition. In maritime countries, the shipping industries having full freedom of operation are efficient and competitive. In India in the post-independence years there were severe restrictions on purchase and sale of ships, restrictions by way of licensing of ships for operation in various trades and routes, and restrictions on chartering-in and chartering-out of ships etc. Indian shipping was therefore operating at a great handicap in international competition. It was Vasant Sheth who took the initiative and campaigned throughout his life for the freedom of operation for Indian shipping. He endeavoured to educate the government and those concerned with shipping—by representations to government, discussions with government officials, Chairman's speeches at the Annual General Meetings of the Great Eastern shareholders—that restrictions on sale and purchase of ships, chartering of ships, licensing of ships for trades and routes etc. were a hindrance to the efficient operation and growth of Indian shipping. Although he did not succeed fully in a government regime riddled with controls, licences and restrictions, there were progressively considerable changes and modifications in government policies which made controls and restrictions less rigorous. Thus Indian shipping benefited by these relaxations in the regulatory regime and its handicap in the international competition was reduced.

Since the installation of the present government there has been a strong trend towards liberalisation of economic policies relating to all economic sectors including shipping. It was Vasant Sheth who championed the cause of removal of controls and regulations and freedom of operation for shipping for over four decades. There is now general agreement that shipping in order to be fully efficient and competitive must have full freedom of operation.

Vasant Sheth was thrice elected as President of the Indian National Shipowners Association (INSA). In 1957, at the age of 29, he was the youngest president of INSA. It was at the Annual General

Meeting of INSA held on 17 December, 1957 that in response to Vasant Sheth's persuasive presidential speech (a copy of which was sent in advance to the Minister of Transport Lal Bahadur Shastri) three important measures of assistance for Indian shipping were announced by Shastri - establishment of Shipping Development Fund Committee (SDFC) for making loan finance available at concessional rate of interest for acquisition of ships, formation of Shipping Co-ordination Committee for preferential employment of Indian ships, and increase in development rebate from 25 per cent to a higher percentage for Indian shipping. It was these three measures of assistance which brought about the substantial growth of Indian shipping.

Entrepreneurship and Vision

As an entrepreneur he not only set up the company and managed it efficiently, but also displayed great innovative skills. He was the first to start a tramp shipping company in India, first to buy a tanker in India, the first to raise foreign exchange loans for acquisition of ships on a self-financing basis, first to employ ships on a regular basis in international cross trades, first to acquire an OBO carrier, first among Indian shipowners to acquire offshore supply ships. Despite controls in India on the sale and purchase of ships by Indian shipping companies, Vasant Sheth displayed the qualities of a genius in securing so many bargains for Great Eastern. Vasant Sheth was perhaps one of the few major entrepreneurs in the classical mould who ran his business on merit without buying patronage from politicians and bureaucrats.

He was a great team leader. He inspired all those working with him so as to draw out from each of them their full potentialities. By his leadership he developed a dynamic and devoted team of managers. It must also be stated that in selecting employees for the company or granting promotions, no religious, provincial or caste considerations ever influenced his decisions, which were merit-based. The composition of Great Eastern staff has always been illustrative of national integration.

Vasant Sheth was endowed with great vision. In the midst of the shipping depression in 1983-84 he was the first Indian shipowner to realise that Indian shipping, like world shipping which was predominantly loan-financed, had to develop a strong equity base with far less reliance on loans. Although the Great Eastern's Board of Directors was hesitant, as it had doubts about the success of the flotation of equity issue and servicing of the increased equity capital in depression, Vasant Sheth persuaded the Board to issue convertible bonds (50 per cent to be compulsorily converted into equity and the balance 50 per cent to be converted into equity later at the option of the bond holders). In view of Great Eastern's track record, the bond issue was oversubscribed even during the depression by the shareholders. Thereafter Great Eastern made a rights issue of equity capital and also obtained an equity-cum-subordinate loan from International Finance Corporation. Thus Great Eastern developed liquidity and could meet its loan-servicing obligations in the depression and could have spare funds for acquiring ships which were available at rock bottom prices during the depression. With the lifting of the depression these ships with low depreciation and interest charges could make substantial profits. Great Eastern was one of the very few major Indian shipping companies which during the depression did not default in loan repayment and interest payment obligations to Shipping Development Fund Committee.

Vasant Sheth, keeping in mind the cyclical nature of the shipping industry, decided to diversify Great Eastern's activities. First the Company diversified into offshore shipping and thereafter into the real estate business.

Dedication to the Cause of Indian Shipping

He consistently and relentlessly championed the cause and worked for the growth of Indian shipping. He was founder-member of India's National Shipping Board and besides being President of Indian National Shipowners' Association thrice, worked on many committees and commissions of INSA and government. As a member of the Planning Group on Shipping appointed by the government, which submitted its Report in September 1987, he attached a Note to the Report which ardently advocated "Abolition or Substantial Liberalisation of Regulatory and Restrictive Regime Essential for Development of Shipping." In the same note he suggested that Shipping Corporation of India, the public sector company, should be required to raise equity funds from the public by tapping the capital markets, that is, stock exchanges in India. This would have the effect of reducing the burden on the Central Government's budgetary funds for providing further equity capital of Shipping Corporation. It would also ensure that the public sector company would have to improve its efficiency and profitability and establish a track record of management in order to attract equity funds from the investors. Both the suggestions, which were opposed at that time, have now found acceptance under the new economic policy of the government.

Vasant Sheth advocated the registration of Indian-owned ships under foreign flags of convenience as part of the process of globalisation of shipping enterprises. A shipping company is organised on a global basis so that it can have access to equity and loan finance in well-developed capital markets internationally and at the same time can have low manning costs of the officers and crew recruited from India. The freedom of operation enjoyed by such global companies' ships will enable them to operate efficiently and further improve their position in international competition. The government and Indian shipping companies were not favourably disposed towards this proposal at that time. After setting up of the second international registry in 1987, by Norway which gave great impetus to the growth of Norwegian shipping, second international registers were established by many maritime countries for growth of their shipping fleets. A second international registry provided all the advantages of registration of ships under flags of convenience and at the same time did not break the genuine link between the country and the ships. Vasant Sheth advocated the setting up of second international register for registration of Indian ships in a paper which was published in two issues of *Indian Shipping* (Vol. 12 of 1988 and Vol. 1 of 1989). Although the government and Indian shipping companies did not approve the proposal, there is now less opposition to the proposal of registering ships either in foreign countries or under the second Indian Register. Incidentally, Vasant Sheth implemented his views on the registration of ships abroad by establishing a wholly owned subsidiary of Great Eastern in the U.K. in January 1985.

In his paper advocating the setting up of a second international register for registration of Indian ships, Vasant Sheth visualised and set for Indian shipping a target of five per cent of world shipping to be achieved by the year 2000. He stated "We must now come out of the narrow grooves of import substitution which is excellent as far as it goes. We must now boldly embark on substantial expansion of shipping by participating in international cross trades. This should enable us to secure a share of five percent (two per cent for own trades and three percent for international cross trades) in the world shipping tonnage by the year 2000." In 1988, when the paper was written, the world shipping tonnage was about 400 million GRT. Five per cent of that figure would amount to 20 million GRT (which does not take into account the increase in world shipping between 1988 and 2000).

It was an observation of a knowledgeable shipping man that what Vasant Sheth advocated, the shipping industry accepted after a time lag of 5 years. What Sir Donald Anderson, P & O Chairman in 1968 assessing the group's tankers and looking forward to delivery of OCL's containerships observed applies to Vasant Sheth's innovative suggestions and methods. Anderson said : "They are first considered laughable, then objectionable and finally obvious".[1]

Other Distinctions

Vasant Sheth was President of Bombay Chamber of Commerce and Industry for the year 1975-76. He was also a Member of the Managing Committee of the Associated Chambers of Commerce and Industry. In recognition of Vasant Sheth's outstanding contribution to the advancement of global co-operation, especially that between Norway and India, the King of Norway bestowed upon him in 1988 the most prestigious award - Knight First Class of the Royal Norwegian Order of Merit.

He was the Director of longest standing on the Board of Directors of Steamship Mutual Underwriting Association Ltd., London, a reputed international P & I Club. As a shipowner of international repute, Vasant Sheth was invited to become its Chairman as well as Chairman of its group from 1988 to 1990. He was the first Indian to hold the high assignment of Chairmanship of an international P & I Club. He was a director on the Boards of a number of Indian companies which included Tata Chemicals Ltd., Rallis India Ltd., Pudumjee Pulp & Paper Mills Ltd.

Passing Away

Vasant Sheth died at Houston, U.S.A. on 13 May, 1992 after

undergoing a heart by-pass surgery, leaving behind his wife Asha Sheth and daughter Ketaki Sheth.

Tributes and Varuna Award

Excerpts from A Tribute to Vasant J. Sheth by Dr. C. P. Srivastava, Secretary General Emeritus, International Maritime Organisation : "In the passing away of Vasant J. Sheth, Chairman of the Great Eastern Shipping Company, Indian shipping has lost a pioneer, a leader and a visionary of exceptional abilities and unparalleled achievements. Fate has now stilled a powerful and persuasive voice which championed the cause of Indian shipping with total conviction, dedication and unremitting perseverance for more than four decades. He had come to be acknowledged and applauded as the doyen of Indian shipping and the courageous and inspired architect and builder of the largest shipping enterprise in the private sector, the Great Eastern Shipping Company, a name which inspires admiration and respect for its glorious successes. Today Great Eastern is the most profitable shipping company in India and is highly regarded in international shipping circles. At several shipping conferences which I had the honour of attending in different countries, I felt so delighted and proud to hear Vasant Sheth's name being mentioned as one of the most dynamic and admired shipowners in the world. Vasant Sheth was a great son of India who demonstrated by personal example that exceptional success can be achieved in business with honest means and with highest integrity. In the history of Indian shipping since Independence the name of Vasant Sheth will be written in letters of gold as one of its towering personalities. He made an enormous contribution to the development of Indian shipping and in the building up of India as a great shipping nation. He was one of the prime movers in the maritime field for many years. After all he was a great gentleman and an extremely warm-hearted friend. And now he has left behind a great name and a unique record for its emulation."

The National Maritime Day Celebrations Central Committee which has representatives of government, shipowners and seafarers with Director General of Shipping as its Chairman, bestowed the prestigious Varuna Award for his distinguished and outstanding contribution to the development and growth of Indian shipping for over four decades. The Award was received by Mrs. Asha Vasant Sheth at the main function of the National Maritime Day Celebrations on 5 April 1993, which was presided over by Dr. P.C. Alexander, Governor of Maharashtra and at which Mr. Jagdish Tytler, Minister of Surface Transport was the Chief Guest. A photocopy of the Citation of Varuna Award is annexed.

Philanthropic Activities

Vasant Sheth was deeply concerned in the welfare of fellow human beings. He devoted a good deal of his resources in the medical and educational fields. He converted the hospital built by his brother, the late Dr. K. J. Sheth, into an institute for medical research in the much neglected field of leprosy. Financed by the Sheth family and the Godrej family, the Foundation for Medical Research is one of the very few private research institutes which is solely devoted to basic medical research in India. It is the only one doing research in leprosy and has gained both national and international recognition.

He also founded with his own sole contribution the Vashketu Foundation, whose charitable projects are: (a) rural and Harijan uplift, (b) educational scholarships and (c) medical assistance. Vashketu Foundation has extended assistance in these fields.

Vasant Sheth also took keen interest in the Eye Hospital and First Eye Bank in India in Ahmedabad established as a result of the donation given by his father and uncle. The Eye Hospital was inaugurated by the late Smt. Indira Gandhi, the then Prime Minister of India.

It has been stated that Vasant Sheth was a role model of what a businessman could and should be. However, his enormous success and wealth never went to his head. His cordiality and warmth not only towards his business and non-business friends but also towards members of Great Eastern staff who dealt with him was remarkable. He was a gentleman to the core, always pleasant, simple in his habits. The following *doha* (couplet) of Kabir may be quoted as applicable to him:

देश देशांतर मै फिरौ, मानुस बड़ा सुकाळ ।
जा देख सुख उपेजे, ताका बड़ा दुकाळ ।

In many a land at home and abroad
I found men are plentiful
But rarely the one whose very sight
made me cheerful

The innate goodness of a man shows up in his face and the heart gladdens on seeing such a person.[2] Vasant Sheth was such a person.

References

1 The Story of P & O by David Howarth & Stephen Howarth published by Weidonfeld and Nicolson London, 1986.

2 Couplets from Kabir (Kabir Doha) - Edited, Translated and Compiled by G.N. Das, 1991, Motilal Banarasidas Publishers Pvt. Ltd., Delhi.

NATIONAL MARITIME DAY CELEBRATIONS COMMITTEE

Presentation of
"V A R U N A A W A R D"

for the year 1993
POSTHUMOUSLY TO SHRI VASANT J SHETH

CITATION

The National Maritime Day Celebrations Committee has great pleasure in presenting the "Varuna Award" for 1993 posthumously to Shri Vasant Jagjiwan Sheth for his distinguished and outstanding contribution to the development and growth of Indian Shipping for over four decades.

Born on December 10, 1927 in Bombay, Shri Vasant Sheth championed the cause of our national shipping which he served with dedication, drive and perseverence. He was regarded as a doyen of Indian Shipping Fraternity and internationally acknowledged as one of the dynamic shipowners of the world.

As a founder Director and later Chairman and Managing Director of Great Eastern Shipping Company Limited, he built up the company as the largest shipping enterprise in the private sector with international reputation for its efficiency and financial strength. He pioneered bulk cargo shipping in dry as well as wet cargo sector in India which presently forms a very large sector of Indian Shipping operations. He was a persuasive and consistent advocate of freedom of operation for Indian shipping, which presently forms part and parcel of Government's economic reforms for healthy and rapid development of our national economy by making it market oriented to integrate it into the global economy.

Shri Vasant Sheth was the youngest President of the Indian National Shipowners' Association and was elected three times to the office. He was a founder member of the National Shipping Board and President of the Bombay Chamber of Commerce and Industry. He was the first Indian to hold the Chairmanship of Steamship Mutual Underwriting Association, U.K. In recognition of his outstanding contribution to advancement of global co-operation in shipping, the Government of Norway bestowed upon him the award of the Knight First Class of the Royal Norwegian Order of Merit in 1988.

Shri Vasant Sheth was keenly interested in promotion of excellence in maritime education, training and research in India. He was actively participating in the management of the Sea Cadet Council which imparts sea training to school students of T.S. "Jawahar". He established the first Cadet Academy for a Private Sector Company for pre-sea training of Navigating Cadets. He was closely associated with Dr. C.P. Srivastava, Chairman of the Committee on Maritime Education and Training and others for establishment of an autonomous organisation for promotion of maritime education, training and research.

Shri Vasant Sheth has thus made very valuable and lasting contribution to the development of our national shipping. He passed away at Houston, U.S.A. on 13th May, 1992, while he was undergoing heart surgery.

In bestowing the 'Varuna Award' upon Shri Vasant Sheth posthumously, the National Maritime Day Celebrations Committee recognises the enormous contribution made to the growth of Indian Shipping by this illustrious personality who will hold an honoured place, as one of the pioneers, in the golden leaves of Maritime History of India.

(DINESH K AFZULPURKAR)
CHAIRMAN

Bombay
5th April, 1993.